R.M. (Dickie) Owen, architect of the historic Welsh victory over New Zealand on 16 December 1905, causing further consternation to the All Blacks at St. Helen's, Swansea, two weeks later.

1905 AND ALL THAT

Essays on Rugby Football,
Sport and Welsh Society

Gareth Williams

First Impression—1991

ISBN 0 86383 758 1

© Gareth Williams

This volume is published with the support of
the Welsh Arts Council.

Printed by
J.D. Lewis & Sons, Ltd. Gomer Press, Llandysul, Dyfed, Wales.

i'm teulu

Contents

ACKNOWLEDGEMENTS:
CYDNABYDDIAETHAU

I am grateful to the following for their ready permission to reprint articles, essays and reviews that first appeared elsewhere. I have taken the opportunity to correct errors, insert some new material, and make various other modifications with the result that no chapter has retained exactly its original form. For allowing me to repeat myself so often I thank:

Cambridge University Press for Chapter 2, which first appeared as 'Rugby Union' in Tony Mason (ed.) *Sport in Britain: A Social History* (1989) pp. 308-32.

Collins Willow for Chapter 3, which was first published in David Parry-Jones (ed.) *Taff's Acre: A History and Celebration of Cardiff Arms Park* (1984) pp. 30-45.

Frank Cass & Co Ltd. for Chapter 4, first published as 'From Popular Culture to Public Cliché: Image and Identity in Wales 1890-1914' in J.A. Mangan (ed.) *Pleasure, Profit, Proselytism: British Culture and Sport at Home and Abroad 1700-1914* (1988) pp. 128-49; for Chapter 7, which first appeared in *The British Journal of Sports History*, vol. 2, December 1985 pp. 248-69; and for in Chapter 10 the review of Godwin, *The International Rugby Championship 1883-1983*, from *The British Journal of Sports History*, vol. 2, September 1985, pp. 203-5.

The Glamorgan County History Trust for Chapter 6 which was first published in Prys Morgan (ed.) *Glamorgan County History*, vol. vi (Cardiff, 1988) pp. 381-400.

Professor K.O. Morgan for Chapter 8, first published in the *Welsh History Review*, vol 9, June 1983, pp. 338-57.

I Wasg Gomer am Bennod 5, a gyhoeddwyd gyntaf yn Geraint H. Jenkins (gol.) *Cof Cenedl* V (1990) tt. 117-45.

I'r Cyngor Llyfrau Cymraeg a Gwasg Cambria am yr ysgrifau ym Mhennod 9 a ymddangosodd gyntaf yn W.J. Jones (gol.) *Enwogion Byd y Bêl* (1983) tt. 109-48.

The reviews in Chapter 10 are re-published with permission, having first appeared in *Book News from Wales*, in The *British Journal of Sports History*, and in the now sadly defunct *Arcade*.

While more specific debts are acknowledged as they arise, I count myself extraordinarily fortunate to have enjoyed over many years the practical help, warm friendship and stimulating company of my fellow historians of sport—and of much else besides—Dick Holt, John Jenkins, Tony Mason and Dai Smith.

Hoffwn ddiolch i Dyfed Elis Gruffydd am ei gefnogaeth frwd i'r gyfrol, ei gyngor golygyddol doeth a'i ofal arbennig wrth lywio'r cyfan drwy'r wasg; ac i'r digymar Gerald Davies am gyfrannu Rhagair.

Dengys y cyflwyniad i bwy y mae fy nyledion dyfnaf.

FOREWORD

The other day I took a return journey.

This is never the wisest course of action that any man can take. There is always a sense of a life being put in jeopardy. Going back to any place which once held a store of experiences, bitter or sweet, is hazardous. Sweet memories can be ruined, bitter ones must once more be confronted. The corner shop, of a thousand gob-stoppers, is closed; childhood jealousies over a broken teenage heart or a stolen cricket bat are ingloriously exposed once more.

Some things, though, never change.

A request had arrived to say that my presence was required. When such an invitation comes from 'yr hen gynefin'—that old square mile of a patch that we all know so well from childhood—there is more, much more, of a tug at the elbow to shift out of a routine, than it might otherwise be from an anonymous caller, unattached to the past. An old pal rings up.

To retrace the steps of what begins nowadays to appear like a former self which barely touches on the present man, is never entirely a comforting experience. Things are never what they used to be. Yet . . . Yet, certain things are always the same. Always as they were. And as you remember them.

'Dafydd is playing for Wales. Could you come down and make the presentation?'

'He's playing for Wales'. The words, as evocative now as they ever have been, first uttered as a modest whisper, grow into an almighty roar of back-slapping acknowledgement of the great deed. And the village and the whole surrounding countryside echoes in glorious salute to the boy. The longing is made good. He will feel as one with the stars.

You notice that the sport needs no mention at all. In Wales, it could be soccer. But it isn't. It just might be cricket. But, hardly. You could, if you really wanted to be obtuse, mention badminton or squash. But you would be letting yourself down.

To play for Wales, whatever the *aficionados* of the other games might think, can only mean Rugby Football. It is not even Rugger which, in this small corner of the world, conjures up something which is not altogether the same thing at all. Rugger is all very well in genteel Roehampton and Blackheath where the bowler-hatted somebody who is something in the City plays.

But in Wales it has to be Rugby. Catch anybody shouting in the four-ale bar in Penygraig or Blaina, Tondu or Treorchy— 'Anyone for a game of Rugger?', and he might as well high tail it immediately out of the locality—although the Treasurer, noticing the accent and the suit from the bespoke tailor, might wish to introduce him to his daughter before the rugger-bugger swishes out of town in the company car. Which, the treasurer will have concluded, is the next best thing to having a Welsh International as a son-in-law; or, if younger, a father-in-law with adjacent debenture tickets for the Cardiff Arms Park.

'He's playing for Wales'. The words have reverberated down the years.

The elderly gentleman meanders down to the local park, raises his head in recognition and hears those words again as he has done so many times before.

The shrewd observer, the devotee, on the 'tanner' bank—at Llanelli's Stradey Park or St. Helen's in Swansea—will brave the January cold and wet for the coming man. He believes it right that he should be there. He has done so over the decades. From one generation to the next, he want to be 'in the know'; no second-hand information will do. He has to be there himself to witness the first blossoming of the talented boy. He can tell class at a glance. His whistle and sharp intake of breath and a slow nod of the head, signal the arrival of the boy who will one day be king of the red jersey.

It is as natural for the boy in the Rhondda to want to side-step lamp posts and to want to play Rugby for Wales as it is for the street urchin of Sao Paulo to kick tin cans and to dream of play-ing soccer for Brazil. Different culture, same dream. The wish is realised on the playing fields; the glory to be found in scoring goals or tries. In Wales, goals are fine, but tries are better.

From North to South, East to West, from the deepest rural hamlet to the helter-skelter, higgledy-piggledy streets of the industrial towns; from the corner shop to factory floor, from playground to boardroom; from the glossy cheeks of the well-fed luncheon face to the chiselled, raw-boned features of the man who has no need to prepare a face to meet the faces he meets, the oval ball beckons and beguiles us all. Even nowadays when Wales has become less, far less, than it should be on that acre of splendid grass, the thrill remains.

Heroes are spawned on the Rugby field; heroes with their feet set in the community, fulfilling other people's dreams as well as their own. A nation's happiness depends on their wellbeing; they despair if they lose, they rejoice in victory. As for the next match, Wales attack on a wave of pessimism.

Each victory is only a preparation for the next; each moment of victory is fleetingly brief. Because there is always a next time when it all has to be gone through again. And again. And again.

For a Welshman, the game defines and dignifies his position in a spare sporting world. He has found, after all, that he is good at it. Sometimes even able to charm the sullen and the unwilling. He can as easily bring a smile to a man's face for his audacious wit as have scorn heaped on his head for embracing such brute force.

There is affection and wit for the rugby's cruel demands. Songs are sung, poems written about a game in which you can find an intoxicating mix of sweet easy elegance and raw intimidating power. You can share in serious drama or giggle at the rich seam of comic relief. There are heroes as well as villains.

And you can talk about it. For all the social, educational, economic, geographical, even political reasons why rugby, of all games, should have caught on in Wales, the humorist may advise that it all depends on something else. That the game appeals to our gift of the gab. There are the professions—the law, education, the church—which Welshmen have always been good at, and they depend on the interpretation of the word.

There is plenty of room for interpretation in Rugby. There is not much doubt as who to crosses the line first in the 400 metres. Not much to dispute—well, not until recently—when a wicket falls in cricket. Or a goal scored in soccer. But who in heaven knows in actual fact quite what goes on in a scrum, ruck or maul. Few of the players themselves know for sure. Conjecture is all. Did he or didn't he touch down? Was the knock-on deliberate or not?

Was it or wasn't it a try at Twickenham in 1974? J.J. did score, didn't he?

Yes, said the Welshman, who lived in hope.

No, said the Englishman, who had spent 13 years for a win.

And No, said the Irishman, whose opinion, as referee, mattered.

The next man is no wiser than the next.

Not even the referee, poor soul, who is the epitome of human frailty. He can whistle for the 3 points for a drop goal. Gareth Edwards did so in Dublin.

Yes, said the biased Welshman who had the referee, an Englishman, on his side this time.

No, said the Irishman who had the television pictures on his side.

Foot up, Ref!

Not in straight Ref!

All the time, Ref!

There's pushing and shoving in the line-out.

He's off-side, Ref!

But 60 different infringements can happen in the line-out at any one time. Goodness me! We can all be right.

It's all so random and chaotic, dark and mysterious, with so many endless interpretations and permutations, so disputable and lovely.

Except, of course, when a couple of All Blacks take a dive from a line-out and the penalty makes Wales lose by a point. Now there's travesty which will keep the home fires burning for ever.

But it all adds up to an imperishable folklore which makes any Welshman's blood race through all of his seven ages: the tries, the tackles, the penalities and the Biblical proportions of the great conversions.

Though they are thin on the ground of late Welsh rugby players are meant to be the enchanted performers. It is the Welshman's game. Boys must wish to travel towards the sun and to listen to the changeless refrain:

'He's playing for Wales'.

It is a rich inheritance but few writers have truly distilled its essence. Gareth Williams is one of them. Times beyond recall I have turned, for refreshment and illumination, to that singing epic he wrote with Dai Smith called *Fields of Praise*. 'The best thing to come out of the Centenary' hymn'd Carwyn; 'the best book ever written about a game', amen'd another late and lamented friend John Morgan. I echo those sentiments.

I am delighted the author has been persuaded to collect together some of the articles and essays he has written over the last few years. Some are more familiar to me than others. I look forward to reading them all, for pleasure as much as for profit.

History, for me, was always something of a mystery. Here it is a delight, pure and unalloyed. A return journey.

Dyma gyfrol y bydd darllen arni am flynyddoedd. Mae'n ddysgedig ac yn ddifyr hefyd. Mwynhewch hi.

Gerald Davies

Why was it that I was so obsessed with rugby football? I was only, after all, one of a community, of a society that for the past century or so had elevated rugby football into becoming a symbol of itself as a nation. It is true that a kind of traditional rough and tumble game had been played in Wales, as in other parts of Britain occupied by the Celts, a game of hacking and hustling an object from one end of the village to the other. Yet the spring for the spate of enthusiasm for rugby was more specific. To win at the game, especially against England, is as important as gaining victory in the long war Wales began fighting for its independence centuries ago.

No one can understand the seriousness that is paid to rugby in Wales unless he views it as a social and political affirmation of its nationhood. For a nation that has existed for many years as subject to a more powerful one it is the sheet-anchor of its self-respect . . .

George Ewart Evans, *The Strength of the Hills*

CHAPTER 1

INTRODUCTION:
SPORT AND THE HISTORIAN

Karenin: Sport has, in my opinion, a deep value and, as is always the case, we see only its superficial aspect.

Tolstoy, *Anna Karenina*, chap. 28

It is generally accepted that a knowledge of its history is essential for a proper understanding of anything in our world, whether politics, religion, art, science, whatever. Sport should be no exception, for given its presence as a global phenomenon, media spectacle, big business and national signifier it is one of the social phenomena of our age.

Yet though sport, like it or not, is everywhere, its historians have been nowhere—until recently. Twenty years ago it could be legitimately complained that 'grandfather clocks, balloons and potatoes have benefited from historical studies that games and sports still lack',[1] but since then there has been a remarkable explosion of interest in the history of sport. In North America and Australia particularly, periodical publications (like *The Journal of Sport History* in the USA, *The Canadian Journal of the History of Sport*, and Australia's *Sporting Traditions*), conferences and departments in institutions of higher education devoted to the serious study of sport's historical development, have proliferated. NASSH (The North American Society for Sports History), CAHPER (The Canadian Association for Health Physical Education and Recreation, with its own History of Sport Section), ASH (The Australian Sports History Society) and HISPA (The International Association for the History of Sport and Physical Education) were all founded in the 1970's, acronymic advertisements for the striking growth of sports history world-wide. In Britain, however, where so many games originated, events moved slower, though the BSSH (British Society for Sports History) founded in 1983, and the *British* (now *International*)

1

Journal for the History of Sport, launched the following year, are by now well-established.

It can therefore come as something of a surprise to realize that it was as long ago as 1801 that Joseph Strutt observed that

> In order to form a just estimation of the character of any particular people, it is absolutely necessary to investigate the Sports and Pastimes most generally prevalent among them. [2]

That is to say, it is in the relatively free context of sport that we can recognize what men and women value when least constrained by their circumstances. Whether the player or spectator *has* genuine freedom, or is unconsciously collaborating in a more subtle form of subordination is a question that much exercises those social scientists for whom sport is not liberating but exploitative. [3]

Sport, however, is too important to be relegated to the position of merely confirming a sociological theory, or illustrating apparently more weighty matters of political or economic history; equally, it is too important—on the analogy of war and the generals—to be left to sportspeople, or for that matter sportswriters. This is not to devalue the contribution of either to the writing of the history of sport. No-one who has ever leafed through newspapers of the years 1880-1930—the period when mass spectator sport became a major focus of national and social communication and identification in much of the western world—can resist the inflated literary style of the new breed of sporting journalist. This was a style consciously designed to reflect and heighten the reader's feelings that the Saturday afternoon ritual was more than just a game: it was a dramatic spectacle, a capsulised eighty minute version of the struggles, conflicts and frustrations of a lifetime—or a nation; a symbolic mass movement with myths, symbols and rituals of its own.

We need only recall that remarkable generation of sportswriters that emerged in the United States in the 1920's, the so-called 'gee-whizzers' whose enthusiasm for sport outran that of even the most perfervid fan. It is an advanatage if a writer can actually write, and inspired columnists like Paul Gallico, Damon Runyon and Ring Lardner certainly could. It was one of that generation, Grantland Rice, who penned the most stirring opening lines in the history of sports writing. After Knute Rockne's backfield (this is American football) had been mainly responsible for Notre Dame's victory over all-powerful Army in 1924, Rice began:

> Outlined against a blue-grey October sky, the Four Horsemen rode again. In dramatic lore they are known as Famine, Pestilence, Destruction and Death. These are only aliases. Their real names are Stuhldreher, Miller, Crowley and Layden. [4]

Transposed to a cold Cardiff December afternoon in 1905, the Welsh three-quarter line of Morgan, Gabe, Nicholls and Llewellyn does not have quite the same resonance. For all that, the tone of a number of pieces in this book will strike the more fastidious reader as being uneasily poised somewhere between history and journalism. They first appeared within the last decade in learned journals, a county history, and various compendia of essays, all written from the conviction that sport is historically important and that it is incumbent upon professional scholars to communicate their findings, formulations and conclusions to as wide and intelligent a readership as possible. Sports history ought to be sober and serious, but it need not be solemn or soporific.

It is, then, only within the last twenty years or so that the gap has narrowed between the increase in the social significance of sport and its historical coverage. There has long been, in Britain, historical writing, of a kind, about sport that was colourful and descriptive, but which fails entirely to relate sport to those economic forces, political structures and social influences which are the preoccupations of the professional historian. It can often be blurred in focus, and lax in critical judgment. Equally, for too long there was no countervailing recognition from the academic side that sport might furnish insights into social patterns, cultural values and economic conditions. This reluctance on the part of historians to recognize the history of sport as an integral part of social and cultural history, and therefore a legitimate subject for scholarly inquiry, arose partly from a misplaced intellectual disdain, partly from an equally mistaken belief that institutions and expressions of mass culture are sufficiently well-understood by the people who participate in them, and partly from the delusion that strenuous research in this particular field might add to the sum of knowledge but do little to further historical understanding.

It was the 1960's, a pivotal decade in so many ways, which saw the rediscovery of social history and stimulated a new awareness of its totalizing potential. Following the trail blazed by pioneer scholars like Christopher Hill, Eric Hobsbawm and E.P. Thompson, other pathfinders began to open up tracts of unexplored, often previously invisible territory. The excavation of everyday life in the past meant that sport, like popular culture generally, would eventually find its historians. It may be that one of the unintended consequences of the new interest was a tendency to view mass culture as an agency of social control, an exercise in manipulation by a ruling class who set the rules of the game (see chapter 4); but at least the subject became a legitimate topic for analysis, research and debate. At the same time, in the sixties and early seventies a new generation of scholars entered academic life from a wide range of social backgrounds who, brought up in the post-war enthusiasm for sport and reared on a diet of commercialised mass entertainment, found it difficult to accept that the *Oxford History of England* could mention Arnold Bennett and G.K. Chesterton, but not Marie Lloyd, brass bands or the Cup Final. [5]

The shift away from the amiably anecdotal (when it was not stupefyingly statistical) kind of sports writing on the one hand, and the restrictive academic approach on the other, could be discerned in the work of Brailsford, Walvin and Vamplew in the late sixties and seventies, [6] but the critical breakthrough came with the appearance in 1980 of Tony Mason's inspired *Association Football and English Society 1863-1915*, a pioneering study which explored hitherto unstudied areas like the background and living standards of the players, the composition of the crowds, and the economic structure of the clubs; in other words, who played, who watched and who controlled the people's game. Hot on the heels of Mason's book came *Fields of Praise* which I wrote with David Smith in response to the Welsh

Rugby Union's imaginative commission to produce an official history that would 'attach itself to the social, industrial and religious life of Wales'[7] and which eventually turned out to be as much an orthodox institutional history as *Moby Dick* is a book about a whale.

More studies appeared which were similarly concerned to identify socio-economic factors influencing the way in which sport developed and in what respects these new forms of leisure reflected both continuity and change, a theme which in the context of the former unitary county of Glamorgan is the subject of chapter 6. In his innovative *Sport and Society in Modern France* (1981), Richard Holt wrote as follows:

> The speed with which traditional patterns of amusement were replaced by new sports in the last decades of the nineteenth century was remarkable, though quite in keeping with the pace of social change as a whole. Within twenty years rugby, which had been the elite preserve of polite schoolboys, had become the collective winter passion of half the Midi. (p. 4)

He could have been writing about late-Victorian Wales. Similarly the focus of Steven A. Riess' *Touching Base* might also have been Welsh rugby rather than American baseball, an instrument of social integration in, especially, migrant-dominated small town communities, and a sport increasingly projected as the national game, a patriotic pastime that 'touched base' with the prevailing attitudes, beliefs and values of Progressive America.[8] Sports whose recent origins were embellished with spurious historical antecedents contributed to the way in which nations imagined themselves: that process of ideological engineering by which the new, generally nineteenth century, constructs of 'nations' homogenized their heterogeneous components and persuaded their members into unity.[9] The critical role of sport in the social construction of a Welsh national identity is examined in chapter 4, and its Welsh version, chapter 5.

The recent appearance of Richard Holt's 'modern history' *Sport and the British* (1989) and the launching of a series of *International Studies in the History of Sport* under the general

editorship of J.A. Mangan, confirm that it is a good time to be a
sports historian. One of those studies concludes that 'the football grounds of England were the Labour Party at prayer'.[10] The
rugby grounds of Wales have never been too accommodating to
the   prayer-mats   of   political   nationalists,   for   all   the
much-canvassed view that rugby is the only real popular
manifestation of Welsh self-consciousness. This common
belief persuaded a man who was 'a strong enemy of Welshness'
in Gwyn Thomas's Rhondda to start a soccer team:

> 'Rugby players tend to talk Welsh' he said. 'I don't want
> them. The oval ball is the symbol of deviousness. A round
> candid ball and no pawing of bodies, that's the honest
> English way'.[11]

He was wrong though: rugby started in England, which is
where Chapter 2 also begins. Moreover, 'the honest *Welsh*
way', if there is one, requires that I include some material that
reflects the awkward fact that the dragon has two tongues.
Welsh rugby has always been for me, as for thousands of others,
a bilingual experience.

Non-Welsh readers who may feel aggrieved that one-fifth of
this book is in a language they cannot understand can be
assured that chapter 5 is in its argument and much of its detail
exactly that of the preceding chapter; the only difference is that
I have been able to quote from primary scources, especially the
Welsh-language Nonconformist press, in the original. Chapter
9, also in Welsh and written for younger readers, consists of
pen-portraits of some of the high priests of a game that is
occasionally claimed to be a second religion. The Welsh have
always known the difference between a religion and a recreation. But for those who still find the metaphor meaningful and
cling to the idea of the National Ground as some kind of holy
space sacralized by the attitude of fans to whom the players
appear as priests in a liturgy, chapter 3 traces the pre-history of
the shrine that is Cardiff Arms Park.

The book ends with an anthology of reviews and shorter
pieces culled from a variety of places. It may be objected that
only someone of great eminence should permit himself such
self-indulgence. Eminent I am not, but Gerald Davies most

certainly is. I am delighted and privileged that he has agreed to contribute a Foreword to this book. If I have required an Introduction, he needs none.

NOTES

[1] Eugen Weber, 'Gymnastics and Sport in Fin-de-Siècle France'. *American Historical Review*, vol. 76, 1971, p. 70. For the belated entry of French historians into the sports arena see footnote 68 of Chapter 3 below.

[2] Joseph Strutt, *The Sports and Pastimes of the People of England* (1801), 1838 ed., p. xvii.

[3] For some observations on the social theory and sociology of sport from Emile Durkheim to Eric Dunning, see Tony Mason (ed.) *Sport in Britain* (Cambridge, 1989) pp. 344-49, and Richard Holt, *Sport and the British: A Modern History* (Oxford, 1989) pp. 357-67.

[4] *New York Herald Tribune*, 19 October 1924, quoted in Benjamin G. Rader, *American Sports: from the age of folk games to the age of spectators* (Englewood Cliffs, N.J., 1983) p. 199.

[5] It was Eric Hobsbawm who made this point with characteristic prescience in Francis Newton (i.e. Eric Hobsbawm), *The Jazz Age* (1956) 1989 ed., p. 7.

[6] Dennis Brailsford, *Sport and Society: from Elizabeth to Anne* (1969); James Walvin, *The People's Game* (1975); Wray Vamplew, *The Turf: a Social and Economic History of Horse Racing* (1976).

[7] Hermas Evans' Foreword to David Smith and Gareth Williams, *Fields of Praise: The Official History of the Welsh Rugby Union 1881-1981* (Cardiff, 1980), p. v. The social history of rugby union in England awaits its historian, but a start has been made by a Canadian scholar, James W. Martens, 'Rugby Union Football and English Society 1871-1914' (University of Manitoba Ph.D. thesis, 1988).

[8] Steven A. Riess, *Touching Base: Professional Baseball and American Culture in the Progressive Era* (Westport, Conn.; 1980).

[9] E.J. Hobsbawm and T.O. Ranger (eds.), *The Invention of Tradition* (Cambridge, 1983); E.J. Hobsbawm, *Nations and Nationalism since 1780: programme, myth, reality* (Cambridge, 1990).

[10] N. Fishwick, *English Football and Society 1910-1950* (Manchester, 1989) p. 150.

[11] Gwyn Thomas, *High on Hope* (Cowbridge, 1985), p. 24.

CHAPTER 2

FROM WILLIAM WEBB ELLIS TO WORLD CUP — THE SOCIAL HISTORY OF RUGBY UNION

1

> I remember William Webb Ellis perfectly. He was . . . gener-
> ally regarded as inclined to take unfair advantages at football.
> Rev. Thomas Harris, a Rugby School contemporary of Ellis, quoted in
> *The Origin of Rugby Football* (Rugby, 1897), p. 21.

The commemorative tablet erected at Rugby School in February 1900 in honour of William Webb Ellis, who in 1823 'first took the ball in his arms and ran with it, thus originating the distinctive feature of the rugby game', tells us more about the late-Victorian mind than it does about the early nineteenth-century beginnings of rugby football.

Ellis's piece of inspired illegality was first resurrected during a flurry of public correspondence between various Old Rugbei-ans in the wake of the formation of the Rugby Football Union in 1871. By the 1890s there were sound reasons for wanting to explain the birth of rugby in this way, especially for old boys—in both senses—who viewed the abolition in 1871 of 'hacking' (the vigorous and apparently character-building kicking of an opponent's shins) as a collective bereavement and who felt aggrieved at the diluting of their manly, mauling game by the effete innovation of passing; after all, no one recalled Ellis actually having *passed* the ball. Their suspicions that the drift towards a more open, faster spectacle would encourage entertaining the gallery rather than playing the game for itself were confirmed when its popularity among the working classes of the industrial north provoked a major crisis in the ranks of the RFU, culminating in the breakaway of half the clubs in it to form the Northern Union in 1895. To memorialise W.W. Ellis, therefore, was to reassert the game's public school amateur origins, and to perpetuate an act of creationism reassuring to an

William Webb Ellis, (1807-72).

age that found a Carlylean 'great man' theory of history more to its taste than Darwinian evolution.[1]

In truth, it took several decades for rugby to evolve from diverse forms of public school football, via the so-called 'Camgridge Rules', the FA rules of 1863 and the RFU's counter-proposals of 1871, into the recognisably modern game of the 1890s. It is also difficult to deny the sociologists Dunning and Sheard's argument that it is 'just not ... plausible that a deeply

entrenched traditional game could have been changed fund-
amentally by a single act', and even more implausible that the
deviant action of a low status day-boy should have been
regarded as commendable rather than punishable. They follow
through with a most cogent case for seeing rugby's separate
development as the byproduct of a conflict between established
and ascendent classes in the public schools. Older, impeccably
aristocratic establishments like Eton, Winchester, Harrow and
Shrewsbury could adopt a 'new' form of popular street football
with impunity, but the headmasters of more recent foundations like Cheltenham, Marlborough, Wellington, Clifton
and Haileybury, as well as re-endowed old grammar schools
like Sherborne, Sedbergh and Tonbridge opted for the game
they themselves had learned as masters or pupils at Arnold's
Rugby, a school like theirs that had come into existence to cater
for a thrusting industrial and commercial middle class anxious
to put as much distance as possible between themselves and the
lower orders from which they might be thought to have
sprung.[2]

The origins of rugby, as of associated football and most of the
other organised sports of Victorian England, lay in the reform of
the public schools. The cults of athleticism and muscular
Christianity acquired a greater seriousness in the face of foreign
threats to England's colonial and commercial dominance.
What J.A. Mangan has dubbed the 'precarious fusion' of Christian gentility and social Darwinism produced a games-field
rhetoric, 'a frame of reference and a rationale for action . . . for
generations of public schoolboys'.[3]

The RFU was summoned into existence in 1871 out of an
urgent desire to rescue the game of rugby from the confusion of
unregulated modes of play into which it was slipping. The FA
was formed in 1863 and the association game was growing in
popularity: it was no coincidence that the RFU was established in the same year as the inaugural FA Challenge Cup
Final. The Rugby School influence was pervasive in the early
years: the RFU's first five presidents, the first captain of
England, and seven of the 15 who constituted the RFU's first
committee were all Old Rugbeians. There were 16 Rugbeians in
the first Oxford XX of 1872, and 10 in the first English side of the

previous year. The old boy network has always counted for a lot in English rugby because that is how it started.

What made the necessity for a unified code of rules even more pressing was the diffusion of the game from the schools and universities to wider society. The mechanics of the process of dissemination are not too hard to envisage. There is a Webb Ellis-like implausibility in the popular picture of clubs springing up overnight once the son of the local squire or factory-owner brought home from his public school an oval ball. Yet something not too dissimilar must have happened when several old boys of the same school living and working in fairly close proximity to each other wished to continue playing the game they had known at school. Old Rugbeians in mid-century Liverpool first selected teams from among themselves on an alphabetic basis, A to M versus N to Z, or by matching the Football Club against the Boat Club. When in 1857 the Gentlemen of Liverpool met the Gentlemen of Manchester at Edge Hill, it was advertised as 'Rugby versus the World'. The social composition of Manchester FC, founded that year, is instructive. Its early players were products of Rugby, Manchester Grammar School, Uppingham, Edinburgh Academy, Fettes, Cheltenham and Oxbridge colleges. Several went on to be capped and they stimulated enough local interest to justify holding seven international matches at their Whalley Range ground between 1880, when the England v. Scotland match drew 8,000 spectators, and 1892. The club, though, was socially 'closed'. The annual subscription was fixed at 10s. 6d. in 1886, when a skilled workman's average weekly wage in Lancashire was 33s. 6d.; the distinction between 'the old nobility' and lesser mortals was expressed in differentiated membership fees and separate stands. It was this social exclusiveness that enabled soccer, which arrived later, to become the popular game in Manchester.[4]

All the nothern clubs had respectable origins. York FC was founded in 1868 by ex-pupils of St Peter's School, Leigh (1877) by a local surveyor, St Helens three years earlier by an industrial chemist at Pilkingtons. Hull was formed in 1865 by the head of a shipping company, a wine merchant, a solicitor and ex-public schoolboys from Rugby and Cheltenham; more significantly, in 1871 a plumber, a glazier and a gas fitter also became members. Rochdale had clear gentry origins in 1867 but by 1881 there were as many as 57 rugby clubs in the district, fielding 80 teams. [5]

Clubs, like the football codes themselves, were not created *ex nihilo*, they were often built on pre-existing formations like schools, churches, places of work and neighbourhoods. Just as Aston Villa, Bolton, Everton and Burnley soccer clubs were familiar offshoots of the church's missionary activity, so were Wakefield Trinity (formed in 1873 by the Young Men's Society of Holy Trinity Church) and Bramley (1879); in Leeds, where there was little soccer until the 1890s, every church had its own rugby club, Leeds St John (1870) actually confining its membership to the church class. Headingley, after a faltering start, was revived in the mid-1880s by Headingley Hill Chapel's Sunday Class. [6]

Nor was this a northern peculiarity. Northampton's sobriquet 'the Saints' dates from the original name of Northampton St James (1873); in the West Country, Newlyn owed its existence to a literary and debating society steered by a local vicar. In the Scottish Borders the Rev Dr James Barclay introduced the game 'to retard the drinking habits of the Canonbie colliers', while examples from Wales might include the Merthyr combinations Penydarren Church Juniors and Dowlais St Illtyd's, and Llanelli's St Peter's Stars and St Paul's United. Places of employment, too, generated their own teams. Camborne (1878) owed its playing strength to the tin workers of the Dolcoath mine, the largest in Cornwall, with some assistance from the ex-public school trainees of the Camborne School of Mines. Pontypridd Chainworks Crusaders and Llanelli's Wern Foundry and Copper Mills Rangers are Welsh examples of works teams. As for neighbourhood or street sides, 'Tinopolis's Prospect Place Rovers and Gilbert Place Rangers could be matched from across the Bristol Channel by Bridgwater's Barclay Street Hornets, Albert Street Dreadnoughts and Bristol Road Rovers. [7]

Finding a permanent field to play on, however, could be a problem even to more formally organised clubs. Coventry lived a nomadic existence from its foundation in 1873 until it acquired the Coundon Road ground, its sixth, in 1916, while a metropolitan side like Wasps, ever-prey to voracious land developers, were forced to move five times in 12 seasons during the 1890s. By contrast Redruth, formed in 1895 on the initiative of some old Marlburians and Cliftonians in concert with the usual assortment of local petty bourgeoisie, managed to secure support, and a ground, from the Redruth Brewery Company. Patronage from this source was reminiscent of the traditional involvement of the drink trade in public amusements, while prominent local landowners and industrialists were similarly pleased to extend their patronage, from motives as diverse as family tradition, civic pride, personal gratification, and even something as uncomplicated as a love of the game.

A common solution to the problem of finding somewhere to play was to put the facilities of an existing cricket club to wider use. Like Derby County, Preston North End and other soccer teams, many rugby clubs had their beginnings in the desire of cricketers to extend their summer association into the winter. Bradford (1868), Wigan (1876) and Oldham (1876) in the north, Moseley and Coventry (both 1873) in the midlands, and Rosslyn Park (1879) in the south, as well as Swansea (1874) and Cardiff (1876), playing on the park behind the Cardiff Arms in Wales, and Gala (1876) in Scotland, all began as cricket clubs. In Belfast, the North of Ireland CC was persuaded by some of its ex-Cheltenham and Marlborough members to play 'football according to the Rugby rules' between cricket seasons, and NIFC came into existence in 1868.[8]

II

From Hell, Hull and Halifax, good Lord deliver us.

Old proverb

The rugby rules underwent a series of modifications throughout the 1870s. Partly from increasing player frustration at a static game of five-minute mauls (ironically, the initial effect of the abolition of hacking was to prolong mass scrummaging), partly through spectator demand for greater entertainment, modes of playing and scoring evolved which made for a more open game. By the late 1870s forwards were expected to heel the ball back and it was to give backs more of the ball and more room to run with it that in 1877 the number of players on each side was reduced to 15 and the forwards whittled down from 10 to 8 by the 1890s. A faster game called for more combination among both backs and forwards and provided for the display of individual skill. With the introduction of a points system of scoring in 1886, standardised throughout the four home countries in 1894, the try began its long march from being merely a preliminary to the more valuable kick at goal, to being equivalent and eventually superior to the conversion. Deciding the outcome of games by points not only simplified the task of keeping score; it also separated winners from losers.

It was the high priority accorded to winning that gave northern, and soon Welsh, rugby its special flavour. As clubs proliferated in the industrial north, to become foci of communal identity and collective achievement, the establishing of the Yorkshire Challenge Cup in 1877 set an example which by 1882 the other northern counties had followed, except Lancashire whose more socially exclusive clubs were averse to this kind of competition. Teams returning with local, district or county trophies were greeted with torchlit processions and boisterous celebrations reminiscent of the unrestrained Wakes of earlier generations—industrialisation had done little to undermine much older habits of carnival and celebration.

Keenly contested cup games also raised the standard of football played, the perfecting of techniques and the elaboration of moves. Strong running centre three-quarters like Bradford's Rawson Robertshaw cultivated the art of carving openings for their wings, and powerfully-built athletic artisan forwards mastered the science of smart footwork, of wheeling the scrum and heeling the ball or dribbling it through in a controlled footrush, a speciality of the great Bradford and then Newport sides of the 1880s and 1890s. Although there were no northerners in the English XXs of the early 1870s, there were eleven of them in the England XV that beat Wales in 1892. [9]

Increasingly, seriousness of purpose allied to working-class strength and stamina saw northern sides inflicting consistent defeats on their southern opponents. Once the Rugby Union's county championship was established in 1888, Yorkshire won it for seven of the first eight seasons. By 1890 the county's affiliated 150 clubs constituted almost half the membership of the RFU. The social complexion of northern rugby was different from its southern counterpart dominated by ex-public schoolboys from the professions, occupationally far removed from industry and unsympathetic to it. The northern game was controlled by self-made men in manufacturing and commerce, who came into frequent contact with their employees and shared their enthusiasm for the Saturday afternoon's activities.

Northern rugby, in addition, was a mass spectator sport. In 1891 23,000 watched Yorkshire play Lancashire at Huddersfield; between 1888 and 1893 the Yorkshire Cup Final attracted on average crowds of over 15,000; in 1893 even a third-round cup-tie drew 27,600 to Headingley, more than had watched the FA Cup Final the previous year. Large crowds brought increased gate money, which might be spent on improving facilities to accommodate yet more spectators, or on making it worthwhile for clubs to induce players to forego a day's work in order to play.

Such tendencies were viewed with deep misgivings among the southern-based RFU , whose committee shared the distrust of their class for big crowds, especially working-class crowds, at a time of growing industrial unrest. Cup competitiveness exerted little appeal in the south. When in 1894 the idea was mooted for Middlesex, only seven entries were received. In the north it was too deeply entrenched to be resisted, but a further acitvely canvassed proposal to form a northern 'alliance' or league of first-class clubs was rejected, on the grounds that this would enhance the priority accorded to commercial considerations and further erode cherished amateur values. Had not the founding of the Football League in 1888 both legitimised and encouraged professionalism? At the RFU's annual meeting in September 1893 a Yorkshire proposal 'that players be allowed compensation for *bona fide* loss of ·time' was defeated. In August 1895 22 clubs seceded from the RFU to form the Northern Union. By 1898 they numbered 98.[19]

The consequences of 'the Great Schism' were profound. The RFU's intransigence preserved its middle-class ethos intact, but at some cost. It crippled itself numerically and financially. By 1903 the 481 member clubs of 1892 had fallen to 244 and not until the 1920s, a decade of triumphant amateurism, was the 1893 figure re-attained. As for Yorkshire, having won the County Championship five times consecutively between 1892 and 1896 England's largest county did not win it again until 1926; Lancashire, the 1891 champions, not until 1935. And England? Their prospects were dashed for nearly 20 years. The English XV did not win the international championship from 1892 to 1910.[11] The power in the land in these years was Wales.

III

> But Cyfarthfa is like a fisherman's net. The fly [-half] has been too clever. He should have passed to his wing long ago, but he is greedy and wants the try himself, and on he goes, tries to sell a dummy, and how the crowd is laughing, for to sell a dummy to Cyfarthfa is to sell poison to a Borgia.
> Richard Llewellyn, *How Green Was My Valley* (1939), ch. 24

It was from England that rugby arrived in Wales, where a centuries-long tradition of festive, unregulated football began to give way from the mid-nineteeth century to the new sports emanating from the recently-formed colleges and revived grammar schools of Lampeter, Llandovery, Cowbridge, Brecon and Monmouth. Old Rugbeians, it is true, were responsible for getting the game established in Llanelli (1875) but the origins of other clubs lay closer: Llandoverians figure prominently in the early history of Neath (1871) and Monmouthians in Newport's (1874).[12]

The spread of the game in Wales depended on two other factors. One was the support of that predictable cluster of upwardly mobile young professional men—solicitors, surveyors, small businessmen and building contractors—who, though constituting still only 3 per cent of the population of Wales as late as 1911, would retain a firm grasp on the running of its rugby. Even in Wales it never became the people's game in the sense of their achieving control over it. In this respect the Welsh experience was no different from that of England.

In the second respect it was crucially different, for the arrival of rugby coincided with the climax of the penetration of South Wales by industrial capitalism. The existing population was quite unable to generate the labour power necessary to meet the growing demand for Welsh steam-raising coal, and the consequent high wage-levels attracted enormous migration into the coalfield, the metal-working centres and the ports. By 1911, when the population of Wales had increased by nearly a million since 1871, one in every three occupied males was a miner, 256,000 of them, concentrated in the southern industrial belt. Nothing has more influencd the outlook and character of Welsh society, making it significantly different from that of the large urban areas of England like Merseyside or Birmingham, than this dependence on the primary production of coal. The observer who drily remarked in 1923 that 'they know all about mining in Wales and they apply their knowledge of it to Rugby Football' was nearer the truth than he knew.[13]

Rugby's arrival in Wales in the 1870s predated that of soccer by 20 years. It met significant needs. It provided dramatic excitement and aesthetic satisfaction. In its appeal to a sense of shared ritual it fulfilled a valuable bonding function; it flourished both as a relief from and an analogue to the work experience, complementing as much as compensating for the sinking of the individual in the collective. At the same time, the aspiring commercial middle class who via the Welsh Rugby Union (1881) sought to control its breakneck growth were able to annex the responsible upper end of the working class as a wedge against the dissolute lumpenproletariat. The game was valued too as a focus for local and communal identity, a prized commodity in the ribbon-developed valleys which lacked appropriate civic foci. But we should never lose sight of the central appeal for an industrial population of a physically vigorous spectator sport: its theatricality, its opportunity for self-expression as well as for entertainment, its affirmation of life after work, of a sense of wholeness denied elsewhere.

What it did not do was instil in the crowd sporting habits or a devotion to clean living, any more than it civilised them or quelled their industrial militancy. It was less an agent of change than of continuity. The public house, for instance, always the favourite milieu of the sporting and sociable, effortlessly adapted itself to new conditions by providing changing rooms, committee facilities, even an early results service. Until they acquired their own premises well into the next century, Pont-ypridd rugby club was based at the White Hart, Rhymney at the Tredegar Arms, Penygraig at the Butcher's and Gowerton at the Commercial. One Merthyr hostelry even ran its own side, the Cyfarthfa Old Ship Rovers.

Proliferating cup competitions, in South Wales as in the north of England, honed local rivalries to a keen edge. The cup-tie between Bridgend and Neath in 1880 was the occasion for 'semi-savagery' and 'wanton biting'; the Llanelli team at Neath in 1883 'were left to the tender mercies of an infuriated mob and had almost to fight their way to the hotel . . . they were hustled and pushed, hooted and pelted with clods, mud and even stones'. Between 1895 and 1900 Neath, Aberavon, Abertillery, Llanelli and Cardiff were among the leading clubs whose grounds were suspended because of rioting spectators. The game was as violent as the society that sustained it. Ferndale's game with Mountain Ash in 1897 was reckoned to be 'a blood bath'. During their traditional Boxing Day derby with neigh-bouring Dowlais that season, 'most of the Merthyr players were maimed'. Little wonder that the first of a local paper's 'Hints for rugby players' at this time was 'Hint 1: Make your will'.[14]

From an early date Welsh rugby was watched by larger numbers of spectators than anywhere outside the North of England. In 1893-4 when 1,000 watched the Scotland v. England international at Raeburn Place, 20,000 saw Cardiff's club matches with Newport and Swansea. The lustrous Swansea side of the early 1900s regularly drew crowds of 20,000 home and away. Welsh clubs also tended to add several thousand to away gates. In 1903 Bristol's steady 5,000 was increased to 8,000 for the visit of Swansea; 15,000 descended on the Devonport Albion ground to watch them in 1904. Receipts were correspondingly larger for Welsh games too. In 1890-1 Coventry's takings were £113 when Cardiff's were £1,233; by 1893-4 Cardiff's gate-money totalled £2,478, while Rosslyn Park's was £2. 5s. 3d. In Wales they charged less and still did better. In 1905 12,000 spectators at Mardyke, Cork, paid £900 to watch Ireland play England, while 40,000 paid £2,000 to see the Irish at Swansea.[15]

Visits from crack northern sides like Dewsbury, Wakefield Trinity and Batley were being reciprocated by Welsh clubs from the mid-1880s, but the distance involved militated against frequent fixtures. Much nearer was English rugby's second heartland, a swathe reaching from the south midlands around the Severn Estuary into Somerset and Devon. The rugby links that were early on forged between the West Country and Welsh clubs anxious to prove themselves against good but also accessible opponents were reinforced by the thousands of immigrants from the metal and coal-mining areas of Somerset and the Forest of Dean, and by the incoming agricultural workers of the western counties attracted by the favourable wages of the Welsh coalfield. Some of the most renowned Welsh players of the period 1890-1914 were West Countrymen by birth. The Hancock brewing family from Wiveliscombe in Somerset, having identified the existence of a large thirst on the other side of the Bristol Channel, in 1883 moved to Cardiff to slake it. In 1884 Frank Hancock played a key role in the Cardiff rugby club's historic decision to field four threequarters and reduce the number of forwards to eight. By 1890 the other countries had also embraced the revolutionary 'Welsh system', a concept as enterprising and innovative as the brash, new, self-confident society that invented it. One of the greatest exponents of the four threequarter system, Cardiff's Gwyn Nicholls, captain of the famous Welsh side of 1905, was born in Gloucestershire.

Chronological priority can play as significant a role as geographical accident in determining cultural preference. Association football, based in northeast Wales near the soccer-playing conurbations of Merseyside and Manchester, began making inroads into South Wales only in the late 1890s. Billy Meredith as yet meant little to South Wales crowds. The name they conjured with was that of Newport's handsome, charismatic Arthur Gould, even to Yorkshire's Frank Marshall in 1893 'the central figure in the football world . . . the greatest centre threequarter that has ever played'. In 1897 Gould, who had by then won more caps, scored more points and kicked more goals than any other player in the game, by his brilliance provoked a crisis as potentially destructive as that of 1893 over broken time. The International Rugby Board, founded by representatives of the four home countries in 1884 but at this stage virtually a puppet of the RFU, sought to expel Wales from the rugby community in 1897 for sanctioning a testimonial organised by Gould's countless admirers. The WRU stood its ground and the RFU was soon persuaded by its own clubs, who resented being deprived of their lucrative Welsh fixtures, to urge the restoration of Wales to the international fold in 1898.

For their part, the middle-class controllers of the game in Wales were equally firmly resolved to resist outright professionalism. They were, however, prepared to condone a certain amount of blindside remuneration in order to maintain amateur rugby's social function in Wales as a focus for a perceived community of interest. If rugby in Wales went professional it would be consigned to being a proletarian game enjoying no more than a regional status. The long-established northern manufacturers who lost no sleep about defying what the *Wigan Observer* in 1895 called 'the thraldom of southern gentry' had a different outlook from the administrators of the Welsh game anxious to assert their national identity within a British framework and to be accepted as equals beyond Wales. To them the creation of the Northern Union provided an avenue for those who wished to play professionally to do so. The activities of 'poachers' seeking to lure players north were less welcome. In 1899 a scout from Wigan was thrown into the sea at Penarth. 'Llanelli in football', wailed a 'Scarlet' supporter in 1897, 'has been to the Northern Union what Rhayader is to Birmingham in the matter of water supply'.[16] But its northern safety valve enabled rugby in Wales to remain firmly under amateur control.

It became indissolubly wedded to ideas of Welsh nationality in the wake of the events of a Saturday afternoon in December

1905, during Edwardian Wales's high noon of optimism and prosperity. The epic nature of that day's encounter is only partially explained in terms of the virtual invincibility of the two sides contending for what a contemporary New Zealand journalist called 'the world's championship in rugby'. Wales, riding the crest of a Golden Era which saw them win six Triple Crowns between 1900 and 1911, had just won their third Triple Crown in five years, while the All Blacks had swept through England, Scotland and Ireland destroying all opposition at club, county and national level, amassing over 800 points to a mere 27. Nor does its centrality pivot solely on Bob Deans' disputed try (conjured up after the match by Harmsworth's sensationalist *Daily Mail*) which, if allowed, would have deprived Wales of a 3-0 victory. It was not even that this was a victory for the kind of rugby played: the hard, unrelenting forward power in intelligent combination with brilliant back play of two smooth-running machines lubricated by well-practised tactical ploys and ruses. What the victory really indicated was a collective national achievement, and if there is any connection between sport and ideas of national character, then 1905 stands out as not merely a landmark in the history of Welsh rugby, or of rugby generally, but as a shaper of a wider set of images about the whole culture and identity of a nation.[17] That December afternoon was a moment in the cultural history of Wales.

IV

I believe that Rugby football ... is the best instrument which we possess for the development of manly character.
H.H. Almond, 'Rugby football in Scottish schools' in Rev. F. Marshall (ed.), *Football: The Rugby Union Game* (1892), p. 56.

The only country able to rival Wales's triumphant advance in the first decade of the twentieth century was Scotland, as difficult to beat at Inverleith (Murrayfield was not opened till 1925) as Wales were everywhere else. While the Scots always had exceptionally able individual players like K.M. McLeod, Mark Morrison, and 'Darkie' Bedell-Sivright, they subordinated the cult of the star performer to the thrill of the skilfully-controlled forward foot-rush. Northing was more calculated to inspire the Scots than the cry 'Feet, Scotland', though this was countered by the shout of 'Brains, Wales' at Swansea in 1900.[18]

It was the Scots, too, who were the hardiest defenders of pristine amateurism, from the Gould dispute onwards taking particular exception to the presentation of mementoes. In 1907 they refused Pontypridd permission to make a presentation to their Scottish international D.M. McGregor. When in 1912 Stade Bordelais, the French champions, advertised in a Scottish newspaper offering a good business situation to a suitable out-side-half, the SRU moved quickly to get the French authorities to impose life suspensions on the president, coach and committee of the offending club.[19]

Scottish rugby conservatism was personified by J. Aikman Smith, who served on the SRU in various capacities from 1887 to his death in 1931. Aikman Smith was a former pupil of Edinburgh's Royal High School and Scottish rugby owed its inception, and for many years its character, to the Scottish Academies whose powerful rivalries extended into senior football. The Scottish Rugby Union, founded in 1873, was established and dominated by a closely-knit group of private schools in Edinburgh like the Academy, Merchiston, Loretto and Royal High where, under the aegis of reforming head-masters like H.H. Almond of Loretto, the Rugby School game was introduced in the 1850s by teachers who had studied at English schools and universities. Almond's pronouncements tended to begin with the ominous 'All boys . . .' All boys in the school had to play rugby unless exempted by the school medical officer; all boys were to be accurately weighed and measured twice a term, for 'nothing makes a boy believe in a good physical system so soon as the increase of his measurements'.[20]

Yet it is not to brawn and bone nor to a Calvinist-induced dour streak that we need look to account for the conservatism of Scottish rugby, but to the simple fact that here was a regime where men at 30 were still playing the same opponents as when they were 15 and in school. This was bound to breed a certain resistance to change. Although the Edinburgh game spread to

Glasgow where the West of Scotland CC, former pupils of east coast schools and Glasgow Academy, began to play rugby from 1865, social exclusiveness was again rigidly safeguarded by charging high entry fees, restricting membership to products of particular schools and by careful choice of fixtures. West of Scotland and Glasgow Academicals, for instance, generally ignored requests for fixtures from new clubs, or, if such games were inadvertently arranged, turned out their second teams. Glasgow rugby remained insular, non-competitive and little publicised, 'a minority activity which confirmed and sustained a well-established, shared fellowship among a particular social grouping'.[21]

A quite different kind of atmosphere prevailed in the Borders where the game, radiating out from schools like Galashiels Academy and Kelso High, began to make serious inroads in the 1880s. While Edinburgh's sides were for former pupils in business there, in Langholm (1871), Hawick (1872), Gala (1875) and Melrose (1877) the game was played by weavers, masons and artisans who for studs barred their working boots with strips of leather from the driving belts in the local tweed mills. The small-town self-awareness of the Borders, with their historic rivalries and less marked class divisions—'it is not too much to say', reported an Edinburgh journalist in 1911, 'that all classes in Melrose from the city fathers and ministers of churches down to the humblest follower have an interest in the doings of the club'—made for communal involvement, fiercely partisan crowds and rough play. By 1890 crowds of 4,000 and upwards, drawn from a population too scattered to support professional football, congregated noisily for the visits of smart-aleck city sides who were often the recipients of excessive vigour which the SRU punished with swift disciplinary measures.[22]

The former pupils of the Scottish Union were by the beginning of the century barely able to conceal their distrust of the working man's involvement in the game. In 1903 the prominent Scottish referee Crawford Findlay expressed surprise that Wales selected miners, steelworkers and policemen for their international teams when such players should really have joined the Northern Union. It was an attitude the Borders had come to live with. Increasing dissatisfaction at the SRU's high-handedness and constant neglect of local players almost percipitated the secession of the Border clubs in the 1890s. Scotland had been playing international rugby for 20 years before Adam Dalgleish of Gala became the first Border cap, and it was another 10 before a Border player, T.M. Scott of Hawick, actually capained the national side. The establishment of the Border League in 1903, reluctantly sanctioned by the SRU, widened the cultural gap between Border and city rugby but it was intimately connected with Scotland's ability to mount a serious challenge to Welsh pre-war dominance: with the emergence of the Border international player, Scottish rugby had found its equivalent of 'the Rhondda forward'.

Another rugby stronghold characterised by the same mix of social inclusiveness and anti-urbanism was the southwest of England, where in the early years of the century thousands of excursionists travelled to see Weston, Tavistock, Bath and Bridgwater compete for the Somerset Cup, and where fighting among players and spectators was a common occurence. Further west, Plymouth Albion, already watched by crowds of 6,000 in the 1890s, could draw 19,000 on a Wednesday afternoon in 1905 for the visit of Oxford University. Clearly the extensively-covered All Blacks tour injected English rugby with new blood, and aggravated old problems. Coventry's 1906 Boxing Day match with Moseley degenerated into unlicensed mayhem between players and spectators. As the west midlands became a soccer stronghold, rugby in the east midlands built up an enduring popular base. At Leicester 16,000 watched the All Blacks and 14,000 the 1906 Springboks. Second only to Leicester for enthusiasm were Northampton's 'Saints', by the century's turn enjoying gates of 14,000 for games with their great rivals the 'Tigers', and away support, especially to London, of up to 3,000 followers.[23]

The evident spectator-orientated nature of West Country and midland rugby did not escape the vigilant eye of the player-orientated RFU. Leicester came near to being suspended for broken-time irregularities in 1908, and Coventry *were* in 1909, when a scrutiny of their account books revealed that illegal payments had been disguised as the cost of lemons and towels.

Coventry were prompty suspended and watched helplessly as they lost their ground and several players to a professional organisation that joined the Northern Union. Factors at work here were the arrival of NU players from Salford and elsewhere to work in the motor industry, and welling interest in the success of Coventry City AFC which had driven the rugby organisation to adopt protective measures of its own. The rapid incursion of Southern League football into South Wales and the West Country was similarly not unconnected to the attempt to establish professional rugby there between 1908 and 1912.[24] There was an audience for football played seriously and skilfully whatever the shape of the ball. It was amateur rugby's middle-class ideologues, and die-hards on each side, who sought to erect sectarian barriers between the various codes.

A more virulent sectarianism coloured the history of Irish rugby from the beginning. Rugby took root there as a colonial reflection of the structure and social context of the game in England. It arrived via old boys of Rugby and Cheltenham at Trinity College Dublin, notoriously the bastion of Anglo-Saxon Protestant culture, and the early members of the Irish RFU established at TCD in 1874 were mostly schools and colleges. At the end of the nineteenth century the wily Irish critic Jacques McCarthy distinguished between the three kinds of football played in Ireland as follows: 'In Rugby you play the ball, in Association you kick the man if you cannot kick the ball, and in Gaelic you kick the ball if you cannot kick the man'. In the south of Ireland rugby would always suffer from the popularity of Gaelic football, whose practitioners, according to McCarthy, 'are a free and fierce community based in Drumcondra, co. Dublin, conveniently situated between Glasnevin graveyard and the Mater Misericordia Hospital'. The Gaelic Athletic Association's foreign games ban introduced in 1886 inhibited the growth of rugby, especially in rural Ireland; 'the pseudo-Saxon game' made more headway in the towns, though only in Limerick did it acquire anything like a working-class following.[25]

A north-south division manifested itself in the organisation of Irish rugby from the outset. The North of Ireland RU founded in 1875 took almost five years to join the Dublin-based union in

1879. The game began in the north in the Protestant and Royal Schools like the Royal Belfast Academy, Portora, Londonderry Academical Institution and Magee College; and from there to the towns. Collegians (1890) were the former pupils of Belfast Methodist College, and Instonians (1919) those of the Royal Belfast Academical Institution, but rugby in that city remained socially exclusive and after the founding of the Irish FA there in 1880 soccer became Ulster's dominant game.

In some of the moderate-sized towns of the north rugby reached beyond its professional base to embrace a wider audience. Dungannon, all but one of whose side in 1873 were graduates of TCD, was well known in the 1900s for its large and partisan crowd, among the most vociferous a number of elderly ladies in shawls. Rugby could on rare occasions even transcend the religious divide, witness the triumphant homecoming in 1908 of the City of Derry team bearing the Irish Provincial Towns Cup and accompanied by a Protestant *and* Catholic flute band. For the most part the game in the north, with its segregated school system and an embattled Catholic community unable to afford the same ambiguity in its sporting affiliations as the professional classes in the Republic, was and remains almost exclusively a middle-class, Anglophile, Protestant activity.[26]

The history of rugby in Northern Ireland, therefore, like most aspects of life there, can scarcely be understood without reference to its political context. Thus, while rugby on the mainland came to a halt just as the 1914-15 season was about to begin, in Ulster the Home Rule crisis had already brought sporting activity to a standstill nine months earlier. In December 1913, NIFC decided 'that in view of the political crisis all matches for the second half of the season should be cancelled so that members who are identified with the Ulster Volunteer Force and the Unionist Clubs might have more leisure to devote themselves to the work of drilling and otherwise preparing for eventualities'. All fixtures were cancelled from 14 January 1914 and 'North's' Ormeau ground given over to the UVF.[27]

By August 1914 even wider issues were at stake, though not to the Irish: Kevin Barry of UCD Rugby Club and Frederick

Browning, President of the IRFU, were both killed during the Easter Rebellion. In Britain the national unions sent out circulars urging all their members to join up. The WRU insured itself against defeat home and away: 'If only every man in every first XV in Wales were to enlist, what a magnificent body there would be at the service of our country and even then there would still be plenty of players left to enable the game to be played as usual'.[28]

Clubs up and down the country surrendered their grounds for recruiting, drilling and other military purposes, and there was no shortage of volunteers. Seven junior clubs in the Llanelli district provided more than 400 men, the Keswick XV presented themselves at their Drill Hall as one body. Leicester's formidable secretary-manager Tom Crumbie personally recruited 4,500, and the WRU's secretary, Walter Rees, was given the title of Captain for his domestic wartime efforts. Rugby was seen by its own as setting a patriotic example that 'others'—meaning the soccer fraternity—might have done better to emulate.[29]

'If the first 100,000 British soldiers in the war had not been sportsmen', asserted a speaker at Bath FC's Golden Jubilee dinner (an event postponed from 1915 to 1919) 'they would not have known how to take defeat and eventually turn back the Germans'. The classic equation between war and sport, familiarly expressed in Newbolt's 'Vitaï Lampada' of 1898, with its juxtaposition of the bumping pitch and the jammed Gatling, reached its apotheosis in the hideous carnage of the Western Front. The English fondness for football was seen as an element in their superiority over the Germans. Two years into the war an Old Malvernian took issue in his school magazine with a suggestion that the school give up rugby: 'Rugger must stay', he protested. 'What a confession of weakness to give it up now'. His letter was dated: The Somme, 1 November 1916.[30] A well-attested expression of the sporting spirit was to kick a football towards the enemy lines and follow it. The annual Mobbs Memorial match between the East Midlands and the Barbarians was inaugurated in 1921 to commemorate Edgar Mobbs of Northampton and England who used to lead his men into attack by punting a rugby ball into No Man's Land and following it up.

This 'preposterous act of bravado', in Paul Fussell's words, terminated his life at Passchendaele at 34 years of age. [31]

Rugby football even had its own Rupert Brooke (himself an old Rugbeian in Ronald Poulton (-Palmer), educated at Rugby and Balliol and holder of 17 caps for England. He scored five tries in his first Varsity match in 1909 and four in his last international appearance in 1914, the year he inherited the Huntley and Palmer biscuit fortune, provided he added the name Palmer to Poulton. This done he joined the 4th Royal Berkshires and was hit by a sniper's bullet in Belgium at 25 years of age in 1915. The flagrant good looks of 'the wondrous Poulton, the fleet and flaxen' seemed an inseparable element of his sporting achievement and he was sonorously lamented in similar terms to Brooke as a Newboltian hero, a 'golden-haired Apollo' who 'stood as a symbol of the heart of England . . . of the golden young men who died faithfully and fearlessly in a war where much that was of value beyond price in an imperfect world perished too'. [32] He was one of 27 English internationals killed, as well as 30 Scottish, 13 Welsh and 9 Irish, excluding those who died of their war injuries later. Bristol, who like many other clubs built a Memorial Ground after the war in tribute 'to those who played the Great Game during season 1914-18', lost 300 players and members; Headingley lost a quarter of its membership. Of the 60 players who turned out in the four teams fielded by London Scottish on the last Saturday of the 1913-14 season, 45 were killed. [33]

V

A man who kicks another intentionally is a blackguard and a coward. Recently a well-known International . . . said that a gentleman kicks another with his instep instead of with the toe of the boot. Personally I think no gentleman ever kicks another.

I.M.B. Stuart, *The Theory of Modern Rugby Football* (1930), pp. 3-4

The sanctimonious tendency to portray rugby's amateurs, who in 1914 had flocked unselfishly to the colours, as more patriotic than soccer's paid professionals, who in 1915 had to be reminded of their duty, was a factor in the pronounced post-war swing towards rugby among 'good' schools and those that aspired to be thought of as such. For a diversity of reasons—disdain for the 'pools and Woodbine' image of professional soccer, desire to revive the public-school ethos, the anxieties aroused by post-war militancy and the perceived 'character-building' quality of the Union game—soccer-playing schools moved over in droves to rugby and to the higher social cachet it brought with it. The drift anticipated from 1910 by Radley, Rossall, Emmanuel and Pocklington soon became a stampede among minor public and socially-ambitious grammar schools: a sample would include Beaumont College (1917), Felstead (1919), Worksop, Wrekin and King's Worcester (1921), Manchester GS (1922), Framlingham and Ipswich (1924), Colchester RGS (1926), Magdalen CS and Wycliffe (1928). This shift took place to a rising accompaniment of literary affectation celebrating 'the rugby spirit'. Public-school fiction, like English rugby whose virtues it extolled, revived in popularity, espcially the late Victorian stories of Talbot Baines Reed, who had regaled *Boy's Own Paper* readers with tales of the Cock House of Fellsgarth: 'Well played indeed, Corder!' cried his captain to the scholarship boy who had just scored the winning try and put the snobs to shame. 'Oh what music is the sound. What would he dare not now!' [35]

Nor was there any lack of practical advice as to how rugger should be played by these post-war Corinthians. Among the precepts listed by a widely-read 1922 compendium of rugby hints were 'Never dispute the referee's decision', and 'Keep your mouth shut: all good athletes breathe through their nostrils'. *A Manual of Rugby Football for Public Schools* that appeared in 1925 addressed itself to graver issues: 'Nothing looks worse than a player to have his stockings about his ankles, and it certainly takes yards off his pace. No player who is too slack to go to the trouble of finding a pair of garters is worth his place in any team'. [35]

During the 1920s English rugby enjoyed a period of prolonged success, as if it were actually thriving on its middle-class tennis-and-golf image of suburban sporting gentility. This decade saw the number of clubs in membership of the RFU increase at the fastest rate in its history, with 231 new clubs becoming affiliated to it as opposed to 45 in the years 1901-9. These years too saw the proportion of public-school educated players in the English side at its highest: 572, compared with 422 for 1902-11 and 262 for 1962-71.[36] England won the Triple Crown four times in the 1920s and another twice in the 1930s. Self-confidence expressed itself in a number of tactical innovations centred particularly on the back-row of the scrum from where W.W. Wakefield led the side in robust fashion. Enormous crowds filled Twickenham on international days. While a modest 18,000 had been present for England's opening game there in 1910, 49,000 watched the Calcutta Cup match of 1924, and 73,000 the England v. New Zealand game in 1936. During the inter-war period big matches at Twickenham were social occasions for 'the grand assembly of the Forsyte commonwealth, the parade of the self-possessive class'.[37]

The distinctive feature of the Twickenham crowd, in rugby terms, was its ignorance. It attracted, as it still does and in far greater numbers than other major grounds, thousands of people apparently willing to shout themselves hoarse at what they would not cross the road to see at their local recreation ground. In A.G. Macdonell's satirical *England, Their England* (1933)—it is noticeable how in the inter-war period rugby began to acquire something of the literary status already gained by cricket—Donald attends the 1930 Varsity Match along with 65,000 others 'of whom about 30,000 appeared to be young men, 30,000 young women, and 5,000 parsons'. In the train afterwards there were two schools of opinion, one believing that Cambridge had won 19-6, the other that Oxford had, by either 15-0 or 24-0. Only the evening paper settled the matter: the game had been a 3-3 draw.[38]

As a success symbol Twickenham was rivalled only by Murrayfield, opened in 1925 with a capacity of 80,000. Scotland won three Triple Crowns and won or shared five championships between the wars, while the official mind of Scottish rugby remained as fearful of change as ever. Since 1927 Wales and England had worn numbered jerseys, but the SRU would have none of it. When George V mildly inquired at Twickenham in 1928 why the Scots did not similarly identify their players, Aikman Smith told him it was a rugby match and not a cattle market. This was also the attitude of senior players like J.D. Bannerman, who brought pressure to bear on socially inferior Border players to resist numbering, which came about only after the death of Aikman Smith in 1931 and Bannerman's own retirement the following year. International occasions at Murrayfield, as at Twickenham, were great middle-class affairs, the Princes Street pre-match parade being, in Allan Massie's words, 'an affirmation of confidence in the rightness in the way the world was ordered'.[39]

That confidence was less in evidence in the Border textile towns, where contracting markets, declining production and rising unemployment made for a harsher environment. The return of the gold standard and changing fashions—a flapper needed a quarter of the cloth required by an Edwardian woman —drove many producers out of work and those employed in textiles in Scotland fell nearly 25,000 between 1924 and 1935. In these years textile-dependent Langholm's rugby fortunes took a sharp downturn, whereas Kelso, to whom farming and agriculture mattered more, enjoyed a much happier period. By contrast, economic malaise affected a community club like Melrose to the extent that in April 1935 it decided that 'damage to dentures during a game would not be paid for in future' and a dentist's estimate was even required for repairs to natural teeth.[40] The late 1930s, when textile manufacturer recovered and knitwear production began to cater for an increasing leisure market, brought a revival of Border rugby, though Scotland's 1938 Triple Crown, like those of 1933 and 1925 before it, was won by a side manned almost entirely by former pupils and Anglo-Scots.

Scottish rugby was dealt no more than a glancing blow by the Depression because unemployment, which stood at 25 per cent of the insured Scottish workforce in 1932, was concentrated in the soccer area of heavy industry in west and central Scotland. The corresponding figure for Wales that year was 40 per cent, and was far higher in the ravaged valleys of Welsh rugby's heartland.[41] During the inter-war years the population of Wales actually fell in absolute numbers for the first time since 1801. The 265,000 miners employed in South Wales in 1920 fell to

138,000 by 1933. With over half the population—56 per cent in 1930—engaged in mining and the metallurgical industries, the fall in the wages bill from 65 million pounds to 14 million eddied out into the furthest reaches of the community. By the early 1930s, when unemployment in the southeast of England was around 11 per cent and the 'self-possessive class' paraded at Twickenham, it stood at 43 per cent in the Rhondda, 59 per cent in Merthyr, 76 per cent in Pontypridd and 85 per cent in Abertillery. Nearly half a million people moved out of Wales in these years, the entire national increase of a quarter of a century and another 93,000 as well. Moreover, 50 per cent of those leaving Glamorgan between 1921 and 1937 were in the 15 to 29 age group, a loss which had miserable repercussions for its sport.

South Wales's whole social fabric took a fearful beating as the collective achievements of the pre-war period—chapels, trade unions, workmen's institutes, choirs and rugby clubs—crumbled. The WRU's takings halved during the 1920s as international crowds fell away and clubs defaulted. The Union was beseiged by requests for help from clubs desperately trying to keep afloat. Cross Keys, Ebbw Vale, Pontypool, Blaenavon and Pontypridd sought financial assistance during 1926-7 in the aftermath of the crippling coal stoppage of 1926. As soup kitchens opened, rugby clubs closed. Cwmbrân had no option when the local colliery laid off 1,300 men within twelve months in 1926-7. By 1928 the work of two and a half thousand men at Senghenydd had been terminated; in 1929, when nearly every member of the team was unemployed, the club disbanded. So, that year, did Tredegar and Treherbert. Steel-making in Ebbw Vale ceased in 1929 too, putting 10,000 out of work. Despite a reduced admission charge and a catchment area of 40,000, gate receipts at Ebbw Vale Park seldom reached one pound, and in 1932 the club was forced into the indignity of seeking public assistance.

Not surprisingly the tensions of these years spilled on to the field. Since joining the constabulary was one alternative to emigration or long-term unemployment, there were more policemen than miners in Welsh sides of the inter-war years. In 1926 six of the Welsh eight forwards were policemen; Cardiff had on average ten policemen in its First XV every year from

1923 to 1939. As sports personalities these gentle giants were held in some affection; in parts of the coalfield there was less admiration for the institution they represented as strikers and strike-breakers settled their scores in the course of murderously violent matches. In a game in the Swansea Valley one constable, recognised as having swung his truncheon too freely during the 1925 anthracite strike, was crippled for life. In the Afan Valley, in one of the single-industry communities north of Port Talbot where a state of virtual guerrilla warfare prevailed, a referee went on to the field with a revolver strapped to his waist.[42]

Its infrastructure grievously impaired, the Welsh XV's performance in these years was disastrous. They won only 9 games out of 32 between 1923 and 1930 as the other countries began achieving their first victories in Wales since the 1890s. A demoralised Wales lost consistently away from home, even in Paris in 1928; it was 23 years before they won at all at Twickenham. Lack of success was cause and effect of selectorial myopia and administrative inadequacy. Tactical bankruptcy on the field reflected financial insolvency off it.

The marked contrast between the Welsh inter-war experience and that of the rugby-playing areas beyond it is underlined by Wales's human repayment of its pre-1900 debt to the West Country. The ten years from 1926 were, by its own reckoning, 'glorious' ones for Torquay RFC who had three international and countless other Welshmen playing for them. Weston RFC enjoyed similarly unprecedented success, not unconnected to the town council's policy of placing adverts in Welsh newspapers offering work opportunities to the unemployed—'more particularly centre threequarters and forwards'—so that by the 1930s, when there were up to twelve exiles in the side, they were known as 'Weston Welsh'.[43]

It was not only the West Country that benefited from the Welsh diaspora. The population of Coventry expanded from 128,000 in 1921 to 220,000 in 1939, making it the fastest growing city in Britain. In 1934 its unemployment rate was 5.1 per cent. By 1937 it was estimated that 21.5 per cent of all immigrants to Coventry were Welsh, as thousands of predominantly young males flooded into the west midlands to infuse local politics, trade unionism and an indigenous but ailing rugby tradition with new life. [44] Further north it was significant that in the Roses county match of 1932 both sides were captained by Welsh schoolteachers, Lancashire by Watcyn Thomas of Waterloo and Wales, Yorkshire by Frank Williams, Headingley and Wales. Williams eventually joined the Rugby League, like sixty-nine other international players capped for Wales in the amateur game—the equivalent of more than four full Welsh XVs—not to mention the endless stream of ordinary unsung players who also 'went north' from a depressed south Wales in the inter-war years. In the Rugby League Cup Final of 1939 half the players on the field were Welsh.

The Welsh in exile brought a quickening of interest in un-expected quarters. In the early thirties Sale increased their gates substantially by urging people to 'come and see the two Welsh centres' Wooller and Davey. [45] In 1935 this pair were the architects of Wales's 13-12 defeat of the Third All Blacks, a victory overshadowed outside Wales by Prince A. Obolensky's two remarkable cinema-newsreeled tries in England's 13-0 win over the tourists the following month. In Wales itself there was no doubting the significance of the narrower victory. Seen as symbolic of a wider process of social and economic recovery, what was gratifying was not merely the manner in which four-teen men had hung on to win, or the open 'schoolboy' rugby they played, but the composition of the team itself, a satisfying blend of college-educated backs and tinplate workers, colliers and policemen in the pack. 'Wales is proud of this victory', declared the conservative *Western Mail.* 'Welsh peers and labourers—with all the intervening stratas [*sic*] of society—were united in acclaiming and cheering the Welsh team. It was . . . a victory for Wales that probably is impossible in any other sphere'. [46]

VI

A first-class Rugby player is a public figure, a public enter-
tainer, a public servant, and a part of the national life of the
country.
Rowe Harding, *Rugby Reminiscences and Opinions* (1929), p. 141.

The return of peace and a lack of alternative outlets for the
release of savings brought a sport-starved nation flocking back
to the football grounds of Britain. The international rugby
tourney was resumed in 1947, to be promptly dominated by Ireland whose slight rugby base had been unscathed by the war. It
is tempting to link the consecutive Irish Triple Crowns of the
late forties to Ireland's political, economic and cultural
transformation in that decade but rugby remained rooted
among the urban, Anglophile, professional sector, reflecting
and maintaining class and status identity in the Republic as
much as in the North.[47]
The rekindled interest in rugby across the Irish Sea was still
no match for the enthusiasm on the British mainland where
club matches, in Wales anway, were watched by crowds equal
only to those on international days in Belfast and Dublin and
comparable to the high attendances at league soccer games in
England and Scotland, whose own rugby clubs could not
approach anywhere near the 20-30,000 crowds that consistently turned up to watch the first-class Welsh sides. Even
Leicester had a total match attendance of only 21,000 in 1949-
50. Bedford, it is true, could show a precisely aggregated figure
of 47,449 for that year, but both were exceeded by the 48,500
that watched one match alone, between Cardiff and Newport,
in February 1951. This world record for an ordinary club match
was not so exceptional at the time; in 1952 40,000 watched
Cardiff at Swansea, and by 1955-6 Newport v. Cardiff derbies
were still drawing 30,000 to Rodney Parade and 35,000 to the
Arms Park.[48] Twickenham attained a record attendance of
75,000 for the Welsh game of 1950, and Murrayfield's 1951
Scotland v. Wales figure of 80,000 remained a record until
104,000 saw the same fixture in 1975, the readiness of 25,000 or

more Welshmen, and women, to travel to away games inflating the size of the crowd on both occasions.

Welsh supporters had begun travelling in large numbers in the 1930s. Post-1945 they had greater incentives and improved means to do so as confidence returned to both their society and its rugby. Full employment, substantial capital investment, government-sponsored advance factories and low-interest loans helped diversify Welsh industry. In 1950 Wales won their first Triple Crown since 1911 and did so again in 1952, thanks to a combination of extremely fit ex-servicemen, teacher-training college products and manual workers, for as late as 1950 coal-mining still accounted for one in four industrial jobs in Wales.

Elsewhere in Britain, changes in occupational structure and rising expectations were more pronounced as average real weekly earnings began a rise which saw them almost double between 1950 and 1980. Rugby could not be immune to these changes and by the early sixties their effect was being registered. Attendances at club matches entered on a secular decline as televised Saturday afternoon sport and changing leisure patterns took their toll. A survey of the leading English clubs in the late fifties showed Gloucester to be the best supported with 5,000 a match, Leicester, Bristol and the Harlequins averaging 4,000, and Bath and Coventry barely two thousand. Their best attendances were generally for Welsh sides who brought their own supporters and pulled in Welsh exiles. Although support in Wales held up, the kind of 35,000 crowd that watched Cardiff play Llanelli in 1958—a confrontation rich in the nuances of Welsh tribal rivalry, east v. west, Anglicised v. Welsh Wales, Cliff Morgan v. Carwyn James—was increasingly the exception as the live televising of international matches brought rugby to its widest-ever audience while sapping its grassroots. When the Calcutta Cup match was shown live in March 1957, Bath's usual crowd of a few thousand for the visit of the United Services was reduced to a paltry 261.[49]

Measures were required to reconcile televised internationals with the demands of regular club fixtures, and to lift the game out of the defensively-minded, low-scoring rut into which it was sinking. One notorious international in 1963 was punctuated by 111 line-outs, while the resurgence of soccer after England's 1966 World Cup triumph finally spurred rugby's administrators into a long-overdue legislative over-haul. The most far-reaching among a flurry of amendments geared to improving the game—many of them borrowed from increasingly televised Rugby League—was the introduction in 1968 of the 'dispensation law' which, by prohibiting direct kicking to touch outside the defending 25-yard line, reduced the number of line-outs, kept the ball in play for longer and encouraged running with the ball. The increased value of the try to four points in 1971 was also in keeping with the liberal-ising tendencies of the period, though its benefits were soon smothered in a blanket of legislative adjustments that made the goal-kicker the most valued member of his side, as he had been a hundred years earlier. Even Harold Wilson's 1960s catchphrase 'the white heat of the technological revolution' rubbed off on rugby, particularly in Wales which in 1967 became the first country to adopt a national coaching and squad system. These innovations, complemented by a gleaming tech-nical vocabulary which soon became the stock-in-trade of every self-respecting pundit, coincided with the emergence—again in Wales and emanating from changes within the national culture[50]—of a handful of astonishingly gifted performers who brought to the game a new and enterprising awareness of its potentialities. Based on the London Welsh club where mobile young graduate teachers and medical students like John Dawes, Gerald Davies, J.P.R. Williams and Mervyn Davies exploited in a freely chosen, stimulating environment the implications of the new laws, and enhanced by the further inputs of such remarkable players as Gareth Edwards, Barry John, Michael Gibson and David Duckham, British rugby acquired some of the panache of the Dutch total footballers of that era. In the early 1970s, it briefly flared as the most attractive and successful in the world.

Scotland's hidebound past effectively prevented it from making more than spasmodic contributions to British rugby until the 1980s. An enduring legacy of the Aikman Smith era was the instinctive response of the SRU to say 'no' to any new proposal and then think about it. The traditionalism of Scottish rugby, in the hallowed form of the elsewhere long-outmoded 3-2-3 scrum formation, survived well into the 1950s as diehards died very hard in defence of a game by then half a century out of date. A demoralising catalogue of 17 consecutive international defeats between 1951 and 1955 impelled the SRU to set up training courses, though not for club coaches—they would have to wait until 1969—but, characteristically, for schoolmasters charged with 'the production of better citizens'. By the end of the 1960s it was clear that FP rugby was in terminal decline as the products of Edinburgh Academy, Heriot's and George Watson's preferred to play in the more competitive atmosphere of Border rugby. From the early 1970s Melrose and Hawick replaced the Academies as the principal feeders of the Scottish team. The players' new demand for squad sessions on the Welsh model was partially met by the appointment in 1972 not of a national coach but an 'adviser', a designation evocative of US military personnel in the Third World. In 1973 Scotland then stunned everyone by instituting a national league which did nothing to strengthen the tenuous hold of rugby on Glasgow (in fact it further weakened it as the city's players gravitated to outlying clubs like Kilmarnock and Ayr) but which did forge new links between central and Highland Scotland and the Borders.[51]

The winds of change began gusting through the corridors of English rugby too in the late 1960s. It was not only a new generation of Welsh players that emerged from a society shaped but no longer dominated by a traditional industrial culture. Fran Cotton was born into a mining community near Wigan in 1948. His father had left school to join his six brothers and their father in the local pit. His nonconformist upbringing was suffused with collective memories of the 1920s when the local weekly wage was two pounds and professional rugby players brought home six pounds after a win. Education was the way out, via the eleven-plus to a rugby-playing grammar-school and Loughborough. It was the game played at school that determined the shape of the ball played by other young lads from working-class backgrounds like Steve Smith in Macclesfield, Ian McLaughlan in Ayr and Willie John McBride in rural Antrim.[52]

With the perks that came in the wake of increased media attention in the 1970s, the attractions of the professional game receded for leading players like these. By the end of the decade rugby players were no longer the teachers and sales representatives of the 1950s or even the 1960s; they were increasingly the financial advisers, building society managers and business executives of a commercial world in which rugby personalities were now marketable assets. As the audience for live televised internationals rose to a consistent 8 million, the benefits of advertising did not go unappreciated by the commercial sector, the national rugby unions, or the players themselves.

The appearance from the mid-1970s of advertising hoardings at national and club grounds indicated that commercialisation was encroaching significantly on amateur rugby. Tobacco companies and soft drinks firms pumped money into cup competitions in England and Wales, and by the 1980s international matches were attracting sponsorship worth several hundred thousands of pounds. Some sponsors seemed well suited to their events: it was Dulux Paints who sponsored the 23-3 whitewash of Wales by New Zealand in 1980, while a £1.6 million deal with Courage brewers to establish a club championship in England in 1987 promted the RFU, mindful of their undistinguished international record over the previous 20 years, to remark that they needed all the Courage they could get.[53] In these circumstances, and where every international match could generate half a million pounds, top players, keenly aware of the vast sums available in other sports, began feeling that the professional standard of performance increasingly expected of them was worth more than generous expenses. The development of sponsorship has accelerated the drive to overt professionalism.

VII

There is practically nothing new to be written about Rugby
Football.

P.C. Adams, captain of Old Edwardians in the 1880s, *A Lecture on Rugby
Football* (Birmingham, 1926), p. 4.

In the last 20 years Rugby Union has transformed both itself and
its audience. But not beyond all recognition. It is still, in
Scotland, a rallying point for the respectable. It is still, in Wales,
a barometer of the national condition, whose sorry state
througout much of the 1980s and into the 1990s was reflected
in debilitating self-doubt and recurrent defeat. Irish rugby
continues, miraculously, to avoid Partition. Politics may never
be far from the surface—when the Ulster troubles spilled over
into the south in 1972, both Scotland and Wales refused to play
in Dublin[54] —but consistency, too, underlies the reassuringly
unpredictable fortunes of Irish rugby: in 1979 34 of Ireland's
45 senior clubs were still town-based, and doctors and civil
servants still dominated the national side.[55]

Stands English rugby where it did? The clubhouse is less of an
aggressively heterosexual male preserve than it once was, even
if the ban on ladies entering one in the northeast was lifted only
in 1971.[56] Changing patterns in family life, the greater
emancipation of women and the attractions of the late-night
disco have combined to erode the ritualist subculture of the
'Zulu Warrior' and his drunken acolytes.[57] Even Twickenham's image as a bastion of male chauvinism was severly
dented in 1987 when the Women's RFU final was played
there.[58] Beyond, rugby in the shires and on the leafier fringes of
suburban England remains little changed from the appearance
it presented in 1960, when a study of Banbury showed its
19,000 inhabitants to be part of a society consciously divided by
class, where stratification was 'a fact of life', and where rugby
was identified with the wealthy professionals in the town and
the wealthy agricultural element outside it—with squash,
tennis, Freemasonry, Conservatism and the Church of
England.[59] This England's spiritual home remains Twickenham, the temple of the lumpenbourgeoise, where it struck one

observer sitting in the stand at an international in 1980s that the men and women sitting around him seemed never to have been to a game before.[60] This England took grave offence at the invasion of the Twickenham pitch by Bath supporters before the end of the 1987 John Player Cup Final. Had rowdyism returned in the late twentieth century to plague a game initially promoted to eradicate it from the public schools of the early nineteenth? It seemed only to confirm that life imitates television, and that the dividing line between supporters' loyalty and spectator participation always was a fine one.[61]

In any case, pitch invasions were hardly unprecedented, even at Twickenham. They had regularly beset the Springboks' tour of the British Isles in 1969-70, when matches were played in a siege atmosphere and rugby grounds took on the appearance of armed camps. During the controversial 25-match tour one game was abandoned, the venues of two others switched and the 50,000 anti-apartheid demonstrators who turned out required more than 20,000 police to contain them. A confrontation between protesters and 'vigilantes' at Swansea produced some of the worst mob violence seen in Britain since the thirties, while the 10,000 who marched on Lansdowne Road

Interested spectators watch Swansea v. South Africa, 1969.

constituted the largest public assembly in Dublin for 50 years.[62]

That Rugby Union should now occupy a central position in the increasingly politicised areas of world sport, a role which rather exaggerates its actual global extent, stems from its imperial past. The great colonising urge of the nineteenth century that saw rugby follow the flag had been supervised by an imperial officer class hardened if not created by keenly contested house matches. The Corinthian attributes of courage, self-control and the exercise of authority and of discipline were learnt on the playing fields of England and Scotland, the training grounds of a colonial command force. 'Public schoolboys of limited academic ability whose compensatory delight was muscle'[63] became governors, commissioners and administrators throughout the Empire, sometimes with unanticipated consequences. Among the more exotic relics of the British colonial legacy in Africa is a Scottish international cap which is one of the most valued items in the ceremonial regalia worn during the installation of the Divine King of the Sudanese Shilluk tribe.[64]

Rugby spread and consolidated its position in the white dominions much as it did at home. The first game to be played in New Zealand under Rugby rules took place at Nelson in 1870, organised by the Sherborne-educated son of the Speaker of the House of Representatives; within ten years there were 78 clubs in the country and in 1892 the various provincial unions came together to set up the NZRFU. It was a game for the elite, not a universal sport like football, and therefore the recreation of a superior social group and the expression of a certain form of civilisation. It demanded the exercise of moral values, and its scope for physical hardness, endurance and shared effort made it an ideal game for pioneers. In South Africa, whose Rugby Football Board was set up in 1889, it came to play both an integrative *and* exclusive role, uniting both white communities but deriving its strength from the ferocious collective discipline of the Boers, whose religious and political distinctiveness it reinforced. Democratic but not common, rugby in white South Africa came to articulate the convictions and aspirations of the Vootrekker past.[65]

The British army, which had introduced early variants of rugby to the Cape in the 1860s, took it to even further outposts of empire. The Welsh Regiment played it in the Khyber Pass in 1893 as well as pioneering it among the Chinese in the 1920s.[66] There has been a more substantial return on the rugby investment in Japan, where the game was introduced by a Cambridge graduate returning to Keio University in 1889. Japan's first rugby fixture took place the following year between Keio and the Yokohama Club, composed of British residents. Evangelical motives took rugby-playing missionaries from New Zealand to Fiji, Tonga and elsewhere in the South Pacific (the Fijian RU was founded in 1913), but it was commercial considerations that impelled British businessmen and railway engineers to Argentina, where the game was played in Buenos Aires in the 1880s and the River Plate RU established before the end of the century.

The British also imported rugby to France where Rosslyn Park were the first side to tour in 1893, playing against the British colony in Paris. The Captain of Racing Club de Paris between 1900 and 1903, and later the French Rugby Federation's first secretary, was a Scot, C.F. Rutherford, who arrived in Paris in 1895 from Epsom College. The spectators at his first game in the Vincennes public park consisted of a few workmen looking at 'un tas d'imbéciles, galopant sur le gazon après un ballon'.[67] Representatives of the wine and coal trades played key roles further south so that by the end of the century there were sides at Nantes, Bordeaux, Lyons and Toulouse. While soccer spread in the ports and industrial towns of northern Fance, it was in the south-west that rugby particularly flourished as clubs like Bayonne and Béziers came to enjoy a popular following similar to that in South Wales and parts of northern England. Middle-class in inspiration thanks to the English influences radiating from Bordeaux, Biarritz and Pau, the small-town sides of Languedoc, Gascony and the Basque region provided a new focus for traditional sociability and, as in Wales, cultural distinctiveness.[68] The hiring of semi-professional Welsh players as coaches to clubs like Bayonne and Perpignan raised standards of play sufficiently for France, who began playing all four home countries from 1910, to beat

Scotland 16-15 in Paris the following year. What finally convinced the *Daily Telegraph*'s correspondent that French sport had come of age was the ten-month long siege of Verdun in 1916 which showed that the French could after all 'stick it out' and therefore succeed at rugby.[69]

Unquestionably they could, better than any of the home countries if France's second place in the inaugural Rugby World Cup held in 1987 was any indication. And the Empire, too, struck back when the first winners of the tournament's William Webb Ellis trophy proved to be New Zealand, demonstrably the finest of more than 100 nations at the end of the twentieth centry playing a game popularly if erroneously attributed to a day-boy at Rugby School who 'was . . . generally regarded as inclined to take unfair advantages at football'.

NOTES

[1] W.J. Baker, 'William Webb Ellis and the origins of Rugby Football: the life and death of a Victorian myth', *Albion*, 13, pp. 117-30.

[2] E. Dunning and K. Sheard, *Barbarians, Gentlemen and Players* (Oxford, 1979), pp. 60-2, 83-6. These views are briskly rejected by Rugby School itself: J. Macrory, *Running with the ball: the birth of rugby football* (1991). Jennifer Macrory is the archivist of Rugby School.

[3] J.A. Mangan, *Athleticism in the Victorian and Edwardian Public School* (Cambridge, 1981), pp. 136, 206.

[4] L. Balaam (ed.), *Manchester Football Club 1860-1985* (Manchester, 1985), pp. 4-5, 19, 28.

[5] T. Delaney, *The Roots of Rugby League* (Keighley, 1984), pp. 3-5; A. Service, *Saints in Their Glory* (St Helens, 1985), pp. 1-3; in general on rugby league, the superb essays of Geoffrey Moorhouse, *At the George* (1989), are essential reading.

[6] Rev F. Marshall (ed.), *Football: The Rugby Union Game* (1892), pp. 430, 439; T.W.J. Auty, *Headingley FC 1878-1978* (Headingley, 1978), pp. 17-18. See also David Russell, ' "Sporadic and curious": the emergence of rugby and soccer zones in Yorkshire and Lancashire, *c*. 1860-1914', *The International Journal of the History of Sport*, 5, 2, September 1988, pp. 185-205.

[7] *Victoria County History: Northamptonshire*, vol. 2 (1906), p. 395; W. Bell, *Langholm RFC 1871-1971* (Langholm, 1971), unpaginated; R. Gethin, *Merthyr Rugby 1876-1976* (Merthyr, 1976), p. 7; M. Rhys (ed.), *Bois y Llan: Llangennech RFC 1885-1985* (Llanelli, 1986); W.J. Robbins (ed.), *Rugby in the Duchy* (Camborne, 1934), p. 24; D. Smith and G. Williams, *Fields of*

Praise (Cardiff, 1980), pp. 11-12, *Bridgwater and Albion RFC 1975-1975* (Bridgwater, 1975), p. 17.

[8] C.C. Hoyer Millar, *Fifty Years of Rosslyn Park* (1929), p. 13; S. Barton (ed.), *The Gala Story 1875-1975* (Galashiels, 1975), p. 15; *North of Ireland Cricket and Football Club 1859-1959* (Belfast, 1959), pp. 9, 13.

[9] J. Griffiths, *The Book of English International Rugby 1871-1982* (1982), pp. 11-14, 58.

[10] Dunning and Sheard, *Barbarians*, pp. 198-200; Delaney, *Roots*, pp. 14-15, 52-82. In 1922 the Northern Union became the Rugby League.

[11] U.A. Titley and R. McWhirter, *The Centenary History of the Rugby Football Union* (Twickenham, 1970), pp. 111-24.

[12] Smith and Williams, *Fields of Praise*, pp. 22-7.

[13] L.J. Williams, 'The economic structure of Wales since 1850' in G. Williams (ed.), *Crisis of Economy and Ideology: Essays on Welsh Society 1840-1980* (Bangor, 1983), pp. 35-47; Col. P.C. Trevor, *Rugby Union Football* (1923), p. 188.

[14] *Bridgend Chronicle*, 2 December 1880; *Llanelly and County Guardian*, 6 December 1883; *Welsh Rugby Union Minute Books*; Gethin, *Merthyr Rugby*, p. 8; *Merthyr Express*, 19 September 1903.

[15] Griffiths, *English International Rugby*, pp. 67, 100; *South Wales Daily Post*, 5 January 1903; B.E. Matthews, *The Swansea Story* (Swansea, 1968), pp. 25-7; J.R. Barker-Davies (ed.), *One Hundred Years of Coventry Blue 1874-1974* (Coventry, 1974), p. 30; D.E. Davies, *Cardiff Rugby Club 1876-1975* (Cardiff, 1975), pp. 35, 39; Hoyer Millar, *Rosslyn Park*, p. 63; *South Wales Daily News*, 13 March 1905.

[16] *South Wales Daily News*, 23 January 1899; G. Hughes, *The Scarlets* (Llanelli, 1986), p. 57, quoting the *Llanelly Mercury*.

[17] Smith and Williams, *Fields of Praise*, pp. 145-71. Cf. J. Clarke and C. Critcher, '1966 and all that: England's World Cup victory' in A. Tomlinson and G. Whannel (eds.), *Off the Ball* (1986), pp. 112-26. The rioters who selectively ransacked Tonypandy High Street in 1910 left untouched the chemist's shop of Willie Llewellyn, who had won the last of his twenty international caps against New Zealand in 1905; D. Smith, 'Tonypandy 1910: definitions of community', *Past and Present*, 87, p. 168.

[18] *South Wales Daily News*, 29 January 1900.

[19] A.M.C. Thorburn, *The Scottish Rugby Union Official History* (Edinburgh, 1985), pp. 26-7, 35.

[20] H.H. Almond, 'Rugby Football in Scottish schools' in Marshall (ed.), *Football: The Rugby Union Game*, pp. 51-66.

[21] P. Bilsborough, 'The Development of sport in Glasgow 1850-1914', Unpublished MLitt thesis, University of Stirling, 1983, pp. 110-13, 209, 254-6, 290.

[22] A. Massie, *A Portrait of Scottish Rugby* (Edinburgh, 1984), pp. 111-25; J. Gilbert, *Melrose Rugby Football Club 1877-1977* (Hawick, 1977), pp. 1-2.

[23] *Weston-Super-Mare RFC 1875-1975* (Weston, 1975), pp. 26-8; *Plymouth Albion RFC 1876-1976* (Plymouth, 1976), p. 10; Barker-Davies, *Coventry*, p. 30; D. Hands, *Leicester FC 1880-1980* (Leicester, 1981), p. 26; *V.C.H.*

Northamptonshire, p. 395; G. Williams, 'Midland manoeuvres: a history of Northern Unionism in Coventry', *Code 13*, 2 December 1986, pp. 9-14.

[24] Barker-Davies, *Coventry*, pp. 57-8; Hands, *Leicester*, pp. 19-22; Delaney, *Roots*, pp. 113-15; see also Chapter Seven below.

[25] J.J. McCarthy in Marshall, *Football*, p. 222; E. Van Esbeck, *One Hundred Years of Irish Rugby* (Dublin, 1974), pp. 14-41; M. O'Hehir, *The GAA: 100 Years* (Dublin, 1984), pp. 16-17.

[26] *City of Derry RFC 1881-1981* (Londonderry, 1981), pp. 31-2; J. Sugden and A. Bairner, 'Northern Ireland: sport in a divided society' in L. Allison (ed.), *The Politics of Sport* (Manchester, 1986), pp. 100-7.

[27] *NICFC 1859-1959*, (see 8 above), p. 17.

[28] Van Esbeck, *Irish Rugby*, pp. 91-2; *Welsh Rugby Union Minute Books*, 27 August 1914.

[29] W.R. Taylor (ed.), *Keswick RUFC 1879-1979* (Keswick, 1979), p. 15; Hughes, *Scarlets*, p. 90; Hands, *Leicester*, p. 33.

[30] *Bath FC 1865-1965* (Bath, 1965), p. 27; Blumenau, *A History of Malvern 1865-1965* (1965), p. 89.

[31] P. Fussell, *The Great War and Modern Memory* (1975), pp. 25-7, 276; Titley and McWhirter, *Centenary History of RFU*, Biographical Section, *s.v.* Mobbs, E.R.

[32] E.B. Poulton, *The Life of Ronald Poulton* (1919); A.A. Thompson, *Rugger My Pleasure* (1955), pp. 34-7, 85; H. Marshall (ed.), *Rugger Stories* (1932), p. 161.

[33] *Bristol FC Jubilee Book 1888-1938* (Bristol, 1938), p. 23; Auty, *Headingley*, pp. 33-5; W.J.A. Davies, *Rugby Football* (1923), p. 159.

[34] F.A.M. Webster, *Our Great Public Schools* (1937); O.L. Owen, *The Growth of a Sporting Venture* (Ipswich, 1952), pp. 39-47; K. Robbins, *The Eclipse of a Great Power* (1983), pp. 158, 254-5; Marshall, *Rugger Stories* (1932); K. Pelmear, *Rugby Football: An Anthology* (1958), pp. 127-34; J. Stevenson, *British Society 1914-45* (Harmondsworth, 1984), p. 387.

[35] E.H.D. Sewell (ed.), *Rugby Football Up-do-Date* (1922), p. 13; R.M. Rayner, *A Manual of Rugby Football for Public Schools* (1925), p. 138.

[36] Dunning and Sheard, *Barbarians*, pp. 235-8. The first rugby match to be broadcast live on BBC radio was the England *v.* Wales game at Twickenham, 1927. Capt. Teddy Wakelam, the commentator, mapped out a plan of squares with his producer, Lance Sieveking, who also supplied a blind man to sit outside the commentary box 'in order that I might imagine that I was describing the game to him'. Wakelam was subsequently informed by a listener in Lancashire 'that I was a complete fraud, that I had been reading from a previously prepared script, and that he would like to hear from me *immediately* what had happened'. H.B.T. Wakelam, *The Game Goes On* (1936), pp. 165-74.

[37] Ivor Brown in Marshall, *Rugger Stories*, pp. 160-1.

[38] A.G. Macdonell, *England, Their England* (1933), chap. 11.

[39] Thorburn, *Scottish Rugby Union*, pp. 27-8; Massie, *Portrait*, pp. 36-7. See also Eric Linklater's novel, *Magnus Merriman* (1934), ch. 12.

[40] C. Harvie, *No Gods and Precious Few Heroes: Scotland 1914-80* (1981),

pp. 42-7; Bell, *Langholm*; A. Hastie, *Kelso RFC 1876-1976, p. 41*; *Gilbert, Melrose*, p. 40.

[41] For what follows, see Chapter 8 below and references there cited. In addition, P.T. Atkinson, *Centenary History of Rhymney RFC 182-1982* (Rhymney, 1982), pp. 41-5; W.G. Boulton, *Senghenydd: The Village and its Rugby Club* (Risca, 1982), pp. 27-34.

[42] Davies, *Cardiff RFC*, pp. 197-7; H. Francis, 'The anthracite strike and the disturbances of 1925', *Llafur*, 1, May 1973, p. 19; T. Lewis, *The Mules: A History of Kenfig Hill RFC* (Pyle, 1973), p. 24.

[43] *Weston RFC*, pp. 44-50.

[44] B. Lancaster and T. Mason (eds.,) *Life and Labour in a Twentieth-century City: The Experience of Coventry* (Coventry, 1987), pp. 24, 67, 265. Several other midland clubs, like Rugby, Moseley and Wolverhampton, had 'excellent seasons' in the inter-war years. G. Holmes, *Midland Rugby Football* (Leicester, 1949), pp. 75-100.

[45] M. Barak (ed.), *A Century of Rugby at Sale* (Sale, 1961), p. 49.

[46] *Western Mail*, 23 December 1935.

[47] T. Browne, *Ireland: A Social and Cultural History 1922-79* (Glasgow, 1981), pp. 171-211; Sugden and Bairner, 'Northern Ireland', p. 103.

[48] Dunning and Sheard, *Barbarians*, p. 250; Davies, *Cardiff RFC*, pp. 117-20; J. Davis, *One Hundred Years of Newport Rugby* (Risca, 1974), pp.; 136-7; Matthews, *Swansea Story*, p. 54.

[49] W.J. Morgan and G. Nicholson, *Report on Rugby* (1959), pp. 148-53.

[50] Smith and Williams, *Fields of Praise*, pp. 373-6, 414-19; J. Davies, 'Wales in the Ninteen Sixties', *Llafur*, 4, 1987, pp. 78-88.

[51] Thorburn, *Scottish Rugby Union*, pp. 45-56; Massie, *Portrait*, pp. 53-4.

[52] F. Cotton, *Fran: An Autobiography* (1981), pp. 34-4; S. Smith, *The Scrum Half of My Life* (1984), pp. 15-20; I. McLaughlan, *Mighty Mouse* (1980), pp. 12-13; \'7.J. McBride, *Willie John* (Dublin, 1976), pp. 13-18. See also D. Hare, *Dusty* (1985), p. 47; P. Wheeler, *Rugby From the Front* (1983), pp. 33-4.

[53] *The Independent*, 10 February 1987. The Welsh XV that played New Zealand in 1980 was on average 2st. 3lbs. heavier, and two and a half inches taller per man than the 1905 side.

[54] In 1954 a crisis arose when southern players refused to acknowledge the British anthem at Belfast's Ravenhill ground so long as the Republican anthem and tricolour were illegal in the North. It was 'resolved' only by transferring all subsequent internationals to Landsdowne Road, Dublin. S. Diffley, *The Men in Green: The Story of Irish Rugby* (1973), pp. 48-50. Although Scotland and Wales declined to play in Dublin in 1972, England did so in 1973, and lost. At the after-match dinner, the English captain John Pullin remarked, 'We may not be much good but at least we turn up.' J. Reason and C. James, *The World of Rugby*, (1979), p. 219.

[55] N. Carroll, *Sport in Ireland* (Dublin, 1979), p. 37.

[56] J. Taylor (ed.), *Middlesborough RUFC 1872-1972* (Middlesborough, 1972), p. 23.

[57] K.G. Sheard and E. Dunning, 'The Rugby Football Club as a type of 'male preserve': some sociological notes', *International Review of Sport Sociology*,

8, 1973, pp. 5-21. The 'Zulu Warrior', the authors remind us (p. 7), is 'the traditional signal for a ritualistic strip by a member of the group . . . usually enacted after the match, either in the club-house bar or, if the team has been playing away, on the coach which is carrying the players home'.

[58] A protest from a leading figure on the RFU that 'Ladies don't play rugby' was met with the rejoinder, 'Women do'. *The Independent*, 13 April 1987. The Women's RFU, comprising nearly 50 clubs in a two-divisional league structure, staged an inaugural international between Wales and England at Pontypool in April 1987. Twelve nations competed for the first Women's Rugby World Cup, held in South Wales in April 1991. It was won by the USA.

[59] Margaret Stacey in R. Frankenberg, *Communities in Britain* (Harmondsworth, 1966), pp. 172-3.

[60] G. Davies and J. Morgan, *Sidesteps: A Rugby Diary 1984-5* (1985), p. 85.

[61] The 'unpleasant' behaviour of Bath, like Gloucester and Somerset's CCC Sunday side, supporters was intriguingly attributed to the absence of any League soccer team in the area, apart from Bristol, 'to filter off the yobbish tendency'. Alan Watkins, *Sports Writer's Eye* (1989) pp. 114, 131-3.

[62] R.E. Lapchick, *The Politics of Race and International Sport: The Case of South Africa* (Westport, Conn. 1975), pp. 156-68; P. Hain, *Don't Play with Apartheid* (1971), esp. pp. 133, 144, 18; Smith and Williams, *Fields of Praise*, pp. 403-5.

[63] Mangan, *Athleticism*, p. 139.

[64] I.M. Lewis, *Social Anthropology in Perspective* (Harmondsworth, 1971), p. 63.

[65] R. Archer and A. Bouillon, *The South African Game: Sport and Racism* (1982), pp. 56-78.

[66] J. Maclaren, *The History of Army Rugby* (Aldershot, 1986), pp. 12-23.

[67] Sewell, *Rugby Football Up-to-Date*, pp. 216-27.

[68] R.J. Holt, *Sport and Society in Modern France* (1981), pp. 68-76; H. Garcia, *Le Rugby* (Paris, 1962), pp. 15-16; E. Weber, *France: Fin de Siècle* (1986) pp. 220-24. 'Sociability', a key concept in modern French historical writing is the theme of the inaugural (1988) issue of the journal *Sport Histoire*. Given the renowned *Annales* tradition of the study of popular mentalities and social structure, it is perhaps surprising that only recently have French historians begun to give the study of sport serious attention. For some idea of the exciting new work emerging from France during the last few years, including important studies of French rugby, see R. Holt, 'Ideology and Sociability: A Review of New French Research into the History of Sport under the Early Third Republic (1870-1914)', *International Journal of the History of Sport*, 6, 2, Dec. 1989, pp. 368-77.

[69] Col. P.C. Trevor, *Rugby Union Football*, p. 9.

CHAPTER 3

TAFF'S ACRE—THE MAKING OF CARDIFF ARMS PARK

'The River *Taff*, sliding downe from the Hills, runneth towards the Sea . . . to Caerdiff, called of the Britains *Caerdid*, a proper fine Towne (as Townes goe in this Country) and a very commodious Haven'.
William Camden, *Britannia*, 1585 (Philemon Holland's 1610 translation).

To begin at the end, a 56,000 capacity crowd at the National Ground can generate £800,000 in International ticket receipts. This is quite an advance on the situation of ninety years ago.

On 18 March 1899 a world record attendance for rugby of 40,000 at Cardiff Arms Park paid record receipts of £1700—though not all of them did—to see whether Ireland could snatch their second Triple Crown of the decade at Wales's expense. The 0-3 final score indicated that Ireland could, denting Welsh pride and, in the process, two of full-back Billy Bancroft's ribs, fractured in the over-affectionate embrace of a whole seminary of green-shirted forwards. We can be sure there were some bruised ribs among the spectators too, for there were at least 10,000 more of them inside the ground that afternoon than it could comfortably or safely accommodate.

Admission in that relatively inflation-free era was what it had been for the previous fifteen years and would be for another ten: field, one shilling (5p), enclosure, two shillings (10p) and three shillings (15p) according to location. Reserved but not numbered ringside seats 'inside the ropes' (some ropes—either steel fencing or strong iron-bound wood palings!) cost three shillings too, while the 1200 reserved and numbered grandstand seats cost five shillings (25p). Until the rotation of International fixtures was introduced in 1973-74 the Irish match was often the Triple Crown decider and attracted massive crowds. 1899 did not see quite the chaotic scenes attending the corresponding fixture in 1914, or especially 1936, when 70,000 defied hell and high water (from the hoses of the local fire brigade) to get into the ground, but graphic eye-witness accounts make it plain that the events of 1899 were the most turbulent yet seen at an International match. They also give us an indication of the physical appearance of Cardiff Arms Park at the end of the nineteenth century.

Within an hour of opening the gates at 1 p.m. there were 20,000 inside the ground, many by rushing the pay boxes and scaling the walls. There were two official entrances in those days—opposite the Angel Hotel (today's entrance number 5) where the path curved around the old cricket ground to the river end, and by the Glamorgan County Club (today's Guildhall Place entrance number 2). Tickets were sold at pay boxes in Westgate Street, and with such unexpectedly large crowds milling about, the sixty uniformed policemen on duty were hard pushed to keep order. From the Angel Hotel entrance to the Post Office ran a fifteen-foot wall, later demolished to make way for the Westgate Street flats. As the impatient multitude surged and jostled around the pay boxes, a 'terrific rush' was made for the wall. 'First of all they were small boys who went over, then the everyday respectable wearer of a bowler hat went over, and finally the high hat and frock-coated gentlemen went over . . . By the gates and pay boxes was a mounted constable but he was more than useless. As the crowd clambered the wall he turned his animal around, which only served as a sign for the dozens behind him to go for the wall . . . the big drop of some fifteen feet from the top of the wall to the ground between the Post Office and the County Club was deemed mere child's play.' According to another account, the crowd swarmed over the pay boxes 'like so many ants on an anthill' and using them as a leg-up 'went for the wall that stood between them and the game in their hundreds . . . altogether it was a most entertaining sight viewed from the street but it must prove a costly experience for the Union.'

Once inside the ground many climbed into the forks and branches of the trees which surrounded it. 'Every tree that was at all possible was thus requisitioned and frequently half a dozen men and youths, one above the other, clung with hands and knees in all sorts of awkward and angular shapes.' Even the distant tower of St John's Church was 'alive with moving pygmies'—presumably pygmies with telescopic eyesight.

Meanwhile those at ground level were in no mood to respect the temporary fencing marking off the variously priced sections of the enclosure. Sheer weight of numbers on the north side caused it to give way 'and the reserve seats in the enclosure were quickly occupied by non-ticket holders who rushed pell-mell for them . . . Hoardings topped with barbed wire were unflinchingly scaled, utterly regardless of sartorial disasters and epidermis wounds.' On the south side, others took up the challenge presented by the heavy square-timbered supports of the grandstand. Though again barbed with wire, these vantage points too were soon commandeered, while the most resourceful actually got up on to the corrugated roof. 'That football enthusiasm will induce usually cautious men to risk life and limb has often been demonstrated at Cardiff, but rash daring was never so amazingly exemplified as on this occasion,' mused one eye-witness, mindful that some blithe spirits had actually crossed the Taff to gain entrance on the west side of the ground.

And of course there were good precedents for this, since the ground itself in a very real sense had come from the river. The landmarks by which the Park is still identified—the Taff, Quay Street, the very name Cardiff Arms—are reminders of an earlier, more tranquil era before Cardiff became the coal metropolis of the world and rugby football captured the imagination of its teeming thousands.

At the beginning of the nineteenth century, it was still a small market town of less than two thousand souls huddled around its castle, an edifice that had seen more centuries borne away by the Taff than changes taking place on its banks. Although the castle was a legacy of their occupation, the Romans were not the first settlers in south Wales. That distinction belongs to the early bronze-age Beaker people, broad-headed, muscular and thirsty. But it was the Romans driving on from their legionary fortress at Caerleon who recognised the strategic potential of a fortification on the Taff, commanding a fordable river and with access to the sea for supplying their fleet. The invaders, moreover, were shrewd tacticians. They made a ball-game and called it *harpastum* and were sufficiently endowed with what certificated rugby coaches would later call 'peripheral vision' to subdue—but only just, as Tacitus confirms—the local Silures, bellicose boyos who had acquired stamina and a side-step among the wooded hills to the north.

It was this fort on the Taff that became the nucleus of the first settlement at Cardiff. What happened between the Roman withdrawal in the late fourth century and the coming of the Normans in the eleventh is unclear, though one of the changes to occur was a shift from a loosely organised tribal society to the creation of a new kingdom extending from the Usk to the Tawe. This was Morgan's land, Morgannwg, and the erratic imprints of Morgan and his descendants lie all over south Wales and not least on the Arms Park. But even Morgan's furious energies were no match for the marauding Norsemen who pillaged the coasts of west Britain from their bases in Dublin, Wexford and Cork Constitution. Liking and settling down in Cardiff they left their mark in places like Womanby (Hundemanby) Street, an axe-throw, or drop-kick, from the Quay Street entrance to the Valhalla of Welsh rugby.

It was left to the Normans, flushed by their 10-66 away victory at Hastings, to revive the neglected Roman fort on the Taff, and Robert Fitzhamon, lord of Glamorgan, acquired control of the settlement that had grown up around it. For the next few centuries south Wales was a cockpit of rebellion and resistance, and its history is illumined by the colourful exploits of various de Clares and Despensers, of Gilbert the Red, first of the men in scarlet, and of Ifor Bach who in 1158 made a daring attack on Cardiff Castle and snatched away to his Senghennydd hideaway Fitzhamon's grandson and all his family. 'Yvor was a man little of stature yet bigg and mighty of heart,' wrote Rice Merrick of him four centuries later, for all the world as if describing the classic Welsh half-back. Ifor, with his bandy legs and evident speed off the mark, was clearly a son of Morgan and forerunner of many subsequent Morgans.

By the end of the thirteenth century Cardiff had become the largest of the Welsh boroughs, with an estimated population of more than two thousand. So it is a remarkable fact that its population was even less—1,870 in 1801—at the beginning of the century which would transform it into the greatest coal exporting port in the world than it had been five centuries earlier. Yet it would be premature to conclude that the only thing moving in Cardiff in the intervening centuries was the Taff. A French roll of 1460 refers to one 'John Derell of Cerdyf in Wales, merchant' taken prisoner in Britanny while forging those Cambro-French links that would be strengthened later by the activities of Percy Bush, vice-consul at Nantes from 1910, and Owen Roe, pirated out of Penarth about the same time to teach rugby to the Bayonnais.

Piracy has long been a Cardiff speciality. Not for nothing did the infant Cardiff RFC sport the skull and crossbones on its jersey, and rejoice in the nickname of 'the Pirates': from the thirteenth to the eighteenth centuries its havens and creeks were the haunts of smugglers, wreckers and illegitimate traders who handled rum, tea and tobacco with all the fingertip rapid-transfer skills of later coaching manuals. There is abundant testimony that infamous freebooters like John Callice (a 'notorious malefactor who hath committed sundry great piracies'), William Herbert, John ap John, John Robert ap Ieuan, John Thomas, Robert Adams, Nicholas Herbert and, inevitably, Morgan the Pirate—a formidable eight by any standards—gave the town's more lawful citizens such a bad name 'that they dare not avow abroad the place of their dwelling at Cardiff lest they be discredited'.

Whether the Tudor peace ever made it a more law-abiding place is an open question: in 1595 Llewellyn David 'did with his sword very cruelly cut and split the nose of [a] woman in such sort as the same hung down over her lip.' Perhaps this was how Elizabethan Welshmen motivated themselves for a brisk bout of *cnappan*, the Tudor ball game alleged by some earnest scholars to be the missing link between *harpastum* and rugby. What is clear from this period is that the material life of at least the town's leading citizens improved. The century after the Act of Union (1536) saw a revolution in housebuilding, and Cardiff's 'many fair houses and large streets' owed much to the activities of gentlemen like Sir Thomas Morgan who in the early seventeenth century built Ruperra Castle (1626) and what was at one time the best known of Cardiff's stately homes, the Red House. In the next century this became the Cardiff Arms Hotel.

In view of the direction which rugby football would follow in the late twentieth century, it is entirely fitting that the Cardiff Arms Park should have taken its name from a coaching inn. The establishment came to prominence with the improved travel facilities of the eighteenth century and the evolution of the mail service and turnpike system, so that 'instead of the quiet of thirty years ago an eternal racket has succeeded at this [summer] season, every bed of this [the Cardiff Arms] Inn being filled and many travellers obliged to go on with tired horses'. The Cardiff Arms was one of several Glamorgan hostelries whose mere names—the Beaufort Arms at Chepstow, the King's Head at Newport, the Angel at Cardiff, the White Hart at Cowbridge, the Mackworth at Swansea—conjure up Christmas-card visions of bustling red-faced porters clumping over cobbled yards, cheery Pickwickian travellers and the aroma of port and brandy.

Whether or not it ever looked quite like that, the Cardiff Arms Inn, demolished for good in 1882, bequeathed to Welsh and world rugby a name as indelible as a watermark. In fact at high water mark its yard flooded over, and coaches and chaises floated out to sea: for the Cardiff Arms stood in Broad Street, a short thoroughfare running at right angles to Angel Street and Castle Street, and the Taff ran behind it. Yet were it possible today to deposit the Cardiff Arms, like Dr Who's police kiosk, magically in its old position, we would find that the Taff was running elsewhere. This is the key to the beginning of the Cardiff Arms Park.

Key, and quay, for even by William Camden's time Cardiff's quay was of ancient origin. Already by mid-sixteen century the town corporation was complaining that it had borne the costs of maintaining it 'tyme out of mynde', for it was being constantly eroded by the river's floods and currents. At the beginning of the nineteenth century the Taff flowed past the ruins of the old Cardiff bridge that had collapsed in the floods of 1792, under the later Canton bridge (completed in 1796 though rebuilt in 1859 and widened subsequently) and then, as it had always done since time immemorial, continued along its north to south course for about four hundred yards before curving sharply east to join the Town Quay. It there ran along the line of modern Westgate Street, with private wharves like the Golate on its eastern bank and the gardens behind St Mary Street sloping down to the riverside. Then it turned off under the site of what is now the general station to rejoin the present river just above Penarth Road bridge.

The Taff had always been an unpredictable creature. In 1614 thirteen people had drowned while crossing it in an open boat and there were plenty of later examples of drownings occurring in the course of fording it. At one time 'a faire Key and a safe harborowe for shippinge' (Rice Lewis, 1596), by the nineteenth century it had fallen into virtual disuse, though small vessels still came up at high tide—the same tide that flooded the yard at the Cardiff Arms.

Indeed, as the century opened it seemed that Cardiff itself was in disuse. Its physical shape was hardly different from what it appeared to Camden's Tudor contemporaries. Even by 1821, when it had a population of three and a half thousand, it ranked only twenty-seventh among the towns of Wales, smaller than Llanelli and Pembroke let alone Merthyr Tydfil. It was still largely unpaved and unlighted and its sanitation little better than in 1750 when a woman drowned falling into the privy of the King David Inn. Although in 1774 it had been the first Welsh town to obtain an Improvement Act, the seriousness with which the Commissioners viewed their responsibility may be gauged from the fact that for many years the venue for their meetings was the Cardiff Arms Hotel.

But after centuries of stagnation, frantic change was imminent, as Cardiff became rapidly transformed from a sleepy market town to a major port with worldwide ramifications. The engine of change proved to be the building, in the revolutionary decade of the 1790s, of the Glamorgan Canal, with a sea-lock at Cardiff, to provide an outlet for the great Merthyr ironworks. By the 1830s the canal was handling annually such a large volume of iron and coal that it was becoming inadequate. The basic problem was that the sea-lock was two and a half miles from low water mark and the canal could not be widened. The second Marquess of Bute, who owned all the land between the town of Cardiff and the sea and enjoyed manorial rights over the River Taff and the foreshore, saw in the predicament of the canal company his own opportunity: a new and wider ship canal parallel to the existing sea-lock and further east. The Bute Ship Canal, or West Docks, opened in 1839, and with the opening in 1841 of the Taff Vale Railway linking Merthyr and Cardiff with connections to the Cynon (Aberdare) valley in 1846, and the two Rhondda valleys a decade later, by 1850 the trade of the Bute Docks had not only overhauled but doubled that of the canal.

The West Docks cost £350,000 and only the Butes could have afforded it, just as only the Butes could raise enough coal from their lands to keep a whole docks supplied and require even more to be built. For not only was Cardiff 'Lord Bute's own town', his estate encompassed its industrial hinterland: in all, 22,000 acres of Glamorgan. The Butes were landlords of the Dowlais ironworks, in the 1840s the greatest in the world; they constructed and owned the Bute Docks, soon to become the greatest coal port in the world; they promoted the mineral exploitation of the Rhondda, the greatest coal valley in the world—and if all that were not enough, they also owned the Cardiff Arms Park, before long the greatest rugby ground in the world. For the Cardiff Arms was a Bute hotel and just as the foundation of modern Cardiff can be laid at the door of the second Marquess, so it is to him that the Cardiff Arms Park owes its existence, for it was he who was responsible for the diversion of the Taff, and at his prompting Isambard Kingdom Brunel undertook it.

Brunel was in the 1840s an engineer with the South Wales Railway Company, and it was to the advantage of the emerging commercial centre of Cardiff to be linked to the line from London to Swansea and beyond. So between 1848 and 1853, to facilitate the entry of the railway, the Taff was diverted into a 'new cut' between Canton bridge and Penarth Road bridge. This amputated the eastward loop sweeping around to run alongside St Mary Street, and left the old quay, at the point where modern Quay Street meets Westgate Street, high and dry, as well as a health hazard in the form of a stagnant channel of foetid water which was not filled in till 1865.

The consequences that followed from the diverting of the Taff were profound. It provided a site for the railway station, removed the recurrent danger of flooding in the town centre, made new land available for redevelopment, and enlarged the meadowland that had existed north of the old loop known as the Great Park. More precisely, the reclaimed land near the old quay, and behind the Cardiff Arms, became the site of Westgate Street—and of the Cardiff Arms Park.

The Great Park was already a favourite recreation area for the citizens of Cardiff and for military and civil celebrations. The eighteenth birthday of Princess Victoria in 1837 was the occasion for a fireworks display on 'the park behind the Cardiff Arms' and in 1856 the ending of the Crimean War was cele-brated there with processions, bands, flags and enough spectacle generally that one eavesdropper could not but over-hear one wide-eyed bystander remark to another 'Dear, dear, did you ever see such a thing in Aberdare?'

Ten years later a long discussion took place in the town council as to whether the Park should be converted into a cattle market. This in turn hinged on who owned it. The land did not formally pass out of Bute hands until 1922, but the third Mar-quess had already virtually conferred it on the town by charging the most nominal rent for its use. The decision not to go ahead with the cattle market was a great relief to the Cardiff Cricket Club, established in 1845, whose members had been playing there since 1848. It has to be admitted that there would be occasions in the next century when intensive usage, allied to deep-seated drainage problems, would churn up the playing area of the Park so badly that it looked as if the cattle market had won after all.

It was the Cardiff Football Club, formed in 1876, that set about the development of the area now reclaimed from the river. Its origins can be traced to the autumn of 1874 when sixty-six members paid a half-crown subscription (12½p) to join the Glamorgan Football Club, and their first practice was held in front of the cricket pavilion on the Arms Park. A number of them were old boys of Cheltenham College who were not above, or below, playing in evening dress, 'and some did not discard their bowler hats'. Several were already members of the Cardiff Cricket Club who had long been playing on the Park, and so a football club was a convenient way of extending their association into the winter months. In 1875 the Glamorgan FC held a sports meeting on the Arms Park, and as well as the usual events there was a prize for the longest drop-kick. The winner was credited with an incredible 145 yards, which reduces acknowledged siege-gun kickers of later years—Brand, Wooller, Bob Scott and Don Clarke—to the level of Subbuteo specialists.

The Cardiff Rugby Club grew out of an amalgam in 1876 of the Glamorgan FC and two local organisations, Wanderers and Tredegarville, whose founder was James Bush, father of the celebrated and irrepressible Percy. It was symbolic that the prime movers in the new combination were W.H. and S.C. Cory, for if any name connoted the bustling world of Cardiff's now booming export and shipping business it was Cory.

As yet the football area of the Park was not enclosed. Its sole facility was the cricket pavilion, and beyond it, for candidates for an early bath, the river. There was no charge for spectators; Newport's Rodney Parade was the first Welsh ground to charge admission and it was an unpopular innovation. When in 1879 the South Wales Challenge Cup Final was played at Sophia Gardens—another Bute bequest—it was because Cardiff Arms Park was not as yet roped off, and unable conveniently to accommodate the expected 3000 to 4000 spectators who duly turned up and paid sixpence (2½p) for the privilege. It soon could. During the summer of 1881, on the strength of the previous season's income of £130, the ground was levelled and re-turfed, and its first grandstand built at a cost of fifty pounds, on the north side towards the Taff end 'for the convenience of the spectators and the ladies in particular'. Cardiff were drawing up to 4000 spectators a game. In 1885-86 there would be still more.

By now the whole town had undergone colossal change quite beyond the control of the Butes who had initiated it. The third Marquess (1847-1900) rebuilt Cardiff Castle and Castell Coch, donated large sums to various charitable and educational institutions, and preserved for the town its many splendid and centrally sited squares and open spaces. His stupendous wealth enabled him to indulge to the full his interest in the mediaeval, the occult and the oriental (so that the much earlier-named suburbs of Canton and Cathays acquired a new exotic relevance) and he travelled widely in Italy, Greece and Palestine. To a man of his tastes and temperament, therefore, it is unsurprising that the pursuit by thirty vigorous young men of a pig's bladder encased in leather exerted as little appeal as the expanding docks and thrusting coal freighters which made his life-style possible. Though Cardiff Arms Park was one of his most famous benefactions, he chose to be buried not beneath it but on the Mount of Olives: less Taff than Acre, for as he said, 'Athens and Assisi have spoilt me for anything else.'

Certainly spoilt him for late-nineteenth-century Cardiff. His desire to get away from 'coalopolis' became urgent as its pop-population more than doubled from 39,000 to over 82,000 between 1871 and 1881; by 1901 it doubled again. This demographic explosion was matched by the doubling of coal exports in the same period to 7½ million tons (from a mere 21,000 tons in 1839), which almost doubled again by 1913. Thousands of immigrants poured in annually to the docks, railways, shops and offices of this El Dorado on the Taff, creating a vibrant, increasingly self-confident community that took drink, religion and rugby in large draughts. Among the thousands of newcomers to arrive in 1883 were the Hancock family from Wiveliscombe in Somerset. The Hancocks were brewers and could recognise a thirst from the other side of the Bristol Channel. The Beaker people were back.

That the West Country was a rugby-playing area largely explains why adjacent, fixture-seeking South Wales adopted rugby rather than soccer in the crucial and explosive decades of the 1870s and 1880s. Some of the greatest players to achieve fame in the scarlet jersey—Arthur Boucher, Bobby Brice, Harry Packer, Dick Hellings, Wallace Watts, Jim Webb and the immortal Gwyn Nicholls—were West Countrymen by birth but Welsh by location, adoption and inclination. Hancock, chunky, skilful, somewhat authoritarian, had already captained his club and county sides in Somerset; he was now ready to try his hand with Cardiff, where tradition and convention counted for less than innovation and enterprise and where styles and attitudes were being fashioned afresh in a buoyant environment whose chief characteristic was its novelty.

Charles Saxton's 1946 Kiwi dictum that the essence of rugby football is fourteen men putting the fifteenth clear had not yet been enunciated, but the Cardiff committee anticipated its spirit when in February 1884 they decided to rearrange the usual formation of nine forwards and three three-quarters to eight forwards and *four* three-quarters. This was to accommodate the go-getting Frank Hancock who, called up at the last moment to make his first team début in a tough away fixture against Cheltenham College the previous week, had scored the only two tries of the match. The committee, reluctant to drop him but equally unwilling to break up their regular three-quarters, included Hancock at centre in a four three-quarter line for the next match with Gloucester on 23 February 1884. It is an historic date.

Cardiff maintained the system till the end of the season but abandoned it for most of the next owing to prolonged injury to their regular full-back. But in 1885-86 Hancock captained the club to one of its greatest seasons when, playing four three-quarters throughout, 26 out of 27 fixtures were won and 131 tries scored to a mere 4 against. The Welsh XV soon adopted the same formation, as did all the other rugby-playing countries, and the four three-quarter system remains to this day Wales's greatest contribution to rugby football.

The outstanding success of Hancock's side attracted a great influx of sensation-seeking spectators, and from that season's income of £900—more than double the previous season's takings—the old grandstand was dismantled and a new one erected. It cost £362 and was first used for the 1885 Boxing Day fixture with Liverpool. A steel rope was put around the ground in place of the previous hempen one, and duckboards put down for the first time to save spectators having to stand ankle-deep in mud. A further temporary stand went up in 1886-87 'to accommodate the ever increasing number of spectators'.

By the early 1890s there were stands on both sides of Cardiff

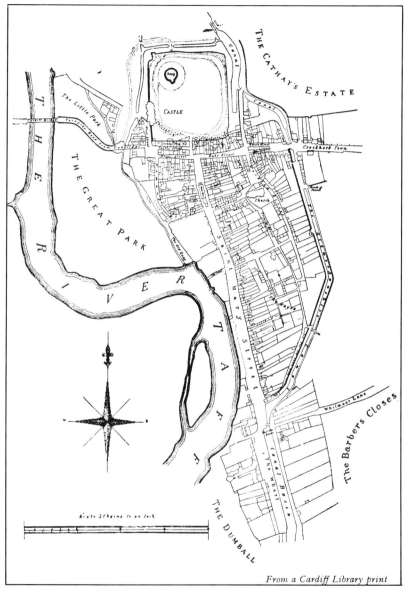

Cardiff in 1828, showing the old course of the River Taff and the position of the Town Quay.

The view south from Cardiff castle around 1870, showing Westgate Street
and the section of Cardiff Arms Park which refused to drain. `

Cardiff Arms Park in 1901.

Arms Park as, in common with many football grounds through-out Britain, it began to acquire the corrugated characteristics and appurtenances of a stadium—though not without expend-iture. In 1891 platforms were laid around the ground at a cost of £21, while more steel fencing cost nearly £150 although 'the purpose for which it was erected, viz. to keep the street urchins from getting into the ground, proved a failure'. Of more value was the provision of a space under the grandstand for the players to hang their sweaters and wraps, a kind of temporary dressing-room. However, until the erection of a new pavilion in 1904, it was the Grand Hotel in Westgate Street that fulfilled that function, and on International days, the Angel.

The first International match played on the Cardiff Arms Park was against Ireland on 12 April 1884 when Wales won by a dropped goal and two tries to nil and supplied their opponents with a couple of players into the bargain. The pride of Erin had arrived two men short, highlighting even then the problem that has wondrously plagued the Irish selectors ever since, of having to choose a team of fifteen from a squad of thirteen. It is a minor curiosity, too, that while Ireland and Scotland played three times at Cardiff before the nineteenth century ran out, England, Wales's first International opponents in 1881, got to play there only once. That was in 1893 and it could hardly have been a more dramatic occasion.

By then Cardiff was a major town with a population of 130,000. The basic problems of water supply, sanitation and drainage had been met. All-night street lamps were in operation. Gas and electricity systems had been installed in the 1870s. Its main streets had long since been laid and paved and were already congested with horse-drawn trams and buses. Imposing buildings designed and constructed in the grand manner were shooting up. Public and private offices, palatial hotels and banks and enticing shopping arcades all proclaimed Cardiff's swelling importance. The 1880s and 1890s saw between them the building of the arcades, the Central Library in the Hayes, the Royal Infirmary, St David's Hospital, the University College, the Cory Hall; the Empire and Grand Theatres and the Theatre Royal (later the Prince of Wales) in Wood Street. It was in 1881, foundation-year of the Welsh

Rugby Union, that the merchant palace of a Coal Exchange went up in Mountstuart Square, and the two institutions symbolished the same headlong growth of industrial South Wales.

A native of Cardiff noted with wide-eyed wonderment in 1884 that its rise 'more nearly resembles that of an American city, of Cincinatti, St Louis or Chicago'. In the momentous year 1905—when Cardiff was granted the status of a city and Wales celebrated by alone defeating New Zealand on the Arms Park—Cardiff was acclaimed for its 'impression of modernity and progressiveness, of spacious streets and buildings, of docks and ships and of great commercial activity, which well merit the epithet "the Chicago of Wales".' In 1893 Chicago staged a World's Fair, where Ben Davies, the Welsh tenor, bought the house down. What meat was to Chicago, coal was to Cardiff, and was itself a spectacle that year, when eighteen tons of it were burnt on the Arms Park to save an International match.

The winter weather of the first week of January 1893 had been severe all over South Wales. There were ice floes on the Taff, the River Rhondda had frozen over, there was even curling in Llwynypia. Cardiff Arms Park was 'as hard as a brickbat' to the *South Wales News*'s 'Old Stager' (who was well accustomed to throwing them). With Saturday's game against England in mind, on the Thursday it was decided to employ 'fire-devils', coal-filled buckets pierced with holes and mounted on bricks to help thaw out the ground. For twenty-seven hours up to 11 a.m. on the morning of the match five hundred 'devils' along with thirty to forty large hot boiler plates were spread over the Arms Park.

So when the correspondent of the London *Morning Leader* arrived in Cardiff with the English team on Friday night, he saw 'a strange, weird, uncanny sight . . . like a scene from Dante's *Inferno*. Imagine if you can an acre or more of ground heaped several feet high with live coal from five hundred fires blazing far up into the dark night. Dozens of dark, ghoul-like figures were threading their way about the fires, heaping on fresh fuel, while the falling snow rendered the scene one of the most unique and romantic ever seen on a football field. Like Wellington at Waterloo your reporter walked over the field at midnight, and found it in a fairly good condition.'

The following day, 7 January 1893, found the Welsh XV in good condition too, and it was England's Waterloo as Wales, spearheaded by the incomparable Arthur Gould and propelled to a 12-11 victory by the unerring boot of Billy Bancroft, laid the foundations for the first-ever Welsh Triple Crown, a triumph that 'sent the population of Cardiff plus the thousands of visitors off their blessed chumps'. In fact it was Wales's only Triple Crown of the nineteenth century, though they would win another six during the first decade of the twentieth.

With rugby now a mass spectator sport in South Wales, it was difficult for Welsh soccer to mount a serious challenge before the turn of the century. At representative level a bridgehead was established in 1894 when the first soccer International to be held in South Wales was staged at St Helen's, Swansea's rugby and cricket ground. It is often forgotten that Cardiff Arms Park, too, was the venue for a variety of South Wales League, Cup and International association football matches between 1891 and the opening of Ninian Park in 1910, about a dozen games in all. The six International matches were, with one exception, played on a Monday. The first against England in March 1896, and though the occasion was graced by the matchless skills of the mercurial toothpick-chewing Billy Meredith, Wales suffered a 9-1 drubbing. Things would improve, and so would attendances, but the very modest 'gate' of £245 taken at that pioneer event of 1896 confirmed that it was rugby that still enjoyed the majority popular support in Cardiff as in South Wales generally at this time. Crowds of 12,000 regularly attended club matches at Cardiff, and there was plenty worth watching—apart from a period of five weeks early in 1897 when the ground was suspended because of the rough handling of the referee in a needle match with old rivals Newport. On 4 February 1893 the great Gwyn Nicholls played his first game for Cardiff, and within eighteen months two wings had to be added to the grandstand, increasing its capacity to 1200.

Already, though, the excellence of the rugby served up was not always matched by the quality of the playing surface. When

Cardiff played the Maoris in December 1888 the ground was 'in a deplorable state, wet, muddy, with pools of water on the pitch'. It was not the first or last time that it would resemble a tributary of the adjoining Taff. The problem was a section of the field on the south side which refused to drain: it was as if the ancient bed of the old river would not lie down. In the summer of 1895 the entire surface was taken up and a network of drain-pipes, a layer of ashes and a thin covering of new soil put down, and the whole area re-turfed at a total cost of over a thousand pounds. Drainage cost the club another £100 in 1896. Not until the massive rebuilding programme begun in the 1960s would the ghost of the old River Taff finally be laid to rest.

By then Wales was about to enter a second golden era. In 1900 it was on the threshold of its first. As if in anticipation of the momentous decade in prospect, in 1900-01 the Welsh Football Union agreed with the Cardiff club, who were themselves anxious to retain International matches at Cardiff, to shoulder three-quarters of the costs of ground improvement. That season, with the great crowd of the Irish match of 1899 fresh in its mind, and a second Triple Crown won in 1900, the Union contributed substantially to a £2000 project for increasing the grandstand accommodation to 1800, and the over-all capacity of the ground to 35,000.

Every inch, every vantage point would be needed during the next decade, when the acre on the Taff staged some of the greatest rugby football ever seen.

This essay was based on the following sources:
(place of publication is Cardiff unless stated otherwise)

C.S. Arthur, *Cardiff R.F.C. History and Statistics 1876-1908* (1908).
E.L. Chappell, *History of the Port of Cardiff* (1939).
M.J. Daunton, *Coal Metropolis: Cardiff 1870-1914* (Leicester 1977).
D.E. Davies, *Cardiff Rugby Football Club History and Statistics 1876-1975* (1975).
John Davies, *Cardiff and the Marquess of Bute* (1981).
J. Howells, 'Reminiscences of Cardiff', *Red Dragon*, V, 1884, pp. 218-232.
J.H. Matthews, *Cardiff Records*, 6 vols. (1898-1911).
J.F. Rees (ed.), *The Cardiff region, a survey* (1960).

William Rees, *Cardiff, a history of the city* (1962).

W.J. Trounce, *Cardiff in the Fifties* (1918).

Glanmor Williams (ed.), *Glamorgan County History*, vols. III-VI (1971-88).

Stewart Williams (ed.), *The Cardiff Book*, vols. 1 and 2 (Barry, 1973, 1974).

Stewart Williams (ed.), *Cardiff Yesterday*, vols. 1-7 (Barry, 1980-83).

Newspapers: *Cardiff and Merthyr Guardian, South Wales Daily News, Western Mail.*

CHAPTER 4

1905 AND ALL THAT: SPORTING SUCCES AND SOCIAL FUNCTION IN WALES 1880-1914

I

Historians are generally distrustful of simplistic generalizations such as that 'the modern age was born in 1900'; and rightly so since it happened in 1905. That year a 25-year-old clerk in a Swiss patent office published three scientific papers which dislodged the two corner-stones of classical physics, the absolute nature of space and time. Albert Einstein's Special Theory of Relativity proposed that space bends: the shortest distance between two points is a curve.

Before the year was out this unlikely hypothesis had received confirmation from an even unlikelier direction. On 16 December, at Cardiff Arms Park, the national rugby team of Wales faced the touring and hitherto invincible New Zealand 'All Blacks'. Some 30 minutes into the game, which would make it around three o'clock, a stratagem which the Welsh players had prepared and practised to a pitch of perfection over the last few days was put to the test. From a scrummage 30 yards outside the All Blacks' goal-line a Welsh attack developed down the right, but the ball was suddenly switched to the left and rapidly passed across field until it reached the diminutive wingman Teddy Morgan, who tore around the converging New Zealand defence on an arcing, curving run that Einstein himself would have approved to score in the corner and win the game.

The following Monday South Wales's leading newspaper carried, amidst acres of match accounts and analyses, an eye-witness description of the occasion in Welsh by 'Ap Idanfryn', alias Gwilym Hughes, for whom this was plainly a new experience. Whatever his initial reservations, they were in full retreat by the end:

A SOUVENIR.

"Y Ddraig Goch a ddyry Gychwyn."

COPYRIGHT.

THE OFFICIAL PROGRAMME.

New Zealand

v.

Wales

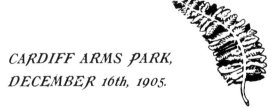

CARDIFF ARMS PARK,
DECEMBER 16th, 1905.

Printed and Published by Rees' Electric Press, Plymouth Street, Cardiff,
in conjunction with the Welsh Football Union.

I had heard about crowds so huge they could not be counted. I saw one today in Cardiff, Wales's principal city, and I have no particular desire to see another like it. Every nation under the sun was represented in this excited throng, black, white, yellow—the clean-living, rustic Welshmen, the self-confident Englishman, the dark-skinned negro, the yellow-complexioned Jap [*sic*] and Chinese—all assembled to watch thirty strong, rugged men play rugby football . . . Who said the [Welsh religious] Revival has killed off football? There's little to suggest that today, and it has to be admitted that this vast crowd is as intelligent, respectable in character and presentable in appearance as any seen anywhere. How many people are there here? Fifty thousand, they reckon . . . Listen to the cheering. Wales has won! What the other nations of these islands have failed to do has been achieved by these sons of the Ancient Britons. The news is going out to the four corners of the earth . . . Tonight is going to be as unforgettable as Mafeking night.[1]

Hailed even at the time as 'the match of the century', the social and cultural symbolic significance of this one rugby game merits as much 'thick description' as any Balinese cockfight.[2] No play was ever deeper than the Wales versus New Zealand match of 1905.[3]

II

The events of that afternoon would reverberate beyond that year and beyond rugby football itself. The epic nature of the encounter can partly, though by no means wholly, be explained in terms of the aura of mutual invincibility which surrounded it. It was not merely that the Welsh XV—at this time enjoying, like the Wales whose offspring they were, a Golden Age of enterprise, optimism and confidence—had proved superior to the all-conquering New Zealanders who had run up over 800 points against a mere 27 in a whirlwind rampage which had destroyed the cream of the other home countries. It was that both XVs were directly representative of a manner of life as much as a style of play, of a social philosophy as well as of rugby thinking, a classic example of the permeation of a game through the interstices of their respective societies so that it was far more than a game, but a factor defining national existence.

For if both were different societies at the start of this century, they also shared a common desire to define themselves on their own terms to the world at large. Neither was unduly hampered by the stays of tradition and hierarchy which corseted the Mother Country; both were continually fertilizing the technical development of the game by devising new ploys and

"Humpty Dumpty Had a Great Fall"

formations, the 'Celts', the pioneers of the four three-quarter system behind the scrum, the 'Colonials' of a seven-man pack in it. But whereas the Antipodeans would surround their victories with the ideology of the life-enhancing challenge of distant untamed lands, Wales' footballing success was deciphered in other terms, as indisputable, even natural evidence of national progress and, more dubiously, of racial superiority. 'In these latter times Wales has progressed phenomenally' announced its main Liberal newspaper in 1909, cataloguing the prominent places occupied by Welshmen in politics, education, the pulpit, commerce and literature, and careful to add that 'in the higher forms of sport our athletes are at once the envy and the despair of other nations'.[4] The Cardiff *Western Mail*, too, after extracing maximum mileage from the idea of Wales 'coming to the rescue of the Empire' by its victory in 1905, concluded that 'The prestige of Wales has been enhanced tremendously as a nation possessed of those splendid [Celtic] qualities—pluck and determination'.[5] When a new edition of George Borrow's *Wild Wales* appeared in 1906, Theodore Watts-Dunton extolled the historic Welsh characteristics of skill and courage as precisely those qualities possessed by the Welsh team that had just defeated New Zealand.[6]

Such ideas were not merely the stock-in-trade of contemporary racial theorists. They had a special resonance in an Edwardian Wales of political self-confidence, cultural creativity, national self-awareness and material prosperity, all to a greater or lesser degree generated by the produce of a coalfield which was approaching its zenith, diffusing its wealth into all areas of Welsh life and keeping the navies of the world afloat. Earlier in 1905, when the Russian Baltic Fleet was despatched to the bottom of the Sea of Japan, the Kaiser mused that Togo's ships had been fired with Cardiff coal.[7] This Cardiff was the chief funnel-port of the world's greatest single coal-exporting region. It had a third of the entire population of Wales within a 20-mile radius; its own population had shot up from less than 10,000 in 1841 to 164,000 by 1901, and was soon to reach 182,000. This was 'noble and squalid' Cardiff, the Welsh Chicago whose economic and political clout was recognized in October 1905 when it was designated a city, soon to become

Lloyd George's 'City of Dreadful Knights'.[8] In December 1905 Lloyd George's own career was launched into the trajectory which would take him to the very pinnacle of power when he was appointed to Campbell-Bannerman's Liberal cabinet. It was Sir Leoline Jenkins, Charles II's Secretary of State (1681-84), who had been the last Welshman to hold such high office; since the later-modern Welsh were as fervently British as their early-modern predecessors, this was an appropriate reassertion of a Welshness that was subordinate to its Britishness. In his celebration of the Welsh victory in cosmopolitan Cardiff in 1905 'Ap Idanfryn' was striking all the dominant key-notes in a Cambro-Imperial fanfare, saluting a Wales confident of its future within the world-wide British polity.

III

It was a Wales ideally respectable, orderly, clean-living, educated, democratic, that was being moulded in its own image by a thrusting middle-class intelligentsia and élite. Their modernization programme involved the reshaping of popular culture, a process which is covered by the umbrella-term 'social control' for the nineteenth century, but which it has become fashionable for early modernists to call 'acculturation'. Historians like R. Muchembled and J. Delumeau interpret the Reformation and Counter-Reformation as a massive missionary crusade aimed at the Christianization of Europe, an attempt to acculturate the masses by their élites.[9] In Peter Burke's definition, this involved 'a systematic attempt by some of the educated . . . to change the attitudes and values of the rest of the population, or as the Victorians used to say, to "improve" them'.[10] The success of the early modern acculturators in turning the inhabitants of Christendom into Christians was, it seems, only partial. By the same token, if late nineteenth-century rugby football, codified in the English public schools and universities and diffused outwards and downwards, was to play a reforming role in the civilizing of the new Wales of surging demographic and industrial growth, then it cannot be pronounced an unqualified success. It did not curb violence and disorderly behaviour: it incited them. The evidence of Welsh rugby confirms the verdict passed on English and Scottish soccer that 'riots, unruly behaviour, violence, assault and vandalism appear to have been a well-established . . . pattern of crowd behaviour at football matches at least from the 1870s'.[11]

Football teams plausibly provided foci for local identity and fulfilled an important bonding function when the division of labour in industrial society worked in the direction of an autonomous individualism; they block-built identity upwards from the level of works, club and street teams, themselves the formalization of gangs and similar 'abbeys of youth' with long-standing traditions of sociability behind them. But just as the standardization and adoption of a uniform set of rules accelerated the growth of regular fixtures, the increasing involvement of working men brought in its train an increased competitiveness. Proliferating cup and league competitions not only reinforced community identity, they also honed local rivalries to a keen edge. There was 'semi-savagery' and 'wanton biting' in a cup match between Bridgend and Neath in 1880; the winning Llanelli team at Neath in 1883 'were left to the tender mercies of an infuriated mob and had almost to fight their way to the hotel . . . they were hustled and pushed, hooted and pelted with clods, mud and even stones'.[12] Grounds were regularly closed for a specified cooling-off period as the Welsh Rugby Union (founded in 1881 in untamed Neath) took a firmer control of its affairs in the 1890s. Neath's own Gnoll ground was suspended in 1895, Aberavon's in 1896, and Abertillery's in 1897. That year the Rhondda club Ferndale's ground was closed after 'a bloodbath' with adjacent Mountain Ash. Even the Cardiff Arms Park was suspended for five weeks that year because of the manhandling of the referee. In 1899 Aberavon's ground was ordered to be closed for, initially, eight months after the crowd had been incited to violence by a committeeman urging his team to 'go for the [expletive deleted], boys'.[13]

Into the new century, old habits died hard. An incident at Llanelli in November 1900, when the referee had been so intimidated by the crowd that he had required a police escort from the ground and out of the district, led to placards being displayed at Newport urging spectators to accept the referee's decision, since to do otherwise by shouting and arguing loudly 'is neither fair nor sportsmanlike'.[14] The referee *was* heeded on a single Saturday in October 1906 when 'discreditable scenes ... fighting and foul play' resulted in five players being sent off at Mountain Ash and another at Brynmawr, while all 30 players took an early bath at Newport when a harassed referee declared a cessation of hostilities well before time; that day there was 'brutal play' at Cardiff too.[15] Whether this continual mayhem is seen in terms of social scientists' typologies of violence,[16] or as merely the domesticated durability of the love of fighting for fighting's sake, what is clear is that rugby football, one of the new model sports, was not, in Wales at least, played or watched with that devotion by working men to the ideals of sporting behaviour which their middle-class acculturators whould have liked. It was not the tranquilizer of unruly proletarian crowds any more than it was the sedative of industrial militancy. In the restless, violent year 1911 enormous crowds thronged to see Wales win its sixth triple crown of the decade, while the domestic Welsh club programme flourished without any diminution of support for its traditional, vigorous rivalries.

IV

It was international success that subdued and eventually reversed the prejudices and, initially, outright hostility of another acculturating agency that did not accommodate within its programme of moral reform anything as conducive to idle living as football, with its attendants evils of drink, gambling and general encouragement to the beast in man—and, it seemed, woman.[17] This was the Chapel. The Church, which had for centuries patronized all kinds of communal events from fund-raising ales to athletic contests, had no such scruples. The Anglican college of St David's, Lampeter, had spearheaded the arrival of rugby in Wales, its peaceful precincts acting as the nursery of tearaway teams that were the very embodiment of the Church Militant; three of the first Welsh representative side were clergymen, including the captain, Bevan; while the

captain of the last pre- 1914 Welsh XV was another, himself a
member of a ferocious pack of forwards known as 'the Terrible
Eight'.

The Noncormist denominations, more puritanical, equated
rugby football with all kind of profanity and intemperance
(before the arrival of the modern club house, teams used the
local 'Arms' to change in; brewers were traditional sporting
patrons). It was not only impressionable young men who were
at risk either: a moral minority—probably of one—in Llanelli
ringingly declared in 1886 that 'the game of football is unfit for
young ladies of both sexes' [sic].[18] Four years later chapel
members at the head of the Swansea valley, having narrowly
lost a public debate as to whether rugby should be played in the
village, sawed down the goalposts on the eve of the newly-
constituted club's first game and solemnly transported them to
the police station.[19] At Pontypridd, at the confluence of the
major coal-producing Rhondda, Taff and Cynon valleys, where
rapid immigration threatened to undermine religion and
morality, a minister denounced football as 'the dullest and
most sensless game the world has seen . . . If young and middle-
aged men wish to frequent pubs, theatres and football fields,
then let them in the name of the living God remain outside the
Christian pale'.[20] Not even the Sabbath itself was safe: when it
became known in 1899 that Swansea intended playing on a
Sunday during their forthcoming French tour, local Baptist
ministers denounced the proposal as 'an act of public dese-
cration and national retrogression which will injure the morality and fair name of the Principality as the most religious
country in the world'.[21]

The Welsh religious revival of 1904-05, which our big-match
eye witness 'Ap Idanfryn' had to acknowledge had not killed off
rugby, almost did so. A final, defiant gesture against the dying
of the light, the anguished cry of a people recently uprooted
from its rural verities and thrown into an industrial melting pot
—a characteristic product of a frontier society, therefore,
uneasily poised between two cultures[22]—the Revival pointed
an accusing finger at rugby. As the evangelists crusaded
through the coalfield, spectacular conversions were recorded,
several, appropriately enough, among the rugby fraternity:

followers ostentatiously tore up their season tickets, players burned their jerseys, clubs closed down from anything from four weeks in south east Wales to four years in the more rural, Welsh-speaking anthracite area.[23] The galvanic, if shortlived, effect the Revival had was encapsulated in the conversion of one veteran footballer in mid-Glamorgan who leapt to his feet during a service to proclaim 'I used to play full-back for the Devil, but now I am forward for God'.[24]

By 1905, however, and certainly afterwards, the future lay with the Devil. It was spectator sport that would now play the role that religion had once enjoyed as a popular mass activity and which the Revival had hoped to regenerate. 'Ap Idanfryn', whose readjustment of his own wrenched sensibility registers like a transplant on a cardiograph, was in truth a Sioni-come-lately by comparison with many who had shared his concerns but who, since the turn of the century, had been persuaded by Wales's striking rugby success to swallow their scruples instead of their blood. 'What is the use of preaching against football?' one deacon 'with a tear in his voice' was heard to remark to another at an international match in 1900. 'We couldn't draw such a crowd as this to a *gymanfa* [hymn-singing festival]'. 'No indeed', replied his companion mournfully, 'but—wasn't that a lovely try!'[25] The Revd. S.B. Williams of Llanelli was, by 1902, condemning 'the attitude of the so-called Christians who objected to going to a football match. He was quite certain that there was less rowdyism among the 12,000 on the occasion of the Swansea match [the speaker was at a club banquet celebrating Llanelli's win] than one would find at a *Gymanfa* or an eisteddfod. Football was a noble game and he did not object etc., etc.'.[26] In 1910 'Play the Game' was the subject of a sermon delivered by a Presbyterian minister in Neyland, Pembrokeshire, in the course of which he rejeced 'the rigid system under which he had been brought up [that] had led him to believe that football matches were of such a character that it was wrong for Christian people to support them'. On the contrary, a game of football taught people good temper, and he proposed that local clergymen and deacons formed a team of their own: his preferred line-up would include the Rev. W.J. Chamberlain (Wesleyan) at forward, the Rev. R.C. Evans at

three-quarter, the Rev. W. Powell at full-back, and himself
—naturally—in the key half-back position. He also advocated
clean play.[29]

It was not only aspirants to religious or moral control who
leapt on to the accelerating anti-rugby bandwagon. In 1895 the
member for Caernarvon Boroughs wrote to his wife from the
industrial valleys of Monmouthshire that his audiences there
were less responsive to his radical politics because they were
'sunk into a morbid footballism'.[2] In 1908, when the member
for Caernarvon Boroughs was president of the Board of Trade
and in Cardiff to receive the Freedom of the City, he saw his
first rugby match. He kicked off the Cardiff v. Blackheath game
at the Arms Park, and pronounced himself intrigued by it: 'It's a
most extraordinary game. I never saw it before and I must say I
think it's more exciting than politics'. Five years later his son
Gwilym was playing for London Welsh.[29]

Thus were the acculturators themselves acculturated, in
accordance with the redefinition of the term 'acculturation'—
that first appeared in American anthropological literature
around 1880—by a later generation of anthropologists as
embracing 'those phenomena which result when . . . individuals having different cultures come into continuous first-
hand contact, with subsequent changes in the original cultural
patterns of either or both groups'.[30] The tailoring of a rough and
ready popular culture that assimilated a robust physical-
contact game like rugby with ease, and fashioned it to suit its
own self-making purpose to meet the requirements of more
ambitious programmes of reform, resulted in rugby becoming
in Wales an annexe of official culture. As a signifier of national
identity, rugby had a valuable role to play within the Welsh-
British imperial framework.

V

'The men—these heroes of many victories that represented
Wales [against New Zealand] embodied the best manhood of
the race . . . We all know the racial qualities that made Wales
supreme on Saturday . . . It is admitted she is the most poetic of
nations. It is amazing that in the greatest of all popular

pastimes she should be equally dinstinguished'.[31] Thus a leading editorial the Monday following the victory which all but stitched rugby football on to the national flag.

Yet this was quite a fortuitous development. Rugby was not intrinsic to the Welsh. How could it be when it was imported into Wales by the familiar diffusionist clutch of headmasters, industrialists, businssmen, solicitors, doctors and clerks? It arrived in Neath via Llandovery College and Merchiston; Llanelli weathered its early days with the products of Rugby and Wellington at the helm; Newport emerged from a conspiracy of Old Monmouthians now in the professions.[32] Athletic exercise, the paradigm national recreation of Victorian England, was canvassed enthusiastically in Wales. 'To take care and develop systematically our physical conditions is not less a duty towards God than ourselves', opined a Welsh sports sage in 1894, 'and the effect is the better development of our mental and moral natures ... the effect of athletic exercise must benefit the whole of man'.[33] There were close links between athletics and rugby in late nineteenth-century Wales. The Welsh quarter-mile champion Richard Gordon died on the rugby field in 1880, while Edward Peake, a member of the first Welsh XV of 1881, had his career curtailed by a hurdling accident at Oxford. Richard Mullock, the Newport impresario who managed that first side, was Wales's representative at the inaugural meeting of the Amateur Athletic Association (AAA) at the Randolph Hotel, Oxford, in April 1880. When, thanks to Mullock, the Welsh Rugby Union was set up the following year, its first president was C.C. Chambers of Swansea, a brother of the famous Llanelli-born John Graham Chambers, 'the architect of modern athletics' who during his 40-year life rowed for Cambridge, became champion walker of England, devised the Queensberry Rules, staged the Cup Final and Thames Regatta, founded the Amateur Athletic Club (AAC) in 1866, instituted championships for billiards, boxing and cycling, accompanied (in a boat) Captain Webb as he swam the Channel, and opened a Welsh shop in Chelsea. C.C. Chambers was succeeded as president of the Welsh Rugby Union (WRU) by the Earl of Jersey, a leading South Wales landowner who was for ten years president of the AAA.[34]

While the Welshness of rugby would be retrospectively legitimized by the publication in 1892 of a standard text of George Owen's *Description of Penbrokeshire* (1603), with its bone-crushing account of the Tudor game of cnappan which conveniently endowed the later game with a plausible Welsh-British pedigree, the development of modern rugby owed more to the initiative and resource of immigrants who found the bracing atmosphere of a new South Wales conducive to the expression of various talents, including sporting prowess. These immigrants—a quarter of a million of whom flooded into Glamorganshire alone in the last quarter of the century—made their mark. James Bevan, the captain of Wales's first national rugby side, was actually born in Australia, while the pivotal figure in the introduction of the four three-quarter back-line ('the Welsh system'), was a scion of the Hancock brewing family who left Wiveliscombe in Somerset to assuage Cardiff's thirst in 1883.[35] It then became the conventional wisdom that Welsh rugby success was due to its classlessness, its capacity to transcend social formations and differences by embracing well-educated, white-collar backs (for their skill) and manual worker forwards (for their strength). That forward strength, which was by no means deficient in skill and technical expertise, was supplied by the formidable likes of Packer, Watts, Boucher, Hellings and Brice, who won 60 Welsh caps among them during the years 1891-1907, but whose Welshness was geographical merely: they had all come to work and live in South Wales from Somerset and Devon. Perhaps the first theoretician of Welsh forward play was the brainy Tom Graham who came from Tyneside to win a dozen caps in the 1890s. In this respect even the heroic team of 1905 was more representative of the game in Wales than of some historic ethnicity, and Watts-Dunton, whose facile Darwinism led him to portray them as the reincarnation of the Welsh bowmen of Crécy, might have done better to reflect that 'Boxer' Harding was born in Market Rasen, and H.B. Winfield in Nottingham, while their captain E. Gwyn Nicholls, had been born in Westbury-on-Severn, Gloucestershire. Nor was this unexpected: by 1911 a third of Glamorgan's population was born outside it.

The self-creating Wales which in turn created these rugby heroes had been looking to the outside world since at least the 1880s, when, in Gwyn A. Williams's words, 'the capital, the technology, the enterprise, the skill and labour of South Wales fertilized large and distant tracts of the world from Montana and Pennsylvania to Chile, Argentina and Russia'.[36] No careers were more global in scope than those of the champion Newport side of the late 1870s, of whom one went to be an army officer in India, another to manage an iron works in Newfoundland, a third to China and a fourth to be a solicitor in Colombo; their captain, W.D. Phillips, went ranching in Texas for 30 years.[37]

This Wales looked out to the world at large and to the Empire in particular. 'Ap Idanfryn' rightly bracketed the jubilation of 16 December 1905 with that of Mafeking night: the Welsh Rugby Union had made several donations in support of the Boer War. Welsh rugby players, especially the professional element among them, are constantly to be found, once their playing careers are over, living—and dying—in the darkest recesses of the Empire. A.J. Gould spent a year in the West Indies in mid-career, while his international brother Bert left for South Africa in 1897 and died in Germiston in 1913. W.B. Norton, who won six caps from Cardiff, died in Old Calabar, West Africa, in 1899; Norman Biggs, also of Cardiff and first capped at 18 in 1888, was fatally wounded by a poisoned dart in Northern Nigeria 20 years later. Strand-Jones of Lampeter and Llanelli, Wales's full back in 1902 and 1903, became an army chaplain in Lahore and elsewhere on the Northwest Frontier.[38] The 1905 team, once again, mirrors this imperial tendency: Harding emigrated to New Zealand where he became a farm-manager in Greymouth, J.F. Williams died of blackwater fever in Nigeria in 1911; less exotically in 1910, Percy Bush followed the imperial coal trade from Cardiff to Nantes, where he became vice-consul. Well might *The Welsh Review* of March 1906, after likening the Welsh to the Japanese, rejoice that 'Wales at last is beginning to give of her best to the Empire and the world'.

It was a deeply, or at least sentimentally, royalist Wales. When the Welsh Rugby Union supplanted the South Wales Football Union as the organising body of the game in 1881, it abandoned the former's brash white leek slashed diagonally across a black jersey in favour of the more circumspect Prince of Wales feathers on scarlet. In 1881 Llanelli flirted, fortunately briefly, with a primrose and rose playing strip, a colour combination that might have been suggested by Victoria herself.[39] This was also a profoundly imperial Wales. Even the quasi-separatism of the Young Wales movement, Cymru Fydd, led in the 1890s by Lloyd George and Liberal Whip Tom Ellis, MP for Merioneth, was aimed at winning for Wales a seat in the imperial sun. They both would have endorsed what a Liberal candidate declared to loud applause at Barry on St David's Day, 1900, that 'proud as he was of being a Welshman, he confessed a still greater pride that Wales was part of the British Empire— the largest and best in the world'. This Empire, claimed a Welsh MP and close ally of Lloyd George, was 'wider, more beneficent than that of Rome, more world-embracing than that conceived by Alexander in his wildest dreams'.[40]

Edwardian Wales seemed to have found that much sought-after seat in the sun: 'in these latter times Wales has progressed phenomenally' so that 'Welshmen take their places with the greatest in the sphere of human activity.[41] Yet educational advance (symbolized by a National University, a National Museum, and, soon, a National Libarary), political maturity and economic progress, significant though they were, were not the only indicators of a national awakening, as the *South Wales News* recognized in 1909: 'In what may in a sense be termed the Renaissance of Welsh nationalism, football is a factor that cannot be ignored. Wales, in a game that demands more skill than strength—that is, even more a 'mental' than a physical pastime—is the equal of, and very often superior to, the other three nations'. It concluded that 'Football is one of the factors that symbolizes individuality in national existence'.[42]

That year Wales won the rugby triple crown for the second successive year, their fifth of the decade, and they had by now gone nine international matches without defeat (Australia had been a further scalp in December 1908). This provided yet further confirmation, if there was still anybody who doubted it, that rugby football marked the Welsh out as a distinctive nation. 'The peculiar qualities of the race may be said to be as distinctly shown in the exponents of the game as in those who lead in other spheres', and it was worth re-emphasizing that it had its mental side, and was 'not a mere exhibition of physical strength or physical skill'.[43]

VI

Imperial Wales' acculturators recognized the potential of rugby as a focus for national aspiration over and above disruptive political-industrial tendencies. They not only realized it but almost marmorealized it, too, when the Herald Bard (T.H. Thomas, R.C.A.) publicly demanded 'some definite acknowledgement on the part of the nation generally' of Welsh rugby success, and proposed 'a memorial column of simple, massive design, treated in the Celtic style, decorated by discs in bronze'. In suggesting a commemorative obelisk he was anticipating the future more accurately than he knew, for the post-war depression would torpedo Welsh prosperity and confidence on, and off, the field: there would be only one more triple crown (in 1911) for the next 40 years. The Herald Bard's scheme did not materialize, but it was not from disagreement with his motives in proposing it:

> Wales is a very small country. The success which has attended her efforts in athletics is therefore a sort of miracle. It has been attained by the exercise of those qualities in which critics of the Welsh declare us to be deficient—hard work, self-control, discipline. The game has been intellectualised by our players. Whatever may happen in the future, Wales is signalised.[44]

An image was being manufactured of Welsh rugby far removed from the reality of the non-ideological excitement and admiration it evoked, the passions it stirred, its ability to conjure artists out of artisans, the sheer theatricality which was at the heart of its popular appeal. Dai Smith has argued that in the face of the destabilizing combination of continuous in-migration, breakneck economic growth and the strident politicization of, particularly, coalfield industrial relations, the concept of Wales as 'an indivisible community, a nation of

St. David's Day.

DEWI SANT: Well, Well! How my tree has grown! There's glad I am to see it.

Saint David and Dame Wales joyfully contemplate their country's sturdy growth and its expression in the highest forms of human endeavour—the arts, sciences and rugby football *Western Mail*, 1 March 1910).

natural origins and organic growth' was a difficult one to sustain.[45] Yet it was strenuously upheld by a two-fold historical presentation of the inevitable, orderly progress of Wales to its present high plateau of achievement, an improving blend of literary bread and literal circuses. The bread came in the form of a determined output of popular history of the *In the Land of Harp and Feathers* (Alfred Thomas, 1896) variety,[46] the circuses by stage-managed extravaganzas like the Investiture of the Prince of Wales at Caernarvon in 1911, and two years before that at Cardiff Castle, a National Pageant depicting Welsh history from the earliest times. The leading roles were taken by Wales's aristocracy, some of them playing their own forbears, but there was an accompanying cast of thousands—five thousand in fact—so that the Pageant, like Wales itself, could be seen to be embracing 'all classes of the community'. Since this was the function of rugby too, it was altogether fitting that the stars of a scene re-enacting the storming of the Norman-held castle by a local chieftain and his followers were well-known international players, including three of those 'heroes of many victories', Harding, R.T. Gabe and Gwyn Nicholls.[47]

The historical and contemporary merging of sporting success and social function made rugby into a badge of national identity in a way that association football, for instance, could not match. Long-established in North Wales through its links with Merseyside, soccer began to make rapid headway in South Wales too from around 1900,[48] but its semi-professional status prevented it from acquiring rugby's cohesive role: it was erroneously but revealingly described in a new journal of 1914 edited by one of Wales's leading figures, Thomas Jones, economist, educationist and later Cabinet Secretary, as 'new and alien ... the game of the alien of the valleys whose immigration and denationalizing tendency is one of the major problems of our country'.[49] Similarly, attempts to establish professional rugby openly in South Wales in these years ran up against a combination of practical obstacles and social prejudices: grounds proved difficult to acquire and fixtures with professional north of England clubs expensive to maintain, while the proletarian, cloth-cap image of Northern Union (later Rugby League) football worked against securing the support of the influential middle class, and a discriminating popular following could not be weaned from a genuine attachment to the fifteen-a-side game.[50]

To the writer of 1914, however, it was not the intrinsic appeal of the game that explained its popularity among 'the democracy' but that it was an agency of acculturation incorporating the people into an idealized notion of a socially-integrated Welsh nation:

> In the sense that nationality is a community of memories so is Rugby football the national game. The names of the giants are on

the lips of the people: there are traditions in Rugby ... Wales possess in Rugby football a game ... which is immeasurably more valuable than the popular code of other countries ... it has made a democracy not only familiar with an amateur sport of distinguished rank but is in reality a discoverer of democracy which acts as participant and patron.[51]

The fit of image to reality was already under strain before the war, while its aftermath ushered in an era when the optimism, confidence and prosperity which had seemed to gild the Edwardian age were in short supply. By the 1930s it had become, in Wales, commonplace to invoke rugby as the integument that could join together diverse interests across a sorely divided social spectrum. With so many other indicators of a distinctive Welsh identity apparently in full retreat as Wales struggles to survive into the twenty-first century,[52] rugby football retains the image—by now a cliché and often a caricature—it acquired in the early years of the twentieth as not merely a prominent constituent of Welsh popular culture but a pre-eminent expression of Welsh consciousness, a signifier of Welsh nationhood.

NOTES

[1] *South Wales Daily News (SWDN)*, 18 Dec. 1905.

[2] Clifford Geertz, 'Thick Description: Towards an Interpretive Theory of Culture' and 'Deep Play: Notes on the Balinese Cockfight' in his *The Interpretation of Cultures* (London, 1975).

[3] The Wales versus New Zealand game is analysed in its total context in D. Smith and G. Williams, *Fields of Praise* (Cardiff, 1980), pp. 145-75.

[4] *SWDN*, 1 March, 15 March 1909.

[5] *Western Mail*, 18 Dec. 1905.

[6] T. Watts-Dunton's 'Introduction' to George Borrow, *Wild Wales* (Everyman ed., London, 1906), p. xxii.

[7] T.K. Derry and T.L. Jarman, *The European World 1870-1945* (London, 1958), p. 112.

[8] For 'the noble and squalid city of Cardiff' see Gwyn A. Williams, *When Was Wales?* (Harmondsworth, 1985), pp. 222-3. More fully, M.J. Daunton, *Coal Metropolis: Cardiff 1870-1914* (Leicester, 1977), and Neil Evans, 'The Welsh Victorian City', *Welsh History Review*, June 1985, 350-87. For an example of the considerable financial clout of the city's business community see A.M. Johnson, *Scott of the Antarctic and Cardiff* (Cardiff, 1984).

[9] For a shrewd conspectus of the literature on social control see F.M.L. Thompson, 'Social Control in Victorian England', *Economic History Review* XXXIV (1981), 189-208. On acculturation, see, e.g. R. Muchembled, *Culture Populaire et Culture des élites dans la France moderne (XVe-XVIIIe siècles)* (Paris, 1978; English trans., Baton Rouge, 1985) J. Delumeau, *Le Catholicisme entre Luther et Voltaire* (2nd ed. Paris, 1979).

[10] P. Burke, *Popular Culture in Early Modern Europe* (London, 1978), p. 20.

[11] J. Hutchinson, quoted in W. Vamplew, 'Sports Crowd Disorder in Britain 1870-1914: Causes and Controls', *Journal of Sport History*, 7 (Spring 1980), 6.

[12] *Bridgend Chronicle*, 2 Dec. 1880; *Llanelly [and County] Guardian*, 6 Dec. 1883.

[13] Examples taken from the Minute-Books of the Welsh Rugby Union. Cf. T. Mason, *Association Football and English Society 1863-1915* (Brighton, 1980), pp. 158-67.

[14] *SWDN*, 26 Nov. 1900.

[15] E.g. Mann and Pearce's FORCE typology, a mnemonic—for frustration, outlawry, remonstrance, confrontation and expressive disorders—adopted by Vamplew, op. cit.

[17] Women spectators were well represented at rugby matches from an early date, e.g. 'Fully a third' of a 5000 crowd at Llanelli in 1884 'were of the gentler sex', *Llanelly Guardian*, 17 April 1884. Moreover, 'football matches are very popular and fashionable places of resort with ladies in other towns', *ibid.*, 25 Nov. 1880.

[18] *Llanelly Guardian*, 9 Dec. 1886.

[19] *Welsh Rugby Magazine*, Dec. 1970 (feature on Ystradgynlais RFC).

[20] *SWDN*, 3 May 1894. The contemporary denominational Welsh language press regularly castigated rugby football as a worthless and dehumanizing

activity, e.g. *Y Dysgedydd* [*The Instructor*] Mehefin [June] 1887, 42-3, *Y Traethodydd* [*The Essayist*] Gorffennaf [July] 1903, 269-74, and the examples in Chapter 5 below.

²¹ *SWDN*, 6 Feb. 1899. There were also protests from the Rhondda and Maesteg, ibid., 12 and 17 Jan. 1899.

²² B.R. Wilson, *Religion in Secular Society* (London, 1966), pp. 27-8.

²³ Smith and Williams, op. cit., pp. 126-7. International match attendances were also affected, e.g. *SWDN*, 16 Jan. 1905.

²⁴ Tony Lewis, *The Mules: A History of Kenfig Hill RFC* (Pyle, Mid Glam, 1973), p. 3.

²²⁵ *SWDN*, 7 Jan. 1901.

²⁶ *Llanelly Mercury*, 6 March 1902.

²⁷ *Western Mail*, 6 Jan. 1910.

²⁸ K.O.Morgan (ed.), *Lloyd George: Family Letters 1885-1936* (Cardiff, 1973), p. 91.

²⁹ *Western Mail*, 27 Jan. 1908; P. Beken and S. Jones, *Dragon in Exile: The Centenary History of London Welsh RFC* (London, 1980), p. 62. Cf. the Mayor of Cardiff, who attended the Wales v. Scotland match in 1902 not because he knew much about it but 'to give countenance to the national complexion it took', *SWDN*, 4 Feb. 1902.

³⁰ R. Redfield, R. Linton and M.J. Herskovits, 'Memorandum for the study of acculturation', *American Anthropology* 38 (1936), quoted in K. von Greyerz (ed.), *Religion and Society in Early Modern Europe 1500-1800* (London, 1984), p. 66.

³¹ *SWDN*,18 Dec. 1905.

³² G. Hughes (ed.), *One Hundred Years of Scarlet* (Llanelli, 1983), pp. 1, 11, 51; Nat. Lib. Wales, Douglas A. Jones Collection (Neath); W.J.T. Collins, *Newport Athletic Club 1875-1925* (Newport 1925), pp. 12-13.

³³ Hughes, op. cit. pp. 60-1, and generally B. Haley, *The Healthy Body and Victorian Culture* (London, 1978).

⁴ B. Jarvis, *The Origins of Chepstow Rugby Football Club* (Chepstow, Gwent, 1978), p. 43 (Peake); *SWDN*, 10 March 1880 (Gordon); P. Lovesey, *The Official Centenary History of the AAA* (London, 1979), pp. 19-23 (Chambers, Mullock, Earl of Jersey).

³⁵ J.A. Venn, *Alumni Cantabrigienses* (Cambridge, 1940), Part 2, Vol. i, p. 253 (Bevan); D.E. Davies, *Cardiff Rugby History and Statistics* (Cardiff, 1973), pp. 26-8 (Hancock).

³⁶ Gwyn A. Williams, op cit., p. 222.

³⁷ 'The Record of Newport Rugby', by 'Dromio', *South Wales Argus*, 25 Oct. 1913.

³⁸ *SWDN*, Jan 1899 (Norton); ibid., 4 March 1908 (Biggs); *The Times*, 10 April 1958 (Strand-Jones); *The Breconian*, Dec. 1911, 54 (J.F. Williams); D.E. Davies, op. cit., p. 65 (Bush).

³⁹ *Llanelly Guardian*, 8 Sept, 1881, 23 Feb. 1882. Hywel Teifi Edwards gleefully explores in Welsh the ultra-royalism of the eisteddfodic élite of Victorian Wales in his *Gŵyl Gwalia* (Llandysul, 1980), and in English in *Planet* 52, 12-24. See also D. Tecwyn Lloyd, *Planet* 32, 36-47.

⁴⁰ *SWDN*, 3 March 1900 (Barry); 24 Nov. 1908 (W. Llewelyn Williams to the Carmarthen Cymmrodorion Society).

⁴¹ *SWDN*, 1 March 1909. The Edwardian high-noon is sympathetically assessed by K.O. Morgan, *Rebirth of a Nation: Wales 1880-1980* (Cardiff and Oxford, 1981), ch. 5.

⁴² *SWDN*, 8 Feb. 1909.

⁴³ Ibid., 15 March 1909.

⁴⁴ Ibid., 16 and 17 March 1909.

⁴⁵ Dai Smith, *Wales! Wales?* (London, 1984), p. 51.

⁴⁶ For this and other examples of a 'Gwaliakitsch of iron-souled feyness that was out to lobotomise all the Welsh on behalf of some of them', see D. Smith, *A People and a Proletariat* (London, 1980), pp. 8-9.

⁴⁷ *SWDN*, 27 July 1909. Other internationals on view were Charlie Arthur, Alex Bland, Bobby Brice, Billy Douglas, Reggie Gibbs, Billy Spiller and Johnnie Williams. The Welsh National Pageant, a cross between a masque and a military tattoo, is exhilaratingly recounted in Welsh by Hywel Teifi Edwards, *Codi'r Hen Wlad yn ei Hôl 1850-1914* (Llandysul, 1989), pp. 239-89.

⁴⁸ B. Lile and D. Farmer, 'The Early Development of Association Football in South Wales, 1890-1906', *Transactions of the Honourable Society of Cymmrodorion*, 1984, 193-215.

⁴⁹ *Welsh Outlook*, Feb. 1914, 18.

⁵⁰ See Chapter 7 below.

⁵¹ *Welsh Outlook*, op. cit., 18-19.

⁵² An almost apocalyptic gloom pervades the conclusion of Gwyn A. Williams' *When Was Wales?* (1985), pp. 296-306.

Y MAES CHWARAE A CHENEDLIGRWYDD YNG NGHYMRU 1880-1914

Ni waeth fod yr hin yn oer a garw, bydd miloedd yn sicr o ddod yno; ni waeth pa un ai glowyr wedi bod yn chwysu trwy yr wythnos fyddant, prydlon ydyw eu hanes; os y tu ôl i'r counter yn sefyll fel delwau am oriau, os cael rhyddid, rhoddant eu presenoldeb yno. Ie, football ydyw Diana Cymru grefyddol heddiw.

Y Tyst, 6 Chwefror 1907

Mae haneswr yn dueddol i amau gosodiadau cyffredinol fel 'Ganed yr oes fodern yn y flwyddyn 1900'. Ac at ei gilydd maent yn iawn, oherwydd fe'i ganed ym 1905. Y flwyddyn honno fe ymddangosodd o law gŵr ifanc pump ar hugain oed a oedd, y pryd hwnnw, yn gweithio fel clerc di-nod yn y gwasanaeth sifil yn Berne yn y Swistir, bapur gwyddonol a chwalodd ddau o gonglfeini ffiseg glasurol, sef natur absoliwt amser a gofod. Gyda'r Ddamcaniaeth Arbennig ar Berthnasedd dangosodd Albert Einstein mai un peth yn unig sy'n sicr—cyflymdra goleuni, sef 186,000 o filltiroedd yr eiliad. Mwy syfrdanol fyth, meddai, nid llinell syth yw'r llwybr byrraf rhwng dau bwynt, ond llinell grom: y mae gofod yn plygu.

Cyn i'r flwyddyn honno gyrraedd ei therfyn, cadarnhawyd y ddamcaniaeth annhebygol hon mewn ffordd annhebycach fyth. Ar ddydd Sadwrn, 16 Rhagfyr 1905, ar Barc yr Arfau yng Nghaerdydd, wynebai pymtheg chwaraewr rygbi Cymru bymtheg gorau Seland Newydd. Yn y saith gêm ar hugain a chwaraewyd ganddynt ers cyrraedd ynysoedd Prydain ym mis Medi yr oeddynt yn gwbl ddiguro. Heblaw cael y gorau ar bob un o'u gwrthwynebwyr ledled Lloegr, yr Alban ac Iwerddon, gan gynnwys timau cenedlaethol y gwledydd hynny (curwyd gwledydd Lloegr ac Iwerddon ill dwy o bymtheg pwynt i ddim), yr oedd rhai o'u canlyniadau yn anhygoel. Gorchfygwyd dwy sir gryfaf Lloegr yn hawdd, Dyfnaint 55-4 a Swydd Efrog 40-0.

Erbyn iddynt gyrraedd Cymru yr oedd tîm Seland Newydd wedi pentyrru ynghyd 801 o bwyntiau ac ildio dim ond 22.

Oddeutu tri o'r gloch y prynhawn hwnnw o Ragfyr, ar ôl hanner awr o'r chwarae, dyma'r Cymry yn rhoi prawf ar dacteg y buont yn ei hymarfer a'i pherffeithio yn unig-swydd ar gyfer y gêm arbennig honno. Ffurfiwyd sgrym ryw ddeg llath ar hugain (deg *medr* ar hugain, hwyrach; yn ddiau yr oedd *medrau* hynod yn perthyn i'r ddau dîm yma) o linell gais y Crysau Duon. Enillwyd y bêl gan Gymru a chychwynnwyd ymosodiad ar yr ochr dywyll i'r dde. Prysurodd amddiffynwyr Seland Newydd i'r cyfeiriad hwnnw. Yn sydyn, dyma'r mewnwr Dici Owen, pum troedfedd ac un fodfedd o wydnwch ac athrylith, yn sefyll yn ei unfan, yn troi ar ei sawdl, ac yn taflu'r bêl dros y sgrym i ganol y cae. Yno yn ei disgwyl yr oedd Cliff Pritchard, torrwr beddau o Bont-y-pŵl a oedd y prynhawn hwnnw â'i fryd ar gladdu gobeithion y Crysau Duon. Trosglwyddodd ef y bêl i Rhys Gabe a rhedodd y canolwr o Langennech yn benderfynol cyn amseru pas berffaith i'r gwibiwr bychan E.T. ('Teddy') Morgan y tu allan iddo ar yr asgell chwith. Rhoes hwnnw ei ben yn ôl a'i gwadnu hi am y gornel. Erbyn hyn yr oedd y Selandwyr

wedi gweld y bygythiad ac yn llifo draw o'r dde—ond yn rhy hwyr! Llwyddodd Teddy Morgan i'w hosgoi trwy wyro i'r chwith, gwibio megis bwa o'u cwmpas, a hyrddio ei hun dros y llinell gais yn y gornel. Dyna unig sgôr y gêm, a sicrhawyd buddugoliaeth hanesyddol. Trechwyd y Crysau Duon am yr unig dro mewn tair gêm ar ddeg ar hugain. A thystiodd rhediad Teddy Morgan i wirionedd sylfaenol gosodiad rhyfedd Albert Einstein, sef mai'r llwybr byrraf rhwng dau bwynt yw llinell grom. Y *mae* pellter yn plygu.

Ymhlith y 45,000 o bobl a wasgwyd i mewn i Barc yr Arfau y prynhawn hwnnw yr oedd Gwilym Hughes yn profi awyrgylch gêm rygbi am y tro cyntaf, ac ni allai fod wedi dewis achlysur mwy cyffrous na mwy hanesyddol. Dan y ffugenw 'Ap Idanfryn', cyfrannai golofn Gymraeg achlysurol i bapur dyddiol mwyaf poblogaidd Cymru, y *South Wales Daily News*, a chan mai ei dystiolaeth ef yw'r unig un sydd gennym yn Gymraeg i'r hyn a ddigwyddodd ar 16 Rhagfyr 1905, buddiol fyddai cofnodi ei sylwadau:

Clywais sôn am dyrfa fwy nag a allai neb ei rhifo. Gwelais hi heddiw yng Nghaerdydd, prif ddinas Cymru, ac nid oes chwant arnaf weld ei thebyg byth eto. Tyrfa llawn asbri ydoedd o bob cenedl dan y nef, yn ddu a gwyn a melyn—y Cymro glân gwladaidd, y Sais hunan-hyderus, y negro croenddu a'r Jap a'r Chinead melyn-ddu, a'r oll wedi cydymgynnull i wyliad deg ar hugain o fechgyn cryf ac ysgythrog yn chwareu pêl droed . . .

Rwy'n deall eisteddfod a chymanfa a ffair, ond y mae rhyw fusnes fel hyn tu hwnt i'm amgyffred . . . Pwy ddywedodd fod y Diwygiad wedi lladd ysfa y bêl droed? Bychan yr arwydd o hynny heddiw, ond gadewch i ni gyfaddef mae y dyrfa aneirif hon mor ddeallgar, mor barchus ei golwg, mor weddaidd ei phryd ag un a welwyd ar faes erioed. Ni chlywais air anweddaidd ac ni welais arwydd y ddiod yn ystod y ddwy awr y buom ar y maes . . .

Faint o bobl sydd yma? Hanner can mil, medda nhw. Wele yn awr pob gwddf yn estynedig, pob safn yn agored, a phob llais yn groch yn llefain â llef uchel eiriau calondid i'r Cymry . . . y mae y brwdfrydedd fel trydan yn ennyn y dorf enfawr

drwyddi draw. Mae yn berwi ac yn ysu . . . Symuda y dyrfa ôl
a blaen fel coedwig ar adeg corwynt, gan faint ei phryder.
Dyma waedd angherddol. Hwre! Mae Cymru yn croesi y
llinell . . . Pwy all ddisgrifio yr olygfa? Hanner can mil o
feidrolion wedi colli eu pennau mewn ton o orfoledd . . .
Clywch y llawen floeddio. Mae Cymru wedi ennill! Yr hyn a
fethodd cenhedloedd eraill yr ynysoedd hyn i gyflawni,
hynny a wnaeth hil yr hen Frythoniaid. Bellach dyna'r
newydd yn cael ei danio a'u bellebru trwy'r bydysawd i gyd
. . . a'r gorchfygwyr yw y lleiaf o deulu y brenin. Mae y bon-
llefau yn fyddarol. Dyma noson fel noson bythgofiadwy
Mafeking. Canwch y clychau! Lluchiwch yr hetiau! Chwif-
iwch y banerau! Cymru annwyl a orfu! Cenir ei chlod trwy
wledydd Cred. Hwre! Hwre! H-W-R-E!![1]

Yr oedd i'r prynhawn hwnnw o Ragfyr 1905 arwyddocâd a
fyddai'n atseinio ymhell y tu hwnt i'r maes chwarae, a thu
hwnt i'r flwyddyn arbennig honno. O ran y gêm ei hun, yr oedd
dim llai na 'phencampwriaeth y byd' yn y fantol, yn ôl un go-
hebydd o ben draw'r byd. Os oedd y Crysau Duon yn ddiguro, yr
oedd y Cymry, hwythau, yn eu hanterth, yn mwynhau cyfnod
eurwych pryd yr enillwyd chwe choron driphlyg rhwng 1900 a
1911, ac enwau Dici Owen, Gwyn Nicholls, Percy Bush a
Willie Llewellyn yn gyson ar wefusau'r genedl. Ym 1905
enillasai'r Cymry'r goron unwaith eto, trwy ddulliau chwarae
beiddgar a chreadigol a oedd yn gwreichioni â'r un hunan-hyder
ag a oedd i'w weld mewn cymdeithas a oedd ei hun, ar ddechrau'r ugeinfed ganrif, yn fwrlwm o fenter ac optimistiaeth.
   Ym 1905 cynrychiolai'r pymtheg mewn coch a'r pymtheg
mewn du ffordd wahanol o fyw lawn cymaint ag unrhyw rag-
oriaeth yn nhechneg chwarae rygbi. I'r ddwy wlad, daethai
llwyddiant ar y maes chwarae i olygu cryn dipyn mwy na dim
ond gêm: yr oedd yn un o'r elfennau hynny a oedd yn diffinio eu
cenedligrwydd iddynt hwy eu hunain ac i eraill. Er mai dwy
gymdeithas dra gwahanol oeddynt ar drothwy'r ugeinfed
ganrif, rhannent yr un awydd i wneud argraff ar lwyfan rhyngwladol. Yn y ddwy wlad, yr oedd apêl elfennol yn y syniad o
ǵuro eu meistri Seisnig mewn gêm a ddysgasant ganddynt, ac
unwaith y cydiwyd yn y gêm o ddifri o'r 1880au ymlaen ni fu'r

naill wlad na'r llall yn araf i ymryddhau o'r ffurfioldeb ffug-
foneddigaidd a oedd yn llyffetheirio'r gêm yn Lloegr, a dyfeisio
ffyrdd o ymestyn ei chortynnau technegol a thactegol. Cyfran-
iad mwyaf y Cymry yn hyn o beth oedd y llinell pedwar tri
chwarter, a olygai leihau nifer y blaenwyr o naw i wyth a
chyfeirio'r chwarae oddi wrth ysgarmesau diddiwedd a diflas er
mwyn trafod y bêl yn fwy agored gan olwyr a oedd â'u bryd ar
ddrysu eu gwrthwynebwyr trwy ysgafnder troed a chyflymder
meddwl yn hytrach na thrwy nerth braich a grym corfforol.
Ymateb y Crysau Duon oedd neilltuo saith blaenwr yn unig i'r
chwarae tyn er mwyn rhyddhau crwydrwr ('rover') i gynnal y
chwarae yng nghanol y cae ac i greu cymaint o drafferth ag yr
oedd modd i'r gwrthwynebwyr.

Ym meddyliau'r sawl ym mywyd cyhoeddus Lloegr a boenai
am ddirywiad y cyff Seisnig, cynrychiolai gwŷr Seland Newydd
bobl fugeiliol iach a oedd wedi darganfod o'r newydd rinweddau
a glendid y bywyd amaethyddol awyr agored; yr oedd y gwrth-
gyferbyniad rhyngddynt a thrigolion llwydaidd trefi diwydiannol gwledydd Prydain yn drawiadol. Mynegid yr athroniaeth
hon yn fynych yng ngholofnau'r *Daily Mail* yn ystod y misoedd
pan oedd y Crysau Duon yn ysgubo fel corwynt trwy Brydain.
Credai'r farn gyhoeddus yng Nghymru, fodd bynnag, fod
llwyddiannau'r tîm rygbi cenedlaethol yn nodweddu cynnydd
mwy cyffredinol mewn addysg a gwleidyddiaeth, ynghyd â
dadeni diwylliannol a llewyrch economaidd.

Yn y blynyddoedd cyn y Rhyfel Byd Cyntaf yr oedd Cymru yn
tasgu ag arwyddion o egni a chynnydd, a'r peiriant a oedd yn
tanio'r holl ynni oedd y maes glo ager yr oedd ei gynnyrch, a'r
cyfoeth a ddeilliai ohono, yn treiddio i bob cornel o fywyd
Cymru ac i rannau helaeth o weddill y byd. Ger Korea ym mis
Mai 1905, mewn brwydr fôr a barodd lai na phedair awr ar
hugain, chwythwyd llynges Rwsia Imperialaidd—a oedd wedi
cymryd saith mis i gyrraedd yno—i waelod Culfor Tsushima
gan longau Siapan o dan Admiral Togo. Pan glywodd Kaiser
Wilhelm yn Berlin y newydd syfrdanol deallodd ar unwaith ei
arwyddocâd: yr oedd gan lynges yr Ail Reich gystadleuydd
annisgwyl, diolch i'r cytundeb diweddar (1902) rhwng Siapan a
Phrydain. 'Taniwyd llongau Togo', meddai Wilhelm, 'gan lo
Caerdydd'.

Yr oedd y Kaiser yn llygad ei le. Porthladdoedd glo Caerdydd, Penarth a'r Barri oedd y prysuraf yn y byd, a thrigai traean holl boblogaeth Cymru o fewn hanner cylch ugain milltir o'u cwmpas. Yr oedd poblogaeth Caerdydd ei hun wedi cynyddu'n syfrdanol o 10,000 ym 1841 i 164,000 ym 1901 ac i 182,000 erbyn 1911. Nid oes ryfedd i Gaerdydd gael ei chymharu â Chicago, canolfan busnes a masnach yr Unol Daleithiau. Ym mis Hydref 1905 dyrchafwyd Chicago Cymru, Caerdydd gosmopolitan Gymreig-anghymreig 'Ap Idanfryn', i statws dinas trwy Sêl Fawr Brenin Lloegr. Ddeufis yn ddiweddarach, ac ymhen deng niwrnod i'r fuddugoliaeth ar Barc yr Arfau, cafodd Cymru gyfan ei chydnabod yn sgil penodi David Lloyd George yn Llywydd y Bwrdd Masnach yng nghabinet newydd Rhyddfrydol Campbell-Bannerman. Pan ddilynwyd hyn ymhen mis eto gan etholiad cyffredinol a welodd y Rhyddfryd-wyr yn cipio'r cyfan ond un o'r 34 sedd seneddol Gymreig, yr oedd y wasg Ryddfrydol ar ben ei digon wrth ddathlu 'Buddugol-iaeth Fawr Arall i Gymru'—goruchafiaeth yr un mor hynod â'r un a gafwyd ar Barc yr Arfau fis ynghynt. Yr oedd 'Ap Idanfryn', felly, yn canu clodydd gwlad esgynnol a ddisgleiriai fel telpyn o lo yng nghoron yr Ymerodraeth Frydeinig fyd-eang.

O ychwanegu'r miloedd a ddibynnai ar y glofeydd am eu gwaith at y ddau gan mil o lowyr a gyflogid ganddynt cyn 1914, yr oedd hanner poblogaeth Cymru—a oedd wedi cynyddu o filiwn er 1881 i bron ddwy filiwn a hanner erbyn 1911—yn ddibynnol ar y diwydiant glo. Ac os oedd unrhyw *un* symbol a safai dros y cynnydd aruthrol yng nghymoedd glo de Cymru, hwnnw oedd Cwm Rhondda, dyffryn coediog lle trigai prin fil o bobl yng nghanol y bedwaredd ganrif ar bymtheg, ond lle'r oedd 152,000 yn byw erbyn 1911 ac yn cynhyrchu dros 20% o'r 56 miliwn tunnell o lo a dynnid o'r 485 o byllau a oedd yng Nghymru y pryd hwnnw, dros hanner cant ohonynt yn y Rhondda ei hun.

Ac nid glo yn unig a ddaeth â Chwm Rhondda i sylw'r byd. Ym 1904-5 ysgubodd diwygiad crefyddol Evan Roberts drwy gymoedd y de, a than ddylanwad ei gyffro hynod, a'r cyman-faoedd grymus a ddaeth yn ei sgil, cyfansoddodd John Hughes o Lanilltud Faerdref, clerc yng nglofa'r Great Western ym Mhontypridd, emyn-dôn i'w chanu ar eiriau mawreddog y Pêr

Ganiedydd, 'Arglwydd, arwain drwy'r anialwch'. Cydiodd y dôn a lledodd ei phoblogrwydd yn fuan; bid siŵr, i'r miloedd a oedd wedi anturio ymlaen o fwynder Maldwyn a Meirion ac o lesni Ceredigion a Phenfro i'r hyn a ddisgrifiodd 'Glanffrwd' fel 'glo, mwg, angerdd a düwch' yr ardaloedd diwydiannol, 'anial-wch' oedd y cyfan oll. Ac eto, ym mhrysurdeb morgrugol y cymunedau bywiog hyn y curai calon y Gymru fodern, a chydnabod hynny a wnaeth John Hughes drwy alw ei dôn 'Cwm Rhondda'.

Cafodd y Diwygiad a ysbrydolodd y dôn honno effeithiau rhyfeddol ar fuchedd a moes rhannau hynny'r wlad a deimlodd ei wres. Er enghraifft, gellir olrhain llwybrau Evan Roberts drwy'r cymoedd trwy weld yr hyn a ddigwyddodd i glybiau rygbi yno. Yn ardal Pontypridd, gwelwyd chwaraewyr rygbi yn llosgi eu crysau a'u cefnogwyr yn rhwygo eu tocynnau tymor; yn Ynysybwl bedyddiwyd yr holl dîm a rhoddwyd y gorau i chwarae am dair blynedd. Cynyddodd Ysgol Sul Capel Noddfa, Treorci, dros nos pan ychwanegwyd ati'r 'dosbarth ffwtbol', sef llond trol o chwarewyr a oedd wedi cael tröedigaeth ac wedi ymdynghedu i ymwrthod â'r gêm am byth. I'r gorllewin, yn y maes glo carreg, lle'r oedd y gymdeithas yn Gymreiciach, bu'r effeithiau'n fwy syfrdanol fyth wrth i rygbi ddarfod yn gyfan gwbl am dair blynedd a mwy ym Mhen-y-groes, Treforys, Casllwchwr, Creunant a Rhydaman.[3]

Gallwn weld erbyn hyn mai math o edifeirwch torfol oedd y Diwygiad gan bobl a oedd newydd eu dadwreiddio o sicrwydd eu cynefin gwledig a'u hyrddio i ganol trobwll trefol, dieithr, lle'r oedd nid yn unig orthrymderau ar bob llaw ond temtas-iynau hefyd, ar ffurf diddanion ac adloniannau nad oeddynt wrth fodd Caersalem. Nid cyhoeddi milflwydd newydd a wnaeth Diwygiad Evan Roberts, ond tynnu'r llen ar gyfnod neilltuol yn hanes crefydd a chymdeithas yng Nghymru. Yr oedd dadansoddiad 'Ap Idanfryn' yn gywir: 'Pwy a ddywedodd fod y Diwygiad wedi lladd ysfa y bêl droed?'

Ond nid ar chwarae bach y byddai'r bêl-droed yn ennill ei phlwyf ychwaith. Yn y Gymru Gymraeg Anghydffurfiol nid mater hawdd oedd derbyn bod i weithgareddau'r maes chwarae le o gwbl ym mywyd y genedl. Adroddwyd hanes trechu'r Crysau Duon mewn papurau newydd o Paris i Efrog Newydd, ond pur ddirmygus oedd *Baner ac Amserau Cymru* o'r hyn a oedd wedi digwydd ar 'y cae cicio yng Nghaerdydd . . . Paham y rhaid i neb golli ei hun ynglŷn â chicio darn o ledr am y gorau, nis allwn ddeall'.[4]

A gosod ei rhagfarn gul i'r naill ochr, gellir priodoli dirmyg *Y Faner* yn rhannol i'w hanwybodaeth am y gymdeithas newydd a oedd yn tyfu yn ne Cymru a'r brif gêm aeaf yno. Fel arall oedd hi yng ngogledd Cymru, lle y teyrnasai pêl-droed. Yn ystod y blynyddoedd cythryblus cyn 1914 pan welwyd herio'r consensws Rhyddfrydol-anghydffurfiol gan dwf sosialaeth, undebaeth filwriaethus a therfysgu yn y cymoedd a'r trefi mawrion, priodolid y tueddiadau 'annymunol' hyn i fewnlifiad cyson pobl o'r tu allan i Gymru, a'u syniadau 'dieithr' ac 'anghymreig'. Amlygwyd y rhain, meddid, nid yn unig yn nherfysgoedd 1910-11 yn Nhonypandy, Tredegar, Llanelli a Bryn-mawr ond hefyd yng nghynnydd pêl-droed yng Nghymru, gêm estron lygredig, faterol, difyrrwch y dosbarth gweithiol, torfol, diddiwylliant a oedd y tu allan i ddylanwad llesol y dosbarth canol, gêm a oedd yn denu teyrngarwch y *lumpenproletariat* diwydiannol difeddwl. Seisnigrwydd proletaraidd y gêm 'ddieithr' hon oedd testun erthygl gyfan yn rhifyn cyntaf *The Welsh Outlook* ym 1914: ynddi, gwrthgyferbyniwyd pêl-droed broffesiynol a'r gêm rygbi amatur a oedd, yn rhinwedd ei hapêl at rychwant eang o ddosbarthiadau, yn falm ar friwiau cymdeithas. Yr oedd ei democratiaeth, meddid, yn dyrchafu gêm a oedd o dras hynafol a Chymreig, tra oedd pêl-droed yn beth newydd a dieithr.

Yr oedd cryn elfen o dwyll, hunan-dwyll ac anwiredd rhonc yn y darlun hanesyddol hwn. Ciciwyd pêl yng Nghymru ers canrifoedd, ac yr oedd pêl-droed 'fodern' wedi ei sefydlu'n ffurfiol yng Nghymru bum mlynedd (1876) cyn i'r awdurdodau rygbi roi trefn ar eu pethau mewn modd cyffelyb ym 1881. Ond yn Wrecsam y ffurfiwyd Cymdeithas Bêl-droed Cymru (yr F.A.W.), nid nepell o lannau'r Merswy a dinasoedd poblog Lerpwl a Manceinion a oedd yn hwylus o fewn cyrraedd ar y rheilffordd. Yno, yr oedd pêl-droed yn teyrnasu. Ar y llaw arall, fe'i cafwyd hi'n anodd iawn i sefydlu'r gêm yn ne Cymru lle'r oedd clybiau llwyddiannus fel Castell-nedd, Abertawe, Llanelli, Caerdydd a Chasnewydd yn bodoli er y 1870au, heb sôn am

y degau o glybiau llai, a'r rheilffordd yn eu cysylltu *hwy* â
Swyddi Caerloyw a Gwlad yr Haf, lle'r oedd pobl yn chwarae
rygbi.

Gwelwyd cynnydd y bêl-droed yng nghymoedd cymysgryw
gorllewin sir Fynwy a dwyrain Morgannwg o 1890 ymlaen. Ym
1890 sefydlwyd Cynghrair De Cymru gan dimau fel Ton
Pentre, Maerdy, Porth a Threalaw yn y Rhondda, Aberdâr ac
Aberpennar yng Nghwm Cynon, a Blaenau a Chaerllion yng
Ngwent. Ond pan geisiodd yr F.A.W. chwarae gêm ryngwladol
'genhadol' yn erbyn Iwerddon yn Abertawe ym 1894 bu rhaid
defnyddio cae Sain Helen gan nad oedd faes pêl-droed addas i'r
achlysur yn y de. Cafodd Caerdydd, hithau, gyfle i lwyfannu
gêm ryngwladol yn erbyn Lloegr ym mis Mawrth 1896, ond dim
ond Parc yr Arfau a oedd yn addas, a bu rhaid chwarae ar ddydd
Llun oherwydd y flaenoriaeth a roddwyd y Sadwrn cynt i'r gêm
rygbi rhwng Caerdydd a Chasnewydd. Ni allodd hyd yn oed
ddoniau diarhebol Billy Meredith wared Cymru rhag cweir o
naw gôl i un y prynhawn hwnnw, ond daeth tro ar fyd a
chynyddodd poblogrwydd pêl-droed oherwydd ei hapêl ddigam-
syniol a'r ffaith fod y mwyafrif o'r miloedd—73% ohonynt yn
dod o'r tu allan i Gymru yn negad cyntaf yr ugeinfed ganrif—a
oedd yn dal i dyrru i dde Cymru yn dod bellach o ganolbarth a
gogledd Lloegr lle chwareid pêl-droed yn bennaf.

Rheswm arall dros gynnydd pêl-droed yn y de oedd y mewn-
lifiad o ogledd Cymru, yn arbennig yn sgil yr anghydfod yn
chwareli'r Penrhyn rhwng 1900 a 1903. Gadawodd y mewn-
fudwyr o Wynedd stamp neilltuol ar ambell ardal fel Bedlinog a
Glyncorrwg. Ym 1894, pan fentrwyd cynnal y gêm ryngwladol
arloesol honno yn Abertawe, nid oedd yr un tîm o Gymru yng
Nghynghrair De Lloegr (y *Southern League*), ond erbyn 1914 yr
oedd un ar ddeg o dimau, sef chwarter y Cynghrair cyfan. Mae'n
gwbl amlwg fod y bêl gron yn denu cefnogaeth gynyddol
ymhlith y Cymry o'r 1900au cynnar ymlaen, ond yr oedd rygbi
wedi achub y blaen arni yn y de er chwarter canrif ac, oddi ar
ennill y goron driphlyg gyntaf ym 1893, wedi dangos y gallai
Cymru gystadlu gyda'r gorau ar y maes rhyngwladol—a'u curo.

Petai'r diwydiannu enfawr a welwyd yng Nghymru yn ail
hanner y ganrif ddiwethaf wedi digwydd yn y gogledd yn hytrach nag yn y de, mae'n ddigon posib mai pêl-droed fyddai ein

'gêm genedlaethol' heddiw, a hynny oherwydd y cysylltiad rhwng gogledd Cymru a gogledd-orllewin Lloegr. Prawf o hynny yw'r ffaith y ffurfiwyd clwb rygbi yn nhref Bangor ym 1876, ond ymhen blwyddyn fe'i gorfodwyd i droi at y bêl gron er mwyn cael gwrthwynebwyr i chwarae yn eu herbyn; yr un modd, ni fu clybiau Abertawe (1872) a Chasnewydd (1875) fawr o dro cyn rhoi'r gorau i'w syniad gwreiddiol o chwarae pêl-droed; troesant at gêm y bêl hirgron a oedd yn lledu drwy dde Cymru o dde-orllewin Lloegr. Erbyn dechrau'r ugeinfed ganrif yr oedd rygbi wedi plannu gwreiddiau dwfn ym mhridd du y de gweithfaol, a'r pymtheg yn y tîm cenedlaethol yn llorio pob gelyn.

Ni welsai Lloyd George yr un gêm rygbi cyn 1908 pan ymwelodd â Chaerdydd i dderbyn rhyddfraint y ddinas a gwylio clwb y ddinas yn chwarae Blackheath ar Barc yr Arfau. 'Mae'n gêm hynod i'w ryfeddu', meddai. 'Welais mohoni erioed o'r blaen a chysytal i mi gyfaddef ei bod hi'n fwy "exciting" na pholitics'; a sicrhaodd fod ei fab yn chwarae dros y Cymry yn Llundain maes o law. Y llwyddiant cenedlaethol oedd yn bwysig, a hyn a'i gwnâi hi'n anodd hyd yn oed i warcheidwaid moesol y genedl wrthsefyll apêl hudol y bêl hirgron.

Ar y cychwyn, wrth gwrs, ac ym mlynyddoedd cynnar y 1900au, yr oedd difyrrwch a ddenai filoedd o bobl i ymgynnull i wylio deg ar hugain o ddynion yn cwrsio pledren mewn cas lledr yn loes calon i selogion y seiat a'r sêt fawr. Brithid y wasg enwadol Gymraeg ar ddiwedd y bedwaredd ganrif ar bymtheg â cholofnau praff yn ceryddu 'ysgafnder', 'gwagedd' a 'phechodau yr oes', gan gyfeirio yn arbennig at y chwaraeon torfol yr oedd eu 'hanlladrwydd yn disodli'r hen eisteddfodau'. Ys gofynnodd y Parchedig John Roberts, Corris, yn *Y Cronicl* (Awst, 1886): 'A glywodd neb erioed fod rhywun wedi derbyn lles ysbrydol wrth gicio y bêl?' Ategwyd ei amheuon yn *Y Traethodydd* ym 1903: 'Mae yr awydd anghymedrol am ddifyrwch gwag wedi cymeryd gafael gref a dwfn ym meddyliau y lliaws yng Nghymru, gwlad y breintiau mawr, gwlad y diwygiadau nerthol, gwlad y capelau a'r pregethau, a gwlad yr Ysgolion Sabothol. Ie, y mae gan chwaraeon ffôl a champau ofer afael ar bob dosbarth, pob oed, pob sefyllfa a phob rhyw'. Pob rhyw? 'The game of rugby football', cwynodd llythyrwr yn y *Llanelly Guardian* ym 1886, 'is unsuitable for young ladies of both sexes'. [5]

Gwelai'r 'young ladies', a oedd yn ffurfio traean o'r dorf o bum mil ar y Strade ym mis Ebrill 1884, ornestau digon garw a gwaedlyd ar brydiau, yn arbennig rhwng trefi neu bentrefi cyfagos pan oedd balchder bro yn y fantol. Mae adroddiadau'r wasg yn y cyfnod hwn yn gyforiog o gyfeiriadau at ymddygiad milain chwaraewyr ar y cae, a mileindra cynddrwng eu cefnogwyr ar y banc. Bu ymladd cïaidd ('semi-savagery' a 'wanton biting', yn ôl y sôn) rhwng Pen-y-bont a Chastell-nedd ym 1880; bu'n rhaid i chwaraewyr Llanelli ymladd eu ffordd i'w gwesty dan gawod o ddyrnau a cherrig ar ôl ennill ar gae'r Gnoll ym 1883, a gorfu i'r awdurdodau orchymyn cau drysau sawl clwb yn y 1890au oherwydd camymddwyn difrifol gan chwaraewyr a chefnogwyr fel ei gilydd, yn eu plith Castell-nedd ym 1895, Aberafan ym 1896, Abertyleri a Chaerdydd ym 1897, ac Aberafan eto ym 1899. Galwyd yr heddlu i'r cae i hebrwng y dyfarnwr oddi ar y Strade ym mis Tachwedd 1900, ac ar yr un prynhawn Sadwrn o Hydref ym 1906 anfonwyd pum chwaraewr o'r cae yn Aberpennar, un arall ym Mryn-mawr, y ddau dîm cyfan yng Nghasnewydd, a chafwyd 'chwarae bwyst-filaidd' yng Nghaerdydd. [6]

Dyma'r union bethau y rhybuddiwyd darllenwyr *Y Dysged-ydd* amdanynt gan y Parchedig W. Thomas, Hendy-gwyn, ym Mehefin 1887: 'Ni bu chwarae mor arswydus a pheryglus o gyfundrefnus ag yw yn awr ymhob man. Cellwair, rhegi, cablu, meddwi, ymladd, dial, hap-chwarae, gwastraff ac ysbeilio. Nid rhyfedd fod trythyllwch, tlodi a thrueni yn canlyn fel dilyw didroi yn ôl'. Yr oedd camweddau o'r fath i'w disgwyl o ystyried y berthynas agos rhwng y maes chwarae a'r ddiod gadarn. Prin iawn oedd y cyfleusterau priodol ar gyfer chwaraewyr gan y mwyafrif o glybiau yn y cyfnod cynnar, a defnyddid tafarnau ar gyfer pwyllgorau, newid dillad a chymdeithasu cyn ac ar ôl gêm. Os oedd gan Bontypridd y 'White Hart' a Chreunant y 'Red Lion', yr oedd gan Ben-y-graig y 'Butcher's', yr Hendy y 'Red Cow' a Phontardawe y 'Gelli Arms'.

Halen ar y briw oedd y ffaith fod Eglwys Loegr yng Nghymru wedi bod yn noddwr traddodiadol i adloniant poblogaidd ers canrifoedd. Gellid disgwyl, felly, i'r Eglwys gefnogi ac, ie, roi arweiniad wrth groesawu rygbi i wlad y diwygiadau nerthol, y capeli, y pregethau a'r Ysgolion Sabothol. Darpar-offeiriaid Coleg Dewi Sant, Llanbedr Pont Steffan, oedd y cyntaf i chwarae'r gêm yng Nghymru, a bu gweinidogion Anglicanaidd yn amlwg yn hanes sefydlu nifer o glybiau. Yr oedd y pymtheg a wisgodd grys coch Cymru am y tro cyntaf ym 1881 yn cynnwys nifer o offeiriaid, y capten James Bevan yn eu plith. Hir y parhaodd y traddodiad. Nid angylion oedd yr 'Wyth Brawychus', fel yr adwaenid pac Cymru ym 1914, a thipyn is na'r angylion oedd eu harweinydd, y Parchedig Alban Davies, curad yn Abertawe a fu farw yn Los Angeles ym 1976. Barn gweinidog yr Annibynwyr yn *Y Dysgedydd* (Mehefin, 1887) oedd bod Hen Eglwys Loegr yn 'cefnogi clybiau ac undebau chwareuol trwy danysgrifiadau sylweddol a chanmoliaeth hudolus' er mwyn 'darbwyllo ieuenctid Ymneilltuol Cymru i ddod drosodd i fynwes yr hen fam yn yr amcan fel y caffont ryddid i chwarae a gwneud y peth a fynont'.

Canlyniad hyn oll, yng ngeiriau 'Enos' yn *Y Tyst* (Chwefror 1907) oedd bod 'yn aros *billiards, cricket* a *football*, a'r mwyaf o'r rhai hyn yw football'. Ceisiodd capelwyr selog Cwm Tawe uchaf ddadwneud hynny ym 1890 drwy fynnu dadl gyhoeddus ar fater sefydlu clwb rygbi yn Ystradgynlais. Yn nannedd taer brotestiadau'r Parchedig W. Moelfryn Morgan, gweinidog Capel Sardis a hen-hen-ewythr i'r Athro Derec Llwyd Morgan, cariodd dilynwyr y bêl y dydd o un bleidlais. Serch hynny, y noson cyn chwarae gêm gyntaf y clwb newydd aeth rhai o'r saint i'r maes i lifio'r pyst i'r llawr a'u cludo i orsaf yr heddlu.

Yn is i lawr y cwm, ddeunaw mlynedd yn ddiweddarach, dal i resynu yr oedd y Parchedig Samlet Williams 'fod bryd ein hieuenctid yn rhedeg ar y peth darostyngedig hwn . . . yr ydym yn gofyn mewn difrif ''Pa hyd, chwi ynfydion, y cerwch ynfydrwydd?'' Drwg gennyf fynegu bod ieuenctid y plwyf hon—dosbarth lluosog ohonynt—yn ymhyfrydu yn yr ynfydrwydd hwn ac yn cynnull gyda'r miloedd yn ein gwlad i weled yr ynfydrwydd yn cael ei gyflawni yn ein trefi ar brydnawn Sadwrn, a hyn oll yng nghanol misoedd y gaeaf'.[7] Llais yn llefain yn y diffeithwch, fodd bynnag, oedd eiddo'r Parchedig Samlet Williams unwaith y sylweddolwyd pa mor llwyddiannus oedd y tîm rygbi cenedlaethol ac, ar ben hynny, mor gaboledig a chelfydd a deallus oedd eu cyd-chwarae. O'r 1900au cynnar ymlaen sylwyd bod coleri crwn i'w gweld yn britho'r torfeydd a ymgasglai i wylio'r gemau mawr, a gyrrai'r wasg ei newyddiadurwyr i blith y cefnogwyr i glustfeinio ar eu sgwrs. 'Pa werth pregethu yn erbyn ffwtbol?' clywyd diacon ym Mharc yr Arfau yn cyfaddef wrth gyfaill tra oedd yn gwylio Cymru yn rhoi crasfa i Loegr ym 1900, 'Fedren ni ddim tynnu tyrfa fel hon i gymanfa'. 'Na'n wir', cytunodd ei gyfaill yn bruddglwyfus, 'ond—dyna i chi gais bendigedig!' Yr oedd sail gwirioneddol felly i alarnad gweinidog yr efengyl ym 1903 oherwydd 'nid yn unig cefnogir y llygredigaethau hyn gan aelodau cyffredin y gwahanol enwadau crefyddol, ond dywedir wrthym fod nifer nid bychan o'u swyddogion, yn bregethwyr a blaenoriaid, ymhlith eu cefnogwyr a'u hyrwyddwyr. Ai peth ysgafn gan broffeswyr crefydd yng Nghymru wneuthur y ffieidd-dra a wnânt yma?'

Ond nid cefnogwyr na hyrwyddwyr y gêm a ddaeth dan lach y Parchedig S.B. Williams, Llanelli, yng nghinio clwb y Sosban ym 1902, ond yn hytrach, 'y Cristnogion honedig hynny oedd yn eu condemnio. Roedd ef yn argyhoeddedig bod llai o drais a chamymddwyn (ymhlith y 12,000 oedd newydd weld y 'Scarlets' yn maeddu Abertawe) nag mewn unrhyw gymanfa neu eisteddfod'. Ac fe aeth bugail gyda'r Hen Gorff yng ngwaelod sir Benfro ymhellach fyth ym 1910. Yr oedd pêl-droed yn meithrin cymeriad da, yn ôl y Parchedig W.M. Williams, ac apeliodd ar weinidogion lleol i ffurfio eu timau eu hunain. Yn bersonol, hoffai ef weld y Parchedig W. Powell yn gefnwr, y Parchedig W.J. Chamberlain (Wesle oedd ef) yn y rheng flaen, ac ef ei hun yn y safle allweddol fel maswr.

Do, fe ddaeth tro ar fyd pan ddaeth cymeradwyaeth yn hytrach na cherydd o'r pulpud a'r sêt fawr. Fel yr oedd y wasg Saesneg yng Nghymru byth yn blino dweud, yr oedd Cymru yn enwog am dri pheth: ei chantorion, ei phregethwyr a'i chwaraewyr rygbi, gyda'r olaf yn gydradd a chyfuwch â'r ddau gyntaf. Coron driphlyg yn wir!

Yr oedd canu a phregethu, fe wyddys, yn ail natur i'r Cymry, ac yn nodweddion cynhenid ers cyn cof. Ond rygbi? Cyn-ddisgyblion bonedd Lloegr a'r Alban a roddodd i'r Cymry eu blas cyntaf o'r gêm newydd y diffiniwyd ei rheolau pan sefydlwyd

Blaenoriaid—neu, yn hytrach, blaenwyr! 'Yr Wyth Brawychus', sef pac Cymru, dan gapteniaeth y Parchedig, Alban Davies, ym 1914. Walter Rees, ysgrifennydd yr Undeb, yw'r ail ar y dde yn y rhes flaen.

Public Notices.

NATIONAL
PAGEANT
- OF -
WALES.
TO - DAY
AT 2.30 P.M.

SOPHIA GARDENS PARK, CARDIFF.

(PROCEEDS TO BE DEVOTED TO CHARITIES.)

JULY 26 to 31—2.30 p.m.   AUGUST 2 to 7—7.30 p.m.

TWO PERFORMANCES on Saturdays, July 31st & August 7th,
and Bank Holiday, August 2nd, 2.30 and 7.30.

The whole of the Episodes and Interludes will be Performed on each occasion.

THE GREATEST EVENT IN THE ANNALS OF WALES.

5,000 PERFORMERS IN ALL.

The SACKING OF CARDIFF CASTLE will be carried out by a GREAT BODY OF
150 INTERNATIONAL FOOTBALLERS, comprising PERCY BUSH, GWYN NICHOLLS,
R. T. GABE, and a host of others in full armour.
GRAND CHORUS OF 250 PICKED VOICES.   COMPANY OF 100 MOUNTED MEN.

Music by the Splendid Band of the Royal Marines, Portsmouth Division.

Hysbyseb i'r Pasiant Cenedlaethol yng Ngherddi Sohpia, 1909.

Undeb Rygbi Lloegr, yr R.F.U. bondigrybwyll, ym 1871. Hen ddisgyblion Rugby a Wellington a gyflwynodd y gêm i Lanelli yn y 1870au. Yn ysgol Rugby, wrth gwrs, y 'dyfeisiodd' William Webb Ellis y gêm ym 1823. Serch hynny, gwnaed ymdrechion yng Nghymru i ddangos ei bod o dras hynafol Gymreig drwy ei holrhain o leiaf mor bell â chnapan yr hen sir Benfro, gêm a ddisgrifiwyd gan George Owen ym 1603: nid cyd-ddigwyddiad oedd y ffaith mai ym 1892 y gwelwyd cyhoeddi, dan nawdd Anrhydeddus Gymdeithas y Cymmrodorion, destun safonol o waith Owen, *Description of Penbrokeshire.* Ymhyfrydai Cymry oes Elisabeth y cyntaf yn eu Prydeindod; daeth y delfryd hwnnw unwaith eto i chwarae rhan ffurfiannol ym meddylfryd Cymreig oes Fictoria, meddylfryd y gwnaeth Hywel Teifi Edwards gymaint i'n goleuo yn ei gylch. Gallod Morris Glaslyn sicrhau Cymreigyddion y Fenni ym 1909 ei fod wrth gwrs yn gresynu at y Seisnigeiddio a oedd yn digwydd yn nhrefi Cymru, ond wrth hynny fe olygai iaith a gwisg, yn hytrach na'r diddordeb newydd mewn rygbi. Oni fuasai'r Cymry—'hil yr hen Frythoniaid', chwedl 'Ap Idanfryn'—yn ben-campwyr gyda'r bêl ymhell cyn dyfod Piwritaniaeth?

Yn oes Elisabeth y Cyntaf heidiai'r Cymry i Lundain. Ond rhwng 1851 a 1914 sugnwyd bron hanner miliwn o bobl i dde-ddwyrain Cymru. Pa syndod, felly, mai yn Awstralia y ganed James Bevan, capten tîm cenedlaethol cyntaf Cymru ym 1881? Clwb rygbi Caerdydd oedd y cyntaf i arloesi'r syniad o ddefnyddio pedwar tri chwarterwr, ond y ffigur allweddol yn y trawsgyweiriad hwn oedd Frank Hancock, un o deulu o fragwyr a groesodd Môr Hafren o Wiveliscombe yng Ngwlad yr Haf i dde Cymru i ddiwallu'r miloedd sychedig a oedd yn gweithio yno. O'r 1890au ymlaen dechreuodd tîm rygbi Cymru seilio'u llwyddiant ar flaenwyr cryf a deallus fel Dick Hellings, Wallace Watts, Arthur Boucher, Harry Packer, Jim Webb a Bobby Brice; rhyngddynt cynrychiolodd y rhain Gymru 75 o weithiau rhwng 1891 a 1912. Ond mater o hap a damwain daearyddol yn unig oedd eu Cymreictod hwy—ganed pob un ononynt yn ne-orllewin Lloegr.

Yn hyn o beth yr oedd tîm enwog 1905 yn ddrych o'r gymdeithas yn ne Cymru ar ddechrau'r ugeinfed ganrif. Hoffai rhai sylwebyddion, fel Theodore Watts-Dunton, yn ei ragair i argraffiad newydd (1906) o lyfr adnabyddus George Borrow, *Wild Wales*, ramanteiddio ynglŷn â dewrder y pymtheg a gurodd y Crysau Duon drwy olrhain eu llinach i'r milwyr o Gymru a fu'n ymladd yn Crécy ym 1346. Buasai'n rheitiach petai Watts-Dunton wedi sylwi ar wir dras rai o'r tîm a glodforai mor frwd. Ganed y cefnwr H.B. (Bert) Winfield yn Nottingham, y blaenwr A.F. ('Boxer') Harding yn Market Rasen, Swydd Lincoln, a'r capten E. Gwyn Nicholls yn Westbury-on-Severn yn Swydd Gaerloyw. A pha ryfedd hynny, o ystyried bod traean poblogaeth Morgannwg, erbyn 1911, wedi eu geni y tu allan i'r sir honno?

Nid trafnidiaeth unffordd oedd hi. Teithiodd y Cymry yn y cyfnod hwn i'r rhannau mwyaf anghysbell o'r pum cyfandir, gyda'u cyfalaf, eu technoleg a'u menter yn canlyn glo, dur, haearn, copr a thunplat i Chile a Phennsylfania, i'r Ariannin ac i Rwsia. Unwaith eto cawn gan chwaraewyr rygbi Cymru enghreifftiau diddorol o'r ansefydlogrwydd o'r chwiw anturus a ddenodd Gymry i ben draw'r byd. Ymhlith aelodau tîm Casnewydd a enillodd Gwpan De Cymru bedair gwaith o'r bron ar ddiwedd y 1870au aeth un yn filwr i'r India, un yn rheolwr gwaith haearn yn Newfoundland, un i China ac un arall i Ceylon (fel yr oedd Sri Lanka y pryd hwnnw). Aeth eu capten W.D. Phillips, i ffermio yn Texas. Gwelir yr un patrwm ymhlith rhai a fu'n chwarae dan yr Awstraliad James Bevan yn nhîm cyntaf Cymru ym 1881: ymfudodd un i Florida, un i'r Ariannin, ac un arall i'r India.

Mae'n amlwg, felly, y bu cryn dipyn o fynd a dod rhwng yr hen wlad a threfedigaethau'r Ymerodraeth, a dyna lle y gwnaeth y Cymry eu hargraff ddyfnaf. O ddarllen ambell bapur newydd fe gredech mai Cymry oedd yn llywodraethu'r Ymerodraeth, fel gweision sifil, gwŷr busnes, peirianwyr, cadfridogion a diplomyddion—yr oedd hyd yn oed Esgob Khartoum yn Gymro! Wrth gymharu'r llawenydd a fynegwyd yng Nghaerdydd ar 16 Rhagfyr 1905 â'r dathlu gwyllt pan gyrhaeddodd y newyddion am godi'r gwarchae ar Mafeking ym mis Mai 1900, yr oedd 'Ap Idanfryn' yn taro tant jingoaidd ac imperialaidd a oedd yn gwbl nodweddiadol o Gymry'r oes.

Daethom i ddeall erbyn hyn mai lleiafrif, mewn gwirionedd, oedd y rhai hynny fel Lloyd George a Herbert Lewis a wrthwynebai'r Rhyfel yn erbyn y Bŵr. Yr oedd Rhyddfrydwyr amlwg fel Brynmor Jones ac Ellis Griffith, a chenedlaetholwyr o frîd Beriah Gwynfe Evans, yn frwd dros yr achos imperialaidd.[8] At ei gilydd yr oedd pobl Cymru o blaid y Rhyfel, a nod arweinwyr y farn gyhoeddus oedd sicrhau i Gymru ei lle haeddiannol yn yr ymerodraeth Brydeinig. Nid yw'n syndod, felly, ddarganfod chwaraewyr rhyngwladol Cymru, unwaith y pylodd eu dyddiau gorau, yn dilyn y llwybrau amrywiol a oedd yn arwain i encilion pellaf yr Ymerodraeth. Ym 1887, er enghraifft, dewisodd W.F. (Bill) Evans, a chwaraeodd dros Gymru ym 1882 a 1883, ymfudo o Rymni i Fremantle, Gorllewin Awstralia. Ym 1891 treuliodd yr enwog Arthur Gould flwyddyn gron ar fusnes yn India'r Gorllewin pan oedd ei yrfa ddim ond ar ei hanner; ymadawodd ei frawd Bert, yntau'n chwaraewr rhyngwladol, am Dde Affrica ym 1887, a marw yn Germiston yn Transvaal ym 1913. Bu farw W.B. Norton (5 chap, 1882-84) yn Calabar yng Nghorllewin Affrica ym 1899. Un o'r chwaraewyr ieuengaf erioed i gynrychioli ei wlad (yr oedd yn 18 oed pan wisgodd y crys coch am y tro cyntaf ym 1888) oedd Norman Biggs, yntau fel Norton yn hanu o Gaerdydd; fe'i lladdwyd gan saeth wenwynig yng ngogledd Nigeria ym 1908. O Lanbedr Pont Steffan y deuai John Strand Jones, Llanelli (5 cap, 1902-03), ond aeth i Lahore ym 1909 yn gaplan i'r fyddin ar y 'Northwest Frontier'.

Unwaith yn rhagor ceir tîm cenedlaethol 1905 yn crisialu gogwydd crwydrol, imperialaidd Cymry'r oes. Bu farw J.F. Williams o dwymyn drofannol yn Nigeria ym 1911; ymfudodd 'Boxer' Harding i Seland Newydd, i orffen ei ddyddiau yn ffermio yn Greymouth. Nid i Nigeria na Seland Newydd yr aeth Percy Bush, y consuriwr o faswr a enillodd ei gap cyntaf yn Rhagfyr 1905, ond i fod yn is-lysgennad yn Nantes yn Ffrainc. Y fasnach lo, wrth gwrs, oedd yn cydio porthladdoedd De Cymru a Ffrainc â'i gilydd mewn cwlwm a gaiff ei goffáu heddiw yn y Boulevard de Nantes yng Nghaerdydd.

Cymru deyrngar, frenhingar, hynod ymerodrol oedd y Gymru hon. Anodd credu'r peth erbyn hyn, ond ym 1881 bu clwb rygbi Llanelli yn ystyried o ddifrif fabwysiadu briallu a rhosyn yn lliwiau newydd, cyfuniad blodeuog y buasai'r Frenhines Victoria ei hun wedi ei gymeradwyo. Perthynai naws ac amcanion imperialaidd i fudiad 'Cymru Fydd': y nod oedd gweld Cymru led-annibynnol yn pefrio yng nghoron yr Ymerodraeth Brydeinig. Byddai Lloyd George a Tom Ellis ill dau wedi amenio'r hyn yr oedd gan ymgeisydd Rhyddfrydol i'w ddweud i fanllefau o gymeradwyaeth yn y Barri ar Ŵyl Ddewi 1900, sef 'er falched yr oedd o fod yn Gymro, yr oedd yn rhaid iddo gydnabod balchder mwy eto bod Cymru'n rhan o'r Ymerodraeth Brydeinig—yr helaethaf a'r orau yn y byd'. Dyma'r Ymerodraeth, meddai W. Llywelyn Williams ym 1908, wrth annerch Cymmrodorion Caerfyrddin (y dref y bu'n Aelod Seneddol Rhyddfrydol drosti o 1906 tan 1918) a oedd yn fwy haelionus nag un Rhufain, yn fwy eang nag a ddychmygodd Alexander yn ei freuddwydion mwyaf ffôl, 'the most stupendous creation of all time'. Diferai'r wasg Rhyddfrydol Gymreig â datganiadau o'r fath. Ar ôl honni, drannoeth Gŵyl Ddewi 1907, bod cynnydd rhagluniaethol Cymru o les i'r Ymerodraeth, aeth y *South Wales Daily News* ymhellach ar yr un diwrnod y flwyddyn ganlynol i haeru bod 'y dadeni Cymreig' yn llesol nid yn unig i'r Ymerodraeth ond, erbyn hynny, i'r ddynoliaeth hefyd.

Dysgasom gan y Prifathro Kenneth O. Morgan fod i'r cyfnod rhwng 1880 a 1914 yn hanes Cymru ei undod neilltuol ei hun. Yn wleidyddol fe'i ffurfiwyd gan Ryddfrydiaeth, ac yn economaidd gan ddiwydianaeth a threfoli syfrdanol. Yn ddiwylliannol cafwyd dadeni ym myd llên, a chwyldro mewn addysg. Gwelwyd sefydlu Prifysgol, Amgueddfa a Llyfrgell Genedlaethol, Adran Gymreig o'r Bwrdd Addysg a rhwydwaith o ysgolion uwchradd. Ac nid dyma'r unig arwyddion o ymwybyddiaeth y Cymry o'u cenedligrwydd. 'Yn yr hyn y gellir ei alw'n Ddadeni cenedlaethol Cymru', meddai'r *South Wales Daily News* ym 1909, 'mae ffwtbol [h.y. rygbi] yn ffactor na ellir ei hanwybyddu. Mewn gêm sydd yn gofyn am grebwyll mwy na chryfder—sydd, mewn geiriau eraill, yn fwy ymenyddol na chorfforol—mae'r Cymry lawn cystal â'r tair genedl arall, ac yn fynych yn rhagori arnynt'. Yr oedd llwyddiant ar y maes chwarae 'yn un o'r ffactorau sy'n dynodi hunaniaeth genedlaethol'. Yr oedd hwn yn fath o gyflyraeth syniadol, yr hyn a elwir gan gymdeithasegwyr yn goddiwyllianaeth *(acculturation)*. Byddai'r Eidalwr Antonio Gramsci wedi ei ddehongli fel ymgais i greu 'hegemoni' gan y dosbarth canol. Yr oedd i rygbi, pe gellid ei gwneud hi'n ffocws i'r syniad o genedl a chymuned, swyddogaeth werthfawr.

Saernïwyd, felly, ddelwedd o gêm boblogaidd, a oedd yn o bell o'r hunan-fynegiant athletaidd, y cyffro cystadleuol a'r gwrthdaro corfforol, sef nodweddion amlycaf y gêm. Lapiwyd mantell ideolegol o gwmpas chwarae yr oedd ei apêl hanfodol yn ddramatig ac emosiynol. Yn wyneb y peryglon y gellid eisoes eu synhwyro yn codi yn yr ardaloedd diwydiannol, a gyda thwf dosbarth gweithiol a oedd eisoes yn ymddiddori mewn syniadau sosialaidd a syndicalaidd, sut y gellid orau saernïo syniad am Gymru fel cenedl a chymuned a oedd wedi cyrraedd ei safle presennol trwy dyfiant naturiol, organig?

Un ffordd o wneud hynny oedd trwy apelio at hanes, a chafwyd sawl ymdriniaeth boblogaidd ar Gymru'r gorffennol yn Gymraeg a Saesneg gan O.M. Edwards, D.A. Thomas, Owen Rhoscomyl ac eraill. Ffordd arall oedd trwy lusgo hanes, megis yn gorfforol, i'r presennol. Dyna a wnaed gan syrcas frenhinol Lloyd George, yr Arwisgo, yng nghastell Caernarfon ym 1911. Ddwy flynedd cyn hynny bu syrcas nid annhebyg yng Ngerddi Sophia, pan gynhaliwyd Pasiant Cenedlaethol, sioe a ddyfeisiwyd gan Owen Rhoscomyl. Yn hwn cafwyd portreadau a golygfeydd dramatig o hanes Cymru, a chymerwyd rhannau blaenllaw gan nifer o foneddigion Cymru, rai ohonynt fel Ardalydd Bute ac Arglwyddi Tredegar, Mostyn a Crichton-Stuart yn chwarae rhan eu hynafiaid eu hunain. Ond yr oedd rhannau i bum mil o bobl i gyd, yn fonedd a gwreng, er mwyn sicrhau bod y Pasiant, fel Cymru ei hun, yn rhychwantu ac yn uniaethu'r gymdeithas gyfan. Gan mai dyna oedd swyddogaeth ddelfrydol rygbi hefyd, yr oedd yn hollol briodol mai'r prif actorion yn yr olygfa a oedd yn ail-greu ymosodiad Ifor Bach a 'gwŷr y Fro' ar y gaer Normanaidd oedd criw o chwaraewyr rygbi adnabyddus, yn eu plith pedwar o arwyr 1905, Gwyn Nicholls, Percy Bush, A.F. Harding a Rhys Gabe.[9]

Felly y gwnaed llwyddiant Cymru ar y maes rygbi, fel ei hanes hi, yn berthnasol ac yn ddefnyddiol. Gwnaethpwyd apêl at y maes chwarae, fel at y gorffennol, i gynnal delwedd o

Gymru unedig, drefnus, ddiddosbarth, flaengar, lle'r oedd pawb yn cyd-dynnu ac yn cyd-fyw fel aelodau o un gymuned genedlaethol gytûn. Tybed a fu erioed Gymru o'r fath?

NODIADAU

[1] *South Wales Daily News*, 18 Rhagfyr 1905.

[2] Glanffrwd, *Llanwynno* (1888), argraffiad gol. Henry Lewis (Caerdydd, 1949), t. 19.

[3] David Smith a Gareth Williams, *Fields of Praise* (1980) tt. 126-7.

[4] *Y Faner*, 23 Rhagfyr 1905.

[5] *Y Cronicl*, Awst 1886, tt. 247-51; *Y Traethodydd*, 58, 1903, tt. 269-274; *Llanelly and County Guardian*, 9 Rhagfyr 1886.

[6] Ceir cyfeiriadau llawn yn y nodiadau i bennod 4 uchod.

[7] W. Samlet Williams, *Hanes a Hynafiaethau Llansamlet* (Dolgellau, 1908), t. 297.

[8] K.O. Morgan, *Wales in British Politics 1868-1922* (Caerdydd, 1963), tt. 178-9.

[9] Ceir ymdriniaeth lawn, a llawn difyrrwch, o'r Pasiant Cenedlaethol, yn Hywel Teifi Edwards, *Codi'r Hen Wlad yn ei Hôl 1850-1914* (Llandysul, 1985) tt. 239-89. 'Roedd y Pasiant', medd yr Athro Hywel Teifi 'i gymryd ei le gyda buddugoliaeth Côr Caradog yn 1873 a darostyngiad yr 'All Blacks' yn 1905 fel trydedd prawf o ddadeni Cymru' (t. 267).

CHAPTER 6

SPORT AND SOCIETY IN GLAMORGAN 1780-1980

INTRODUCTION

Pre-industrial England appears to have enjoyed a rich diversity of sports and games, intimately connected to a small-scale communal way of life whose recreations were heavily ritualized and bound by the seasons, but linked also to a wider pattern of social life in which all were expected to participate according to their status.[1] The recreational life of pre-industrial Glamorgan, however, is an elusive quarry for the historian. Today, the face of the three counties of modern Glamorgan is freckled with leisure centres, playing fields, and sports facilities, but no such landmarks and occasional eyesores were apparent to the late eighteenth-century tourist—a numerous breed between 1780 and 1830. It is not merely that the recreations of that age had yet to develop specialized locations beyond the open fields, the churchyard and the public house, but that gentlemen travellers were little inclined, through upbringing and temperament, to do more than glance casually at popular pastimes that derived their vigour from an unlettered, communal involvement in an oral tradition with few written records.

The historian seeks to overcome these difficulties by combing the writings of diarists and antiquarians, local government records and the contemporary press for passing references to sports and pastimes. In addition, the diatribes of moral improvers and religious reformers can be unwittingly revealing in describing the activities they so roundly condemn. In so far as godly culture and popular culture were mutually hostile, a colourful source of life in eighteenth-century Glamorgan is the journal kept by William Thomas (d. 1795), a schoolmaster of Michaelston-super-Ely, whose puritan attitudes were still in advance of an agrarian society to whom the seasonal cycle of economic and ecclesiastical activities was of continuing relevance.[2] It clearly emerges that the major recreational events of the year were the *mabsantau*, the wakes or revels whose original purpose of celebrating the local saint had become the pretext for boisterous festivity of all kinds. They varied in length from a day to a week, and while they ought not to be overladen with symbolism they may still be regarded as one of the ways in which the parish defined itself as a corporate group and territorial unit.

Their prevailing atmosphere of pleasure-seeking and profanity was deplored by William Thomas. He condemns as pagan—or worse, popish—the erecting of *y fedwen haf*, the beribboned summer birch, in many villages in the Vale; it pains him to recount the attempts made by the youth of St Nicholas to steal the idolatrous maypole of St Fagan's ('their wooden painted god') in 1768.[3] Today we are inclined to identify such adolescent high spirits as a classic rite of passage. It has been plausibly argued, too, that the fierce competitiveness of these festivals may have derived from tensions engendered by contemporary poor-law legislation. This imposed pressure on parish funds for the maintenance of the poor and illegitimate, and disputes over the settlement or removal of those dependent on the parish spilled over into the bruising inter-village rivalries of eighteenth-century Glamorgan.[4]

The *mabsant* and the *taplas haf*, summer dances whose apparent informality again concealed a pattern of structured relationships and rules of precedence, were the occasions of athletic contests that provided for all sorts of ball games, races, and animal sports. 'Revels', to William Thomas, were synonymous with 'riots', which only confirms that spectator sports and violence have always accompanied each other: the line between merriment and mayhem is easily crossed. The deeply-rooted inclination to let off steam is age-old, its form conditioned by the changing historical context. The *mabsant* itself was not traditional in any sense of its having originated in the mists of time: William Thomas observed in 1764 that the revels in St Andrews were a mere 50 years' old, and St Fagan's only 38 years' old.[5] Nor was it common throughout Glamorgan as a whole: it was not a feature of west Glamorgan or of the upland *Blaenau* but specifically of the Vale (*Bro Morgannwg*), the lowland area between the Rhymney and Afan rivers, at a particular time, the 'long eighteenth century' from the seventeenth-century Acts of Settlement to their abolition in 1834.[6]

THE EIGHTEENTH CENTURY

While the county, like Wales and indeed Europe, was a collection of separate regions, fragmented as much by local traditions and customs as by geography, there were, nevertheless, certain élite sports characteristic of the landed classes wherever they lived. The newly ascendant gentry families of eighteenth-century Glamorgan were all the keener to live up to artistocratic traditions of recreation and leisure. So when John Byng noted in 1787 that he was passing 'not far distant from Cowbridge race ground' he was acknowledging the fame of the town's race meetings, which had grown in status from a mere family occasion in mid-century to being 'the Glamorgan races', attracting horses from as far distant as Yorkshire. One regular racegoer was the Rev John Carne, whose expenses at the 1770 races, reckoned to exceed a labourer's annual wages, remind us that there remained a deep-seated sympathy for such pleasures amongst the gentry and clergy. The Spread Eagle Inn, where the horses were shown, with its assembly-room milieu of dinners and balls, was the focal point of the gentry's social life, and Cowbridge is Glamorgan's best example of the role played by eighteenth-century towns in servicing the increased demand for gentry status as gentlemen invested much time and money on stock breeding, horses and hounds.[7]

The most socially-exclusive of all sports was of course, hunting, with the justices in the van: George Borrow noticed that 'all that was required of a Glamorgan squire was that he should be a justice of the peace and keeper of a pack of hounds', and the preoccupation with hunting of the Glamorgan gentry was reflected in its commissioned paintings and verses in both languages extolling a squire's horses and hounds—and fowl, Mansel Talbot introducing the pheasant to Glamorgan in the 1770s. It was not only the outlay on guns and the hunting establishment that made this pursuit the preserve of the landed class, but also the Game Laws and the high freehold qualification which prohibited most of the inhabitants of Glamorgan's countryside from being able to shoot on their own land. The social tensions thus engendered led to the possible poisoning of the Talbot Hounds at Hensol in 1733. There was malicious glee in Iolo Morganwg's lament for horses that 'sometimes in breaking down a five-barred gate break their own necks'.[8]

Foxhunting, though, was not among those lists of customs and holidays that Iolo, the brilliantly creative self-educated stonemason of Flemingstone, industriously compiled in support of his assertion that Glamorgan was 'the most old-fashioned county in Wales'. A great believer in, if not the inventor of, *mwynder Morgannwg* (the suavity of Glamorgan), he reckoned the three things most easily come by in the county to be 'liberality, pleasure, and learning', and its pleasures included the kind of sports and games held over three days in 1780 in Llangyfelach near Swansea, and sponsored by those perennial patrons of conviviality, the local publicans. The activities Iolo exhaustively lists include sack- and pony-racing, cockfighting, shooting at a mark, bar-throwing, footracing, bando, a badger hunt, football, and bull-baiting, for all of which the prizes were nicely graded: a gun worth ten guineas for the champion marksman, a bottle of brandy for the bando players, and gin for the winners at football.[9]

Bando (bandy) is the first mass spectator sport of Glamorgan and Wales, and Iolo was ambivalent in his attitude to it, here celebrating it as a characteristic of hoary bardic tradition, there urging its suppression in the name of social reform and agricultural improvement. A traveller *en route* from Cowbridge to Pyle in 1797 noted 'the extraordinary barrenness' of the locality in ash and elm, hard woods ideal for bando bats, and came across hordes of people hastening to the sea shore not to despoil a wreck but to watch a game of bando.[10] Baglan, Aberavon and Margam—where, according to Edward Matthews of Ewenni, no-one above a twelve month would be seen without a bando stick—were as fierce rivals in the west, as Pyle, Kenfig, and Llangynwyd in mid-Glamorgan, while to the east Llantwit

Major in the early nineteenth century acted 'exceeding hoity-toitily among the neighbouring villages and carried everything with a high hand'. As ever, the apparently lawless and haphazard aspects of pre-industrial game like bando can deceive: when one village challenged another, free-for-all informality was subordinated to the laying of wagers which demanded agreement on rules, an agreed number of players (usually 20 to 30) and a fixed area of play (about 200 yards long with the goal markers ten yards apart, according to Matthews). There is no doubting its appeal—3,000 spectators watched red-and-white Margam—nor its close links with local brewers, who rolled casks of ale down to the beach to keep everyone well-lubricated.[11] It survived in the Aberavon area until the last quarter of the nineteenth century, when the death in 1876 of Theodore Talbot, captain of the Margam Bando Boys and heir to the Margam estate, coincided with the arrival of the Mansel, Avon Vale, and Taibach tinworks, which sealed the fate of bando as their employees turned to a new game: in 1876, under the patronage of the manager of the Mansel works, Aberavon R.F.C. was founded.[12] But local patriotism had only shifted its focus. Just as older games made like distinction between participants and onlookers caught up in the collective frenzy, fighting remained an integral part of the whole experience: Aberavon's rugby ground was closed for a month in 1896, and 1899, because of the intrusion of spectators on to the field.[13]

If bando, like Breton *soule*, was 'little more than a ritualized battle between parishes ... part of a coherent set of under-standings and part of normal life',[14] pugilism, too, was a long-standing social reality. Fist-fighting attracted a wide spectrum of support and a free flow of money-betting as it became increasingly subject, from the late eighteenth century, to formal rules and championship matches organized by gentlemen promoters and publicans. The renowned Daniel Mendoza fought an exhibition in Swansea in the 1790s, and in 1819 Tom Cribb and Tom Spring 'exhibited their willing talents' on a tour of Glamorgan.[15] One of the county's homegrown champions was George Heycock, 'the Bruiser', who eventually renounced mixing it for Methodism. In his heyday in the 1820s he was an ungainly fighter in that he had one leg shorter than the other, a handicap that prevented him from wholehearted participation in his real loves, football and bando.[16] Meanwhile, in the raw iron communities of upland Glamorgan, prize fights attracted large crowds and wagers. Shoni Sgubor-fawr, emperor of Merthyr's notorious 'China', had an awesome reputation as a fighter before his involvement in the Rebecca Riots got him transported to Van Diemen's Land in 1844. The arrival of the Taff Vale Railway in Merthyr was celebrated by a bare-knuckled contest between Shoni and Nash of Cyfarthfa in 1840. Fist-fighting made the transition to industrial society with little effort.[17]

Other athletic diversions recognizable after two centuries included *taflu'r bar*, bar-throwing. Glamorgan's champion was George Williams of Aberpergwm (d. 1796). Iolo's son, Taliesin, described a contest in the late eighteenth century between the musclemen of Aberavon and Cadoxton (Neath) at Coed Iarll, where the latter's reputation was saved by the late appearance in the lists of the aged squire of Aberpergwm to win the match with a colossal throw.[18] Owing to their links with the more informal lower-key relaxations of everyday life, varieties of bowls, skittles, and quoits receive notice only when they fell foul of the law. In 1744 Joanna Lond of Swansea was accused of 'maintaining a certain common gaming house for a certain unlawful game called shuffleboard and for one other unlawful game called [struck out] billiards . . . and a certain unlawful game called fives and another place called a skittle alley for the play of bowles and skittles'.[19] Peter Roberts refers in his *Cambrian Antiquities* (1815) to 'the game called in Wales Fives' but this was really a genteel term: what English upper-class rugger was to Welsh rugby, fives was to handball. Byng noticed it in Pyle churchyard in 1787, Matthews of Ewenni refers to it in his biography of Jenkin Thomas, 'Siencyn Penhydd', of Goytre above Pontrhydyfen, and it was played in the Swansea Valley, but it is particularly associated with east Glamorgan. It involved playing a hard, leather-cased rubber ball with the hand against the pine-end of a house, church or, later, in an open-backed squash court generally near a public house. It was played for money prizes and attracted keen wagers. Thanks to Glanffrwd's history of Llanwynno (1880) we know that it was a speciality of the Ynysybwl district, which threw up a whole clutch of skilled exponents. The more aristocratic Eton fives played at Cowbridge and Pengam grammar schools was socially a world away from the proletarian, often professional, handball played at Cowbridge's Tennis Court Inn and the Royal Oak, Nelson, where the game was popularly revived during the depressed 1930s and 1980s.[20]

Ineradicably associated with pre-industrial Glamorgan, and with Llanwynno in particular, is the fleet-footed Guto Nyth Brân (Griffith Morgan, d. 1737), whose malodorous pre-race habit was to sleep in compost to ensure muscular suppleness and secure the maximum distance between himself and his opponents. Guto was only the most legendary of several footracers whose feats attracted heavy betting. 'Siân o'r Siop' was one devoted backer who took hundreds of pounds on the outcome of Guto's famous race with Prince, and it was her overhearty back-slap that killed the breathless victor after he had covered the 12 miles from Newport to Bedwas in 53 minutes.[21] Running for wagers was the essence of footracing, or pedestrianism: promoted and patronized initially by the gentry, who generally backed their own servants—footmen being professional runners engaged to carry messages—by the second half of the eighteenth century it had moved out from the club and mess to the tavern and taproom. Twm Emwnt (Thomas Edmunds, d. 1785) of Vaenor earned his living as a professional runner: his failure in a crunch race in London led one mortified backer to set fire to Twm's house.[22]

Runners who developed their muscles and stamina pounding the moors of the uplands found their skills amply rewarded in the iron districts. In 1814 Thomas Llewellyn of Penderyn raced Howell Richard along the Taff Vale tramway, drawing spectators from twenty miles to watch and gamble on the result. As Merthyr's remembrancer writes, 'These people had a passion for games . . . they'd bet on anything, one man streaked naked through a wedding procession in Merthyr High Street for sixpence'. Where there was sport there was gambling, which offended against morality and obstructed the traffic: at Aberavon in 1843 several runners were fined because their supporters blocked the turnpike, but this failed to diminish the high popular regard for local heroes like John Davies (y Cyw Cloff) of Bryncethin, who became virtually county champion after beating Wil Bevan of Pontrhydyfen for a £20 prize the following year, and the subject of innumerable songs and ballads after he went on to defeat the English champions, Tetlow and Cox. [23]

However, given the strong disposition to manipulate animal life for 'sporting' purposes, sporting endeavour was no more confined to human beings in Glamorgan than it was anywhere else. Bull-baiting, to William Thomas, was a regrettable event in the St Fagan's revels of 1764, and featured—without comment—in Iolo's three-day olympiad at Llangyfelach in 1780. Swansea had a corporation bull-ring from 1723 to 1769, and Cardiff's was located between the modern Kingsway and the Hayes. Cardiff town council paid towards its upkeep in the early eighteenth century ('Paid to the slipkeeper 2/6', 'for washing the Bull Rope 1/8', are two entries for 1717) but such provision had already ceased before the passing of the Cruelty to Animals Act of 1835. Similarly, certain publicans in Kenfig were granted their licences in 1822 on condition that their premises were not used for 'cockfighting and the baiting of bulls, bears and badgers'. Prohibitory legislation served only to divert the human propensity to humiliate animals into obscure channels: in mid-century a man from the Vale of Neath used to wrestle with bulls at Margam Park. His technique was to wrap the bull's tail around his arm and bludgeon the wretched animal senseless with the club he wielded in the other. This clown was hailed even in America as 'the Wild Welshman'. [24]

Equally unsavoury, and far more common, was cockfighting, which cut across class lines. Glamorgan's game-cocks were sought after from as far afield as the Caribbean. Contests were fought on a regional or county basis: John Harris, the Cornish Cocker (d. 1910), remembered a 'great main' between Glamorgan and Worcester, the main being a contest by 32 pugnacious fowls paired off until there was one survivor. The anti-cruelty legislation of 1835 and 1849 did not achieve its ends overnight: Harris recalled a main between Bristol and Aberdare in the eastern valleys where over a thousand colliers and furnacemen insisted on counting in Welsh, tried to fix the result, and were inclined to be generally nasty. [25] Such spectacles are not edifying in any language, but we might remember that the campaigns against blood sports were often led by men whose own recreations were no less cruel. It was thought somehow morally damaging for the lower orders to enjoy blood sports but perfectly acceptable for their superiors to shoot, hunt, and fish. Legislation and deference kept the common people firmly on their side of the recreational divide.

It would be a distortion, however, to emphasize class conflict at the expense of the considerable degree to which the gentry in Glamorgan as elsewhere patronized popular recreations. We ignore the symbolic and psychological value of such involvement at our peril. Poised midway between a robust local culture and the cosmopolitan sophistication of urban life, the gentry retained a tolerance of popular culture out of paternalism and traditionalism as well as self-interest. When Charles Wesley bridled at seeing a revel at Whitchurch in 1741 'honoured with the presence of the gentry and clergy', and when William Thomas railed against cockfighting in the Vale that 'such work brings but the curse of God upon the generation', they merely deepened the suspicions of the squierarchy towards a meddlesome puritanism that was ethically rigorous and unsympathetic to the traditional, more permissive outlook. A Tory clergy shared these reservations. Entirely typical was the Vale of Neath parson who took part in churchyard ball games, keeping the score and helping to drink the beer afterwards; while a St Athan clergyman could hardly wait to get his surplice off before joining the Sunday bando players on the shore. [26]

But by the late eighteenth century that upper-class desertion of popular culture which had been characteristic of much of Europe for at least a century was also making itself felt in a Glamorgan whose country governors had come to resemble their counterparts elsewhere in social and intellectual assumptions, in social and economic morality, in culture, and in language. The gentry ceased to patronize Welsh literature and popular pastimes simultaneously. [27] Previously-held attitudes of sceptical tolerance towards brutalizing sports were under assault from a dual sense of moral conviction and social respectability, and the accelerating rate of economic change completed the transformation of leisure.

THE NINETEENTH CENTURY

The mass spectator-sports of industrial Glamorgan did not supplant a buoyant, still-vigorous 'traditional' culture. In many respects they filled a void, for much of the internal strength of the customs of the old, face-to-face community was ebbing in any case. The pace of decline varied, but the overall pattern is unmistakeable and can be seen in microcosm in the Vale.

Llantwit Major's *Annwyl Day* was a traditional May festivity linked to both the expulsion of winter (death) and the lynching of the Irish pirate, O'Neal, whose execution was celebrated by a procession and the burning of his effigy. By 1858, when it was taken over by the Oddfellows, a friendly society like the Ivorites that emerged in the wake of the New Poor Law legislation of the 1830s, the *Annwyl Day* parade was already on its last legs. Similarly, the last May-eve beltane fires were kindled in the Vale in the 1830s.[28] The changing face of Cowbridge registered the intrusion of new economic and social forces: its first bank opened in 1835, it had a professional police force from 1842, in the 1850s it was provided with gas, and a branch of the Cardiff to Swansea railway reached it in 1865. Significantly, stealing the painted god, once the expression of inter-village rivalry, was no more than 'an amazing frolic' between Cowbridge and Llantrisant in 1842.[29] The simultaneous atrophy of the *mabsant*, which 'old and venerable though it was, . . . did not end in good odour', was attributed out of deliberately innocent nostalgia to the morally deleterious effects of adjacent new towns and industries, where fresh-faced country lads allegedly picked up undesirable habits and even less desirable company. Clearly, these 'rougher elements' were in truth symptoms of more complex changes: the social differentiation caused by the greater concentration of wealth in fewer hands, the growth of a landless proletariat, and of a more class-conscious society generally were undermining the tightly-knit

organic community which, though never static, was characterized by ties of kinship, long residence, and an oral, ritual
framework of recreations.[30] These dislocations might have led
to conflict had it not been for the gravitational pull of the
country's industrial growth.

That growth did not transform popular culture overnight.
Mabsantau and maypoles were already in decline, but the *cwrw
bach*, *ceffyl pren* and *Mari Lwyd*, and the fairs and the festivals,
survived awhile in all their collective disorderliness. The
evidence from Merthyr in the first half of the nineteenth
century where *twmpath* and *taplas* interacted with fairground
fighting and footracing is of a lusty plebian culture transplanted
to the quasi-tribal immigrant quarters where 'the champions of
Tregaron and Cil-y-Cwm would do battle on the Glebeland of a
Sunday in ritual conflict which would easily end in riot'.[31]

While Merthyr had the oldest industrial workforce in Wales,
a new town like Barry, transformed from a rustic village of 500
inhabitants in 1881 to a booming port of 33,000 by 1911,
spawned recreations appropriate to its newness. Local customs
like the *Mari Lwyd* and ritual wedding processions were
swamped by the incoming immigrant tide. New entertainment
had to be devised. Local drama and music societies sprang up
and the myriorama and bioscope vied with visiting circuses,
menageries, waxworks and fairgrounds, 'which were a link with
the greater and more exciting new world developing in
America'. On the outskirts of the mushrooming town,
informal and sometimes illicit prize-fighting and foot-racing
hung on till the end of the century, to be finally displaced by
proliferating newly-codified club games: quoits (1886), rugby
(1887), cricket (1890), cycling (1891), soccer (1892), as well as
tennis (1891), rowing (1892) and golf (1898).[32]

Late nineteenth-century industrial Glamorgan was a sporting hothouse where a bewildering range of recreational and
sporting activities sprouted. Some, like billiards, ping pong and
gymnastics, were characteristically urban phenomena, others
like weightlifing, wrestling and hockey were adaptations of
older forms, spiced now by the ingredient of national and international competition. Wales, effectively Glamorgan, played
England at waterpolo in 1900 (in front of 700 spectators at

Penarth Baths), lacrosse in 1907, and baseball in 1908. The South Wales Baseball League dated from 1893, becoming the Welsh Baseball Association in 1912, but in Wales it was almost exclusively a Cardiff sport, based on the working-class areas of Splott and Grangetown (Grange Albion being formed in 1904 from the Penarth Road Methodist Club) where it continues to exert a powerful appeal. If baseball's origins were American, quoits was a game with historic Welsh roots. *Chwarae koeten* appears in John Walters of Llandough's dictionary of 1794 and it became popular in Bridgend, Merthyr, and Rhymney where Thomas Jones remembered watching 'the pond'rous quoit obliquely fall': Llwynypia in the Rhondda was a favourite venue for quoits internationals between Wales and England before 1914.[33]

Yet another age-old sport that underwent formalization was athletics, the model rational recreation. Cardiff's Roath Harriers (1882) was the first purely athletic club to be formed with no connection with any other winter sport. Professional running, practised on old railway tracks and tramways, appealed to the constant urge to gamble. Named after the Edinburgh stadium where the famous 130-yard handicap was run professionally, the Welsh Powderhall was established at Pontypridd in 1903, with a prize of £100 for the same distance. Located at the confluence of the eastern valleys of Glamorgan, it was a significant venue: two years earlier the Welsh Professional Union had been established there to promote and control professional foot-and-cycle-racing in south Wales. The cultural contrast between the studied amateurism of the coastal towns and the semi-professionalism of the valleys, where there was little tradition of amateur running, was noted by George Ewart Evans, a native of Abercynon, who was embarrassed to win £15 in 1927 when such a sum was a collier's seven weeks' wages: 'Amateurism flourishes only in a stable environment, and it was useless in the Twenties to discuss with a miner who was involved in frequent strikes and was earning a bare subsistence wage the niceties of the debate between professionalism and amateurism'.[34]

Beneath the common experience of industrialization lay a multitude of local differences. What baseball was to Cardiff,

World champion cyclist Jimmy Michael (1877-1904) of Aberaman.

Jimmy Michael and the Linton brothers, with their manager 'Choppy'
Warburton.

cycling was to the Cynon Valley, which prided itself on its
'knights of the wheel', in fact two wheels. Cycle-racing as a
mass commercial spectacle began in, and remained identified
with, France, following the invention of the modern chain-
driven bicycle with wheels of equal size and inflatable tyres in
the late 1880s.[35] In the 1890s the middle-class mania for
bicycles resulted in a dramatic fall in prices that brought them
within the purchasing power of working men, or at least single
young men. Public houses, as ever, played a pivotal role, and
the training facilities at 'The Swan' and 'Lamb and Flag', Aberaman, helped produce a group of professional world champions. The ramshackle racing tracks that were laid in several
parts of Glamorgan in the 1890s could hardly compare with the
vélodromes of France, and it was there and in America that

Arthur and Tom Linton and Jimmy Michael broke several world records. Arthur Linton's death aged 28 in 1896 evoked a poignant and massive response from the community that had nurtured him; Jimmy Michael's funeral in 1904 was the largest seen in the Cynon Valley since that of the great choral conductor 'Caradog'.[36]

The correlation between industrial and recreational development was rarely straightforward. For many years old and new coexisted. In 1897 there was a prosecution for cockfighting in Abernant, Aberdare; in 1880 twenty men were fined for organizing a footrace on Hirwaun Common, blocking off the road to compete over a hundred yards for five pounds. Up on the moors, areas remote from the authorities became the locations of fist-fights: these were 'the bloody spots'. In 1885 the *Aberdare Times* condemned them as 'an outrage to decency', urging severe punishment on 'the brutes who take part'.[37] Harry, who won three gold sovereigns for licking Flannery in an 1880s moutain fight in Jack Jones's Merthyr novel *Black Parade* (1935), was drawn from life. It was on one of the 'bloody spots' between Merthyr and Aberdare that Twm, brother of Wil Jon Edwards, in 1894 fought a Blaengwawr man for forty-two ultimately fatal rounds before 200 spectators. 'The suppression of pugilism' was one of the aims of the Trecynon Nonconformist League in 1908, but it could not be realized at a time and in a place where a working-class society required champions to articulate their collective identity and, where possible, represent them on the world canvas.[3]

The transition from informal, bare-knuckled mountain fighting to formal gloved contests under Queensberry Rules, graded according to weight so that science and skill counted far more than brute strength, occured in the 1890s. As ever, middle-class patronage attached itself to a working-class sport, and at London's dinner-jacketed National Sporting Club, 'the temple of the Fancy', Welsh boxers became the big crowd-pullers. In the first thirty years of the twentieth century the Rhondda Valleys and Pontypridd produced more boxing champions than any other area of comparable size in the world. Tom Thomas (Penygraig), Percy Jones (Porth), Jimmy Wilde (Tylorstown), Freddie Welsh, Frank Moody and Franco Rossi

Freddie Welsh (Pontypridd), Tom Thomas (Penygraig), and Jim Driscoll (Cardiff) belt up, Lonsdale-style.

(Pontypridd), George Williams (Treherbert), Harold Jones (Ferndale), Billy Hughes (Dinas), and Tommy Farr (Tonypandy) all fought in the 'Welsh style' of standing erect and punching fast; all proceeded from the pit, *via* the fairground booths of the likes of 'Black' Jack Scarrott and the fistic tutorship of such 'Professors' as Frank Gess and Harry Cullis, to Welsh and British titles; Percy Jones, Freddie Welsh and Wilde became world champions.

Boxing became as much a part of the regional culture as rugby football. Its attraction lay in its immediacy. For sheer spontaniety and unpredictability nothing could match it, and its working-class followers held an especial regard for physical courage, the reckless gesture, and stylistic insolence. Hence the tumultous homecoming accorded Freddie Welsh and Cardiff's Jim Driscoll on their return from triumphant American tours in 1909, which perpetuated the carnivalesque traditions of the wakes and revels, just as their electrifying long-awaited clash at the American Roller Rink in Westgate Street, Cardiff, the following year, stirred the fierce loyalties of 10,000 of the valley Welsh and the Cardiff Irish.[39] Such collective heroes throve on a reciprocal complicity with their communities that never compromised their swaggering independence. None was more insouciant than Tom Thomas (1880-1911). Of Cardiganshire stock, he retained the close instincts of that county in the solitude of his farm above Penygraig, where he rode bare-back and fought bulls to avoid the expense of sparring partners. Frederick Hall Thomas, after a richly symbolic change of name to Freddie Welsh, went off to Philadelphia at 17 years of age. World lightweight champion from 1914 to 1917, he eventually became a director of a Long Island health farm where one of *his* sparring partners—for three rounds—was F. Scott Fitzgerald.[40] Welsh embodied that American Wales that was at the same time intensely local and enterprisingly Atlantic in its outlook.

MADDING CROWDS

It is teams rather than individuals, however, who embody their followers' idealized perception of themselves and their communities, and the one team sport that has paralleled the development of a full-blown industrial economy and become part of the cultural matrix of modern Welsh society is rugby football. Its early growth in the 1870s relied on two key factors. One was the support of the Victorian middle class, whose aspirations were summed up by H.A. Bruce at Cardiff in 1855: 'Next to the deep-pervading sentiment of religion, I know nothing of more importance to the well-being of a people than well-ordered amusements'.[41] Rugby football in Glamorgan became the gospel of a thinly-spread layer of upwardly-mobile young professional men—solicitors, surveyors, doctors, land agents and clerks—who founded typical clubs at Neath (1871), Cardiff (1875), Mountain Ash and Pontypridd (both 1876). The middle-class imperatives of respectability, discipline and self-improvement then fused with the imperial ethic: in 1900 the headmaster of Cowbridge School, having defined a sportsman as 'one who takes the rough with the smooth, shows "grit" in adversity, sinks self and is modest in triumph', went on to weave a more complicated tapestry, since 'the sport thus engendered has borne fruit in the grim valour of our soldiers on the death-strewn slopes of Spion Kop and Magersfontein'.[42]

The second key element was the massive immigration into the industrial crucible of 'Greater Glamorgan', if we so designate the area south of the Beacons and Black Mountains, between Newport and Llanelli, whose one and a half million people by 1911 included two out of every three persons in Wales. They adopted rugby because it met significant needs: in its appeal to the gregarious instinct and collective sense of shared ritual it provided excitement, drama, and aesthetic satisfaction. Like baseball in urban America, rugby was portrayed 'as a valuable source of community integration because it instilled civic pride',[43] a desirable commodity in the ribbon-developed valleys which lacked appropriate civic foci. Yet the middle class had no need to convert the working class since the latter were already enthusiasts, as older parochial rivalries could be continued and legitimated on the playing field and the popular bank. Just as pre-industrial football was never entirely haphazard or barbaric, so were its newer versions remarkably bruising. Spectator behaviour changed little: gang warfare was part of the complete social event, and it was in some of the smaller towns and villages that rugby was most disorderly. Nor was it an antidote to drinking or rowdiness but a stimulant to both, for public houses, the traditional foci of sport and sociability, provided all kinds of facilities, from an early results service to committee- and changing-rooms: Pontypridd were based at the White Hart, Rhymney at the Tredegar Arms, Gowerton at the Commercial, Penygraig at the Butcher's, Penclawdd at the Ship and Castle, Creunant at the Red Lion.[44]

Clearly, football was less an agent of social change than a force for cultural continuity. Spectator sports were a feature of pre-industrial popular recreation, and undue concentration on football may obscure the fact that other sports had acquired a surprising level of spectator support, organization, and even formalization since the eighteenth century. *Weatherby's* published lists of race meetings several years in advance and the Glamorgan (Cowbridge) races had long figured in a complex quasi-national race circuit. Those who played and followed cricket, too, were possibly more mobile in the pre-railway age than is generally recognized: certainly the history of Glamorgan cricket as a recreation and a spectator sport predates the industrial changes which so transformed football and boxing.[45] Rugby clubs like Cardiff and Swansea came into existence to perpetuate the companionship of a summer recreation into the winter months.

Swansea Cricket Club—founded in 1785 (according to the 5 May issue of the *Hereford Journal*)—had a membership of nearly seventy by the early nineteenth century. In 1831 they played Merthyr twice, though it is not cricket that makes that year a significant one for Merthyr. Cardiff had a cricket club from 1819, and Maesteg, where the game was introduced by syrveyors of the local iron works, in 1826. By 1850 there were cricket clubs in Bridgend, Neath, Cowbridge, Aberdare and Taibach, from where it was reported in 1843 that the game 'has had a most beneficial effect upon the habits and morals of the young men, withdrawing them from the neighbouring tap-rooms and other places of disreputable resort'. It is likely that cricket developed more easily in the metal-working towns of west Glamorgan because the topography to the east made landscaping good pitches difficult. An English, or at least public-school-educated, middle class was also a precondition. Cricket was introduced to Cwmavon by 'some gentlemen from Kent' employed at the local works, and the side that played Maesteg in 1858 included William Gilbertson, works manager and benefactor of recreation in Pontardawe. In the 1860s the legendary W.G. Grace turned out for the nomadic and well-heeled South Wales Cricket Club, founded in 1859; in 1868, playing for a South of England side at Cadoxton (Neath) he found himself facing two generations of Bancrofts, father and grandfather of W.J., Glamorgan C.C.'s first professional in 1895 at £2 per week and equally legendary Swansea and Wales rugby full-back. A combination of the missionary exploits of W.G. Grace, the role of local gentry, and a new phase of industrial development led to the formation of a club at Gowerton in 1880. The first team it put into the field comprised managers, accountants, clerks, and storekeepers who had moved in from England: they were known locally as '*y starch*'. In parallel with developments in rugby, a South Wales Cricket Challenge Cup was instituted in 1879 and contested on a regional basis, while smaller clubs participated in their own local competitions: the Swansea and District League, including Singleton, Penllergaer, Pontarddulais, Sketty, Clydach, and Ynysygerwn, was the strongest in Glamorgan. Upper-class patronage remained crucial: Ynysygerwn played on Llewellyn land and Briton Ferry on the Earl of Jersey's, just as in Cardiff, St. Fagan's were indebted to Lord Windsor. And while Sir John Llewellyn, on the demise of South Wales C.C. in 1886, presided over the inaugural meeting of Glamorgan C.C. in July 1888, one of the county's early secretaries was J.H. Brain of the famous brewing dynasty, like the rugby Hancocks a further reminder of continuing links with the pre-industrial past.[46]

The arrival of the Hancock family in Cardiff in the 1880s heralded the invention of the four three-quarter system by the Cardiff rugby club's selectors in order to accommodate the dashing Frank, soon to be captain of his club and country—now Wales. This underlines both Glamorgan's historic Severnside links and the readiness of its new industrial society to innovate.

Glamorgan had never been introverted or isolated, and across the Severn Estuary it had long forged durable family, commercial, and political links, bonds reinforced in the late nineteenth century by the thousands of immigrants into Glamorgan from the rugby strongholds of the west country.[47]

By the beginning of the twentieth century it was apparent to outsiders that it was in Welsh clubs that 'rugby is to be found in its most highly developed condition'.[48] This superiority was based on a vigorous social mix and the blending of a wide variety of physical types that provoked fits of indignation from socially superior non-Welsh critics. Quick-witted, nimble-footed, sure-handed backs were acceptable, if a little too clever by half, but the application of working-class stamina and physical strength to ripping the ball away from mauls and scrummages was deuced unfair: here was the sharp end of the dominance that the dangerous classes were already attaining in mass democratic and industrial politics. The worth of a community idol was clearly appreciated in November 1910 by the Tonypandy 'rioters' who deliberately spared the chemist's shop of Willie Llewellyn, rugby hero of Penygraig and twenty times capped for Wales. It was as national heroes, rather than mere rugby players, that the Welsh XV (including Llewellyn) that beat the 1905 New Zealand All Blacks were depicted by opinion leaders and propagandists who were anxious to invest the game with a mythical Celticism, and to preserve its amateur status, the guarantor of social harmony.[49]

This studied determination to promote the classless and national image of rugby football (at this time exclusively, in Wales, a phenomenon of 'Greater Glamorgan'; and hugely successful) secured for it the crucial middle-class support that enabled it to withstand the challenge of association football to its position from the 1890s as Glamorgan's chief winter game.[50]

In 1894, when the Welsh soccer authorities, from their north-eastern base, sought to fly the flag in Glamorgan, they were forced to play an international on Swansea's rugby ground since there was no suitable soccer field anywhere in south Wales. Though a South Wales League—an east Glamorgan and Monmouthshire organization—had been in existence since

1891, there were no Welsh teams in the English Southern League. By 1914 a quarter of the whole Southern League was Welsh, and its Second Division was almost entirely a Glamorgan preserve, comprising Pontypridd, Swansea, Barry, Mid-Rhondda, Caerphilly, Maerdy, Ton Pentre, Aberdare and Trelewis, while Cardiff and Merthyr were in the First. These were all areas with a strong immigrant element from industrial England, reinforced, as in the Aber Valley and neighbouring Bedlinog, by a distinct north Wales presence, after the long drawn-out dispute of 1900-03 in the slate quarries of Caernarfonshire.[51]

The first decade of the century saw soccer make significant headway in Glamorgan. Despite some propagandist sniping from diehards on each side, it is likely that soccer evoked much of the same spectator appeal as rugby, and drew increasingly on the same followers. They were complementary rather than alternative to each other: Walter Rees, secretary of Neath R.F.C. before occupying the same position in the W.R.U. for 52 years, chaired the founding meeting of Neath A.F.C.[52] It was a portent of things to come when in 1903 Aberaman became the first southern side to reach the Welsh soccer Cup Final, and a sign of the times when in 1912 it was contested between Cardiff and Pontypridd. By then, Riverside F.C. had become Wales's first professional side as Cardiff City in 1910 (sport as a vehicle for *civic* identity) and the South Wales F.A. had seen its affiliated clubs rise from 74 in 1906 to 262 four years later. Most spectacular of all was the rise of soccer in Merthyr. It was the independent-minded, old industrial communities at the heads of the valleys, at some distance from the influence of coastal administrators, that were least inhibited about experimenting with maverick sports like professional cycling, professional rugby, and soccer. Merthyr played rugby league in the Northern Union between 1907 and 1911, and soccer from 1908. Within seven years they were playing Arsenal in the first round of the F.A. Cup; in 1920, with Aberdare Athletic, they joined the Third Division South. But to paraphrase a son of Dowlais, they ran out into an economic blizzard that killed football stone dead, at Penydarren Park and in many other places in interwar Glamorgan.[53]

SPORT DURING THE DEPRESSION

Though bankruptcy would become the keynote on and off the field, the immediate post-war period augured well. Glamorgan C.C., who had been playing minor county cricket since 1897, were in 1921 admitted to first-class status; in that year, too, Cardiff City entered the First Division, making, with Swansea, Merthyr, and Aberdare, four Glamorgan sides in the Football League. Club and international rugby throve, and Jimmy Wilde was still the flyweight champion of the world.

But the travails of the coal industry, followed by a world-wide slump that resounded from Wall Street to Wattstown, disembowelled whole communities and undermined Glamorgan's sporting confidence as perniciously as it sapped the vigour of its collective institutions, from chapels to unions. [54] The National Sporting Club became the graveyard of Welsh boxing hopes. Merthyr's Billy Eynon, wartime champion of both Army and Navy, failed to lift the British bantam title there in 1921: 'Peerless' Jim Driscoll, tubercular and needy, ill-advisedly fought Charles Ledoux at the same venue and was defeated after 17 rounds. Jimmy Wilde lost his world title to Pancho Villa in 1923; Percy Jones went into the war as a world flyweight champion and came out of it with horrendous injuries to die in 1922 aged 30. Three years later Driscoll himself died, and two years after that Freddie Welsh was found dead in a dingy New York hotel. Tommy Farr (Tonypandy) and Jack Petersen (Cardiff) were the popular idols of the thirties but a world title eluded them as it did Ronnie James (Pontardawe) in 1946 and Dai Dower (Abercynon) in 1957. It was Howard Winstone in 1968 who at last fleetingly revived former glories by bringing the world featherweight title back to Merthyr, one of those classic areas of limited economic opportunity like London's East End, Glasgow, Belfast, and the Bronx, that seem made to produce boxing heroes. In 1979 there were still enough licensed boxers in Glamorgan to give it 'the dubious distinction of being Britain's premier boxing region'. [55]

With Glamorgan losing over a quarter of a million of its population in the interwar period, half of them in the 15 to 29 age group, a game as closely identified with its society as rugby union particularly felt the chill. Clubs collapsed like cards. Rhymney R.F.C. ceased to exist between 1924 and 1933; both Senghennydd, which produced coal, and Barry, which exported it, had disbanded by 1925; for Skewen, 1926-7 had been 'the worst season in the club's history, mainly due to unemployment in the district for a period of two and a half years'. In 1929 Treherbert in the Rhondda, and Nantyffyllon in the Llynfi Valley, saw their finances dwindle to nothing, and closed down; Abercynon wound up in 1934, Taibach in 1937. In the beleaguered coalfield, tensions between the militant unemployed and the Glamorgan Constabulary flared into violence on the rugby field: one referee armed himself with a revolver before a game at Glyncorrwg. As social conflict sharpened, the perceived integrative role of amateur rugby was increasingly canvassed by educational (grammar school) and civic leaders. When the 1935 Welsh team, a skilful and satisfying blend of manual forwards and varsity backs, beat New Zealand at Cardiff, the *Western Mail* applauded a victory for social harmony 'that probably is impossible in any other sphere'. Compared with the dire situation elsewhere, the relative prosperity of the Swansea area was reflected as much in the 'Boys Own Paper' exploits of the Gowerton schoolboys, Haydn Tanner and W.T.H. Davies, as in the creative artistry of Dylan Thomas and his circle.[56]

The period, or at least the 1920s, was a good time for Swansea soccer, too, and especially for Cardiff City, who won the F.A. Cup in 1927 with an inferior side to the one which narrowly failed in the Final of 1925. From then on Cardiff's support and its league placing plummeted together: by 1934 the City were at the very bottom of the League. Though Welsh international soccer was able to flourish in these years because the cream of its players represented English clubs, domestic soccer in Glamorgan suffered as acutely as its rugby. Ton Pentre, Maerdy, and Porth had to withdraw from the Southern and the Welsh Leagues in the 1920s. Cwmparc F.C. folded in 1926 and Mid-Rhondda in 1928. Aberdare Athletic quit the Football League in 1927, followed three years later by Merthyr. Gone were the Saturdays when 'miners would rush from the day's toil at the Bedlinog, Cwm Bargoed, and South Tunnel pits, travelling from work on the "cwbs", anxious to get to the game in time for the kick-off. Black faces everywhere, food boxes and tin jacks bobbing about; colliers making from Caeharris Station through the High Street in their hundreds, making towards their goal'. No more: in 1934, with unemployment in the borough at 62 per cent, Merthyr F.C. closed its doors.[57]

It was a fate that almost befell Glamorgan C.C. in those locust years. The county's admission to first-class status in 1921 could not have been worse timed. A debt of £97 soared to £6,000 by 1923; by 1927 its financial situation was 'disastrous', in 1928 it propped up the whole championship and risked disbandment. In sum, 'between the years 1921 and 1939 . . . bankruptcy was never far from the Welsh cricket scene'.[58] It is a fitting epitaph to sport and society in Glamorgan during the Depression.

CONCLUSION

Though the difficult 1980s would evoke memories of half a century earlier, the three post-1945 decades of recovery, stability and relative prosperity were mirrored in an increasingly diverse range of sports. A sports-starved populace thronged to Glamorgan's rugby and soccer stadia in the late forties, even in Swansea whose crowds were always reluctant consistently to patronize first-class sport. A phoenix of remarkable soccer talent arose from the rubble of that bomb-stricken town, and names like Allchurch, Charles and Ford stirred a wider pride. So did the Glamorgan cricet eleven that won the 1948 championship and returned from the decisive match at Bournemouth to a boisterous hymn-singing reception (repeated in 1969) of the kind generally associated with the triumphant homecomings of rugby teams and boxers at the beginning of the century. Historical continuity took another form, too, when a centuries-old interest in athletic competitions under-pinned the enormously successful Sixth Empire and Commonwealth Games at Cardiff in July 1958, and made a worldwide impact when Lynn Davies leapt from coal-scarred Nantymoel to Olympic gold at Tokyo in 1964. These selective achievements confirm that the history of sport, at any period of time, should always be located in its social context: they reflect in this case a greater affluence and sophistication in training and coaching techniques, a larger school population, and a generally healthier people than Glamorgan had ever known.

What of the future? Already it would appear that changing tastes and leisure patterns, more free time (too often enforced), rising incomes and increased mobility are eroding old allegiances. Fewer people are prepared to spectate and more inclined to participate in a wide variety of indoor and outdoor sports. The growth of field studies and adventure sports has reinforced the trend towards greater individualism, though local and regional tradition remains as powerful a determinant of sporting preferences as age, gender and social class.[59] What is certain is that sport, like all other forms of social behaviour, will continue to provide a reflection of wider issues and relationships in society at large, just as it always has been an aspect of the interconnectedness of social experience in the past.

NOTES

[1] R.W. Malcolmson, *Popular Recreations in English Society 1700-1850* (Cambridge, 1973). For the seasonal and ecclesiastical calendar in Wales, see Philip Jenkins, 'Times and Seasons: the Cycles of the Year in Early Modern Glamorgan', *Morgannwg*, 30, 1986, pp. 20-41.

[2] G.J. Williams, 'Dyddiadur William Thomas o Lanfihangel-ar-Elai', *Morgannwg*, I, (1957), pp. 13-30; *idem*, 'Glamorgan Customs in the Eighteenth Century', *Gwerin*, I, (1957), pp. 99-108, where Thomas is described as 'a perverted Calvinist' (p. 99).

[3] G.J. Williams, *Morgannwg* (1957), p. 21.

[4] R.F. Suggett, 'Some aspects of village life in eighteenth century Glamorgan' (Oxford B.Litt. thesis, 1976), pp. 99-108.

[5] G.J. Williams, *Iolo Morganwg* (Caerdydd, 1956), p. 41; *idem*, *Morgannwg* (1957), p. 21; Suggett *op. cit.*, pp. 147-8.

[6] Suggett, *op. cit.*, p. 179.

[7] J. Byng (ed. C.B. Andrews), *The Torrington Diaries* (London, 1934), I, p. 289; P. Jenkins, *The Making of a Ruling Class: the Glamorgan Gentry 1640-1790* (Cambridge, 1983), pp. 263-8; L. Hopkin James, *Old Cowbridge* (Cardiff, 1922), pp. 106-7; B.Ll. James and D.J. Francis, *Cowbridge and Llanblethian Past and Present* (Barry and Cowbridge, 1979), p. 67.

[8] G.J. Williams (1956), p. 26, fn. 24; *idem*, *Gwerin* (1957), pp. 101-2.

[9] G.J. Williams (1956), pp. 35-40.

[10] *Ibid.*, pp. 54-6.

[11] Henry Lewis (ed.), *Morgannwg Matthews Ewenni* (Caerdydd, 1953), p. 22, *The Cambrian*, 7 June 1817; C. Redwood, *The Vale of Glamorgan* (London, 1839), p. 175; T. Vaughan Jones in *Y Faner*, 18 March 1983; I.C. Peate, *Diwylliant Gwerin Cymru* (Caerdydd, 1966), pp. 64-5.

[12] A. Leslie Evans, 'Some reflections on local sport', *Trans. Port Talbot Hist. Soc.*, III (1981), pp. 22-49; (ed.), J. Dolan, *Aberavon Rugby Football Club 1876-1976* (Aberavon, 1976), p. 7.

[13] Welsh Rugby Union, Minute Books, March 1896, March 1899.

[14] T.J.A. le Goff and D.M.G. Sutherland, 'The Revolution and the Rural Community in Eighteenth Century Brittany', *Past and Present*, 62, p. 107.

[15] D. Rhys Phillips, *History of the Vale of Neath* (Swansea, 1925), p. 467; *The Cambrian*, 17 Sept. 1819.

[16] Henry Lewis, *op. cit.*, pp. 35-7; *Y Traethodydd*, 1858, pp. 397-414.

[17] D. Williams, *The Rebecca Riots* (Cardiff, 1955), pp. 247, 286-7. A reliable survey is D. Brailsford, *Bareknuckles: a Social History of Prize Fighting* (Cambridge, 1988).

[18] D.R. Phillips, *op. cit.*, p. 588; A.L. Evans, *art. cit.*, p. 38.

[19] J.H. Matthews, *Cardiff Records*, III, (Cardiff, 1901), p. 226.

[20] P. Roberts, *The Cambrian Popular Antiquities* (London, 1815), p. 123; Glanffrwd (ed. H. Lewis), *Llanwynno* (Caerdydd, 1949), pp. 75-6; J. Richards, *The Cowbridge Story* (Bridgend, 1956), pp. 96-7; T. Vaughan Jones in *Y Faner*, 15 April 1983, 9; D.R. Phillips, *op. cit.*, p. 587; J.H. Davies, *History of Pontardawe and District* (Llandybie, 1967), p. 256.

[21] Glanffrwd, *op. cit.*, pp. 61-2, 103-8.

[22] P. Lovesey, *The Official Centenary History of the AAA* (London, 1979), pp. 14-18; W. Morgan, *The Vaynor Handbook* (Merthyr, 1893), pp. 15-19.

[23] G.A. Williams, *The Merthyr Rising* (London, 1978), p. 28; *idem*, *When Was Wales?* (Harmondsworth, 1985), p. 187; A.L. Evans, *art. cit.*, p. 39; B.B. Thomas, *Drych y Baledwr (Llandysul, 1958)*, pp. 117-8; T. Vaughan Jones in *Y Faner*, 6 May, 1983, p. 18.

[24] P.D.G. Thomas in D. Moore (ed.), *Wales in the Eighteenth Century* (Swansea, 1976), p. 19; William Rees, *Cardiff* (Cardiff, 1962), p. 106; J.H. Matthews, *Cardiff Records* IV, (Cardiff, 1903), p. 187; A.L. Evans, *art. cit.*, p. 22.

[25] Malcolmson, *op. cit.*, pp. 49-50; P. Jenkins, *op. cit.*, pp. 268-9; G.J. Williams, *Morgannwg* (1957), p. 22; G.R. Scott, *A History of Cockfighting* (London, 1957), pp. 172-6; 'The Life and Letters of John Harris the Cornish Cocker' in H. Atkinson, *Cock Fighting and Game Fowl* (Liss, 1977), p. 204.

[26] Malcolmson, *op. cit.*, pp. 67-9; G.J. Williams (1956), p. 40; *Morgannwg* (1957), pp. 16-17; *Gwerin* (1957), p. 100; D.R. Phillips, *op. cit.*, p. 587; Edward Matthews, *Hanes Bywyd Siencyn Penhydd* (Pontypridd, 1851), p. 133; J. Howells in *The Red Dragon*, V, (1889), p. 133; R. Denning, 'Sports and Pastimes' in S. Williams (ed.), *Saints and Sailing Ships* (Cowbridge, 1962), p. 46.

[27] P. Burke, *Popular Culture in Early Modern Europe* (London, 1978), pp. 270-81; P. Jenkins, *op. cit.*, pp. 193-216.

[28] M. Trevelyan, *Folk-lore and Folk Stories of Wales* (London, 1909), pp. 26-7; B.Ll. James, 'The Vale of Glamorgan 1780-1850' (Univ. of Wales M.A. thesis, Cardiff, 1971), p. 193.

[29] B.Ll. James and D.T. Francis, *op. cit.*, p. 100.

[30] B.Ll. James, thesis, pp. 150-3, 193-4; J. Howells, *op. cit.*, pp. 136-9.

[31] G.A. Williams in Glanmor Williams (ed.), *Merthyr Politics* (Cardiff, 1966), p. 17.

[32] B. Luxton, 'Ambition, Vice and Virtue: Social Life 1884-1914' in D. Moore (ed.), *Barry, the Centenary Book* (Barry, 1985), pp. 271-331. For the impact of industrialization on the recreational and social life of an agricultural comunity in west Glamorgan, see Denver Evans, *Bont: the Story of a Village and its Rugby Club* (Pontarddulais, 1980), pp. 69-141.

[33] *South Wales Daily News*, 18 Oct. 1901, 20 Oct. 1902, 21 and 25 Feb. 1907, 12 Sept. 1904, 10 Sept. 1900; T. Vaughan Jones in *Y Faner*, 10 June, 1983; I. Beynon in Wyn Williams (ed.), *Sport in Wales* (Denbigh, 1957), pp. 78-80; A.L. Evans, *art. cit.*, pp. 42-9; R. Huws, *Bro*, 17, (1981), p. 22; Thomas Jones, *Rhymney Memories* (Llandysul, 1970), p. 54.

[34] *South Wales Daily News*, 5 Sept. 1908, 7 March 1901; George Ewart Evans, *The Strength of the Hills* (London, 1983), pp. 39-40, 55.

[35] R.J. Holt, *Sport and Society in Modern France* (London, 1981), pp. 81-103.

[36] W.J. Edwards, *From the Valley I Came* (London, 1956), pp. 12-13; *Western Mail*, 24 July 1986, *Aberdare Times*, 1 August 1896, *Aberdare Leader*, 3 Dec. 1904; R. Ivor Parry, 'Sidelights on Aberdare', in S. Williams (ed.), *Glamorgan Historian*, X, (1974), p. 69; for west Glamorgan see J.H. Davies, *op. cit.*, p. 256 (Pontardawe), Denver Evans, *op. cit.*, p. 113 (Pontarddulais).

[37] *Aberdare Times*, 26 Dec. 1885, quoted by M. Barclay, 'Class and Community: Aberdare 1880-1920' (Univ. of Males M.A. thesis, Cardiff, 1985).

[38] Jack Jones, *Black Parade* (London, 1935), pp. 187-93; W.J. Edwards, *op. cit.*, pp. 21-25; *Aberdare Times*, 18 Jan. 1908. For examples of mountainside fighting 'to avoid interference at the hands of the police' above Glynneath, see *South Wales Daily News*, 17 Sept., 10 and 18 Oct. 1902.

[39] *Western Mail*, 2 March 1909, 21 June 1909, 21 Dec. 1910; A. Cordell, *Peerless Jim* (London, 1984).

[40] *Western Mail*, 17 Dec. 1955; G.J. Thomas in *Y Cardi*, 1972, pp. 7-10; Alun Richards, *Days of Absence* (London, 1986), p. 32.

[41] Quoted in H. Cunningham, *Leisure in the Industrial Revolution* (London, 1980), p. 120.

[42] Iolo Davies, *A Certaine Schoole* (Cowbridge, 1967), p. 226, quoting *The Bovian*, Nov. 1900.

[43] Steven A. Riess, *Touching Base: Professional Baseball and American Culture in the Progressive Era* (Westport, Conn., 1980), pp. 18-19.

[44] Much of the documentation bearing on this and the summary discussion of rugby football that follows, can be found in Chapter 4 above.

[45] D. Brailsford, 'The Locations of Eighteenth Century Spectator Sport', in

J. Bale and C. Jenkins (eds.), *Geographical Perspectives on Sport* (University of Birmingham, 1983), pp. 27-60.

[46] G.B. Buckley, *Fresh Light on Pre-Victorian Cricket* (Birmingham, 1937), pp. 12, 107, 150; Brinley Richards, *History of the Llynfi Valley* (Llandybie, 1982), p. 215; *The Cambrian*, 3 July 1830; A.L. Evans, *art. cit.*, 33-35; J. Hywel Rees, *One Hundred Years of Cricket in Gowerton 1880-1980* (Gowerton, 1981), pp. 1-3; W. Wooller, *Glamorgan Cricket* (London, 1971), pp. 9-15. The standard work now is A. Hignell, *The Centenary History of Glamorgan County Cricket Club* (London, 1988).

[47] R.A. Griffiths, 'Medieval Severnside: the Welsh Connection' in R.R. Davies *et al.* (eds.), *Welsh Society and Nationhood* (Cardiff, 1984), pp. 70-89; *Glamorgan County History*, IV, (Cardiff, 1974), pp. 58-74, 311-373, and see Chapter 3 above.

[48] F. Champain in A. Watson (ed.), *English Sport* (London, 1902), pp. 253-71. The basic text is D. Smith and G. Williams, *Fields of Praise* (Cardiff, 1980).

[49] D. Smith, 'Tonypandy: Definitions of Community', *Past and Present*, 87, p. 168; *idem*, *Wales! Wales!* (London, 1984), pp. 33-7; D. Smith and G. Williams, *op. cit.*, pp. 171-5;

[50] B. Lile and D. Farmer, 'The Early Development of Association Football in South Wales 1890-1906', *Transactions of the Cymmrodorion Society*, 1984, pp. 193-215.

[51] Walter Haydn Davies, *Ups and Downs* (Swansea, 1975), pp. 70-75.

[52] *South Wales Daily News*, 9 Sept. 1893.

[53] D. Watkins, 'Merthyr Tydfil AFC 1908-1934', in Huw Williams (ed.), *Merthyr Tydfil: Drawn from Life* (Merthyr, 1981), pp. 70-89; G.A. Williams, *When Was Wales?*, p. 251.

[54] My treatment of boxing owes much to two suggestive programmes made by Dai Smith for B.B.C. Radio Wales in 1985 called *Fighting Class*. See now his 'Focal heroes: a Welsh fighting class' in R. Holt (ed.), *Sport and the Working Class in Modern Britain* (Manchester, 1990), pp. 198-217.

[55] J. Bale, *Sport and Place* (London, 1982), pp. 149-52.

[56] P.T. Atkinson, *One Hundred Years of Rhymney Rugby* (Rhymney, 1982), pp. 41-2; W.G. Boulton, *Senghenydd: the Village and its Rugby Club* (Risca, 1982), pp. 3-31; Peter Stead, 'The Swansea of Dylan Thomas' in *Dylan Thomas Remembered* (Cowbridge, 1978), pp. 8-25. See also Chapter 8 below.

[57] *Merthyr Express*, 30 June 1934; D. Watkins, *op. cit.*, pp. 87-8. The 'Martyrs' re-formed in 1945.

[58] J.H. Morgan, *Glamorgan* (London, 1952), pp. 27-8; Wooller, *op. cit.*, pp. 98-9.

[59] *Sport in Wales—i. Facilities, ii. Participation* (The Sports Council for Wales, Cardiff, 1975) *s.v.* 'Angling', 'Canoeing', 'Caving', 'Gliding', 'Surf-Board Riding', 'Water Skiing'; *Sport in the Community: The Next Ten Years* (The Sports Council, London, 1982); *Sport in the Community: Into the 90's* (Sports Council, 1988).

CHAPTER 7

HOW AMATEUR WAS MY VALLEY: PROFESSIONAL SPORT AND NATIONAL IDENTITY IN WALES 1890-1914

It must be candidly stated that the troubles of the Union commenced with the advent of the working man. [1]

Arthur Budd, President of the Rugby Football Union 1888-89

I

The chief characteristic of the growth of organized sport in the late nineteenth century was its diffusion from the middle class downwards. This is not to deny the vigour and spontaneity of a constantly renewed popular culture, but it was the middle class who created, modified and standardized the new model football games of soccer and rugby.

Their motives for doing so were diverse, and the notion of social control has been subjected to close scrutiny in recent years. If the spread of games was intended to be one of the 'noncoercive agencies in the process of social conditioning' in order 'to uphold a social fabric congenial to the holders of power', then the intentions of these middle-class organizers and administrators—'improvers and reformers . . . socializers rather than controllers, peddling recipes for better survival in a changing environment rather than weaving webs of sub-ordin-ation'—ran up against life-styles, value-systems and expectations that had themselves been conditioned by urban living, commercial entertainment and industrialism. [2] In particular, the whole ideology of amateur sport, with its emphasis on character-building, desirable behaviour, playing the game for the game's sake and the rejection of money prizes, did not square easily with lower-class values, where physical prowess was literally highly prized and where even less strenuous forms of recreation, like dog- and cock-fighting, bowls and quoits, had long been pursued for financial reward and accompanied by gambling, backers and spectators.[3]

The rift between the middle-class exponents of sport for sport's sake and working-class practitioners more concerned with material rewards began to deepen in the 1880s and can be seen as part of a wider working-class hostility to middle-class ideals that found expression in the rise of New Unionism and renewed class conflict. The last two decades of the nineteenth century were years of mounting anguish over the growth of professionalism in British sport. This was less true of cricket, where professionals had been in existence for more than a century and were accommodated within an established, albeit still deferential, career structure.[4] An amateur, however, was a gentleman. Early definitions of the word in a sporting context come from rowing: in 1835 *Bell's Life* defined an amateur as anyone who rowed and was not a waterman or otherwise engaged in rowing for a living. By mid-century it had come to signify those members of the middle and upper class who practised sports that were also indulged in by the lower orders. The *Rowing Almanack* of 1861 defined amateurs by listing the universities, schools and comparable institutions that nurtured these superior beings, and absolutely excluding 'tradesmen, labourers, artisans or working mechanics'.[5]

It is significant that the majority of first-class cricket professionals came from the north of England in the late Victorian period. Keith Sandiford regards the seriousness with which professional cricket was taken in the north as a reflection of the much harsher realities that followed in the wake of the cotton depression of the 1860s.[6] That same seriousness was behind the formation in 1879 of a Northern Counties Athletic Association in defiance of the hidebound and southern Amateur Athletic Club.[7] It was the two codes of association football and rugby, however, that bore the brunt of what the sociologists Dunning and Sheard have identified as 'a change from the relatively harmonistic perception that had characterized class relations between 1850 and 1880 to a more conflictual perception',[8] and it is with amateur rugby's resistance to open professionalism in its working-class heartland of South Wales in the period 1890-1914 that this chapter is concerned.

The monetization of both football codes was an inevitable result of their increasing popularity and competitiveness. As cup competitions local, provincial and national proliferated from the 1870s—both the South Wales and the Yorkshire Challenge Cup (T'owd Tin Pot) were first contested in 1877-78, the latter quickly followed by Northumberland, Durham and Cumberland by 1882 [9]—they fostered a keen competitiveness which bred, among things, a certain violence ('probably nothing but a team of neo-Platonists could pay a rugby union cup-tie without roughness' thought one contemporary) [10] because there was a premium on victory. It was the emphasis on winning that was most at odds with the amateur ethos of merely playing for its own sake. After all, if the result was unimportant, why bother to keep the score? The urge to win cups and leagues also nurtured local pride and civic identity which typically found expression in torchlit processions and boisterous celebrations in honour of victorious home-coming teams. It brought in its train a heightened interest, the charging of admission to improve facilities and attract even more spectators and, soon, to demands from the players for a share of the gate-money.

Irrespective of who the first professionals actually were, it is clear that professionalism was widespread in soccer in the 1880s. [11] Prejudice conveniently identified them as Scotsmen who had migrated south to play in Lancashire, just as it was imported Welshmen, supposedly, who led the campaign in northern rugby circles for payment above and beyond broken-time compensation, the rationale being that having uprooted themselves they had more to lose. [12] With cup games popularized by the press attracting large crowds, material reward became a financial reality. Underhand payments to soccer players of a pound or more per match were common knowledge in Bolton in the early 1880s. In 1884 the president of Preston North End FC was summoned before the Football Association (FA) and accused of making financial inducements. Instead of denying it he caused some consternation by his frank admission that his club paid its players, and that he could prove that nearly every important club in Lancashire did the same. When the FA tried in 1884 to outlaw professionalism, the

Lancashire clubs openly seceded. The following year a reluctant FA sanctioned professionalism and in 1888 the Football League was established.[13]

In English soccer, complaints about growing professionalism had emanated from outside the areas in dispute and became more strident in proportion to the size and regularity of defeats inflicted by northern teams on those from the south. It is well known that the historic victory of Blackburn Olympic over the Old Etonians in the Cup Final of 1883 announced that the days of the part-timers of the south of England were numbered.[14] In rugby terms, similarly, once the Rugby Union's county championship was established in 1888-89 Yorkshire won it during seven of the first eight seasons, Lancashire winning it in the other, 1890-91. The England XV that beat Wales in 1892 contained eleven northerners, including all but one of the forwards.[15] What made the north different was that the game there was less socially exclusive and its clubs allowed working men to become playing members. Whereas the southern rugby establishment consisted of ex-public schoolboys from the professions, occupationally far removed from industry and unsympathetic to it, their northern counterparts were self-made men in industry and commerce who came into direct and frequent contact with their employees and shared their identification with their towns and communities. While their much-invoked bluntness ('Yorkshire grit') disposed northern administrators to recognise a spade for what it was, their southern equivalents could genuinely claim they had never seen one. Nor had they in all likelihood seen money change hands in rugby, for they were not interested in cup competitions. When in 1894 the idea of a challenge cup was mooted for Middlesex, only seven entries were received. That the division between north and south was as much social as geographical was apparent to northern visitors who accompanied their teams south. 'The followers of the game in the South were evidently ''swells'' ' according to one.who had 'never seen as many top hats at a score of matches in the North as he saw at Richmond on this one day'.[16]

The issue which brought the dispute over professionalism to a head was broken-time payment, i.e. compensating working

men for the wages lost through travelling and playing. The
attitude of the Rugby Football Union, which was not prepared
to sanction professionalism as the FA had done, was crystall-
ized in the reply of Arthur Budd, RFU President 1888-89, 'to
those who urge that working men ought to be compensated for
the ''loss of time'' incurred by his recreation . . . if he cannot
afford the leisure to play the game he must do without it'.[17]
H.H. Almond, the renowned headmaster of Loretto, saw
professional football in the critical year 1893 as injurious to the
paid player's moral welfare and rejoiced that the RFU's opposition prevented the game from 'becoming a byword for money-
grabbing, tricks, sensational displays and utter rottenness'.[18]
Five years later Ernest Ensor articulated the deep middle-class
hostility to professionalism in some unpleasant but revealing
remarks about the 'warped sporting instincts' of the professional footballer who, he said, was an 'idler . . . [who] cannot
help but be brutalised'.[19]

II

The events surrounding the split of rugby into union and professional between 1893 and 1895 are familiar enough.[20] The
Rugby Union had steadfastly withstood pressure from
Yorkshire and Lancashire to form 'alliances', or leagues: in its
view the founding of the Football League in 1888 was both a
recognition and further encouragement of professionalism. In
1892-93 there had been a rash of suspensions and widespread
allegations of money payments in northern rugby. At the RFU's
annual meeting in September 1893 the Yorkshire Union's
proposal 'that players be allowed compensation for *bona fide*
loss of time' was defeated by a counter-motion intended to
'crush any attempt to establish professional cells'[21] that was
carried by a majority swollen by 120 proxy votes, mainly from
Oxford and Cambridge colleges. Within two years the breakaway had taken place. The Northern Union (NU) was born on
29 August 1895 at the George Hotel, Huddersfield, but it had
been conceived at the same venue the previous January when
'the premier clubs of Lancashire and Yorkshire as here repre-

sented do form themselves in a Union for the . . . furthering . . .
of rugby football in their two counties'. The fatal decision
originated, according to Yorkshire RU President J.A. Miller, 'in
the snubs and unfairness meted out to the Northerners generally by the Rugby Union'. [22]

It did not take long for the RFU to forbid the proposed union.
Early in August it drafted new draconian rules on amateurism,
and for the rest of that month there was a series of anguished
meetings on both sides of the Pennines as to whether the NU
should be proceeded with, and whether broken-time payments
should be permitted. This indicates that the RFU had failed to
appreciate that the proposed union, far from condoning professionalism, was considered by many northern officials like
Miller as the only way to prevent full-time professionalism on
the soccer model. Rule 1 of the NU rules of October 1895
roundly declared, in fact, that 'Professionalism is illegal', and
players were allowed broken-time at six shillings per day and
called amateurs until 1898. [23]

The repercussions of 'the Great Schism' [24] went far beyond
the inferior playing record of an English XV whose social
composition was now far more narrowly circumscribed. In
Wales the controversy surrounding the Gould testimonial of
1897 can be fully understood only in the context of the events of
1895.

A.J. Gould yields only to W.G. Grace as the eminent Victorian Lytton Strachey left out. [25] Athlete and footballer supreme,
his handsome features were seen on matchbox covers and his
fame was celebrated in the papers and the music halls. To the
Rev. Frank Marshall, Arthur Gould was simply 'the central
figure in the football world . . . the greatest centre three-
quarter that has ever played'. [26] By January 1896 Gould had
played more matches, scored more tries and dropped more
goals than any other player in the history of the game. He had
also been capped for Wales more times than any other
international. That month his admirers organized a national
testimonial in his honour 'after the manner of that raised for Dr
Grace whose position in the cricket world coincides with that of
Mr Gould in the sister sport'. It was mooted and administered
independently of the Welsh Football Union (WFU), who

Arthur Gould

nevertheless supported it to the tune of £50.[27] The fund, attracting contributions from as far afield as America, Australia and Africa, soon exceeded ten times that figure and it was decided to present Gould with the deeds of the house in which he lived in Newport.[28] The RFU, however, decided in April 1896 that 'the giving of a house is tantamount to the giving of a monetary testimonial' and in November the WFU withdrew their subscription and sanction of the fund. In season 1896-97 Gould continued playing for Newport and Wales, and the RFU prohibited any of its clubs or players from playing against him, lest in so doing they professionalized themselves. In February 1897 the International Rugby Board (IB), the governing body of the game which was numerically dominated by English representatives, unsurprisingly sided with the RFU, and Wales withdrew from the Board, thereby voluntarily excommunicating themselves from the international rugby community.[29]

Throwing Down the Gauntlet.

A TALE WITHOUT WORDS.

    The nub of the issue was not the Gould case as such but the
attitude of the Welsh to the payment of players, of which the
testimonial was seen to be symptomatic. The WFU for their
part pointed to the case of W.E. Bromet, captain of Richmond
and an English international who had received plate worth
£100 from his admirers in 1895. They might have, but did not,
draw attention to the fact that W.G. Grace himself, an amateur
and a gentleman, had scooped over £9,000 in three benefits,
which aroused little condemnation and prompted his admirers
to lobby for a knighthood for him—'and Mr Gould has . . . done
as much for rugby football as Dr W.G. Grace for cricket'.[30]
According to the RFU's own historians the deadlock, had it
continued, would have been 'a disaster to Wales and would
bear very hard on the Welsh committee who admittedly were a

body of sound amateurs'.[31] In fact, the disaster would have been to English clubs who much regretted the loss of the Welsh fixtures: Rockliff FC protested their own 'debt of gratitude to Newport. They had met the Welsh clubs during the past few years and always found the Welshmen true footballers and perfect sportsmen and what was more in all those matches, unlike many others, they had not suffered any financial loss'.[32]

There was widespread sympathy for the Welsh position from outside Wales. A correspondent to the *Daily Chronicle* who had seen Gould play at Bristol, where the thousands lined up and formed a passage for the great player, defended a national testimonial 'to one who is acknowledged to be the finest footballer of the age'. The *Pall Mall Gazette*—'our sympathy must go out to the Welsh people'—seemed to rank the Gould affair with a colliery disaster. The *Birmingham Post* saw it as 'another historic piece of mismanagement' and wondered whether 'the settlement of a freehold property upon a distinguished footballer' was so degrading after all.[33] Others in 1897 accused the RFU of sour grapes after England's 11-0 defeat at Welsh hands in January, when secretary G. Rowland Hill, usually voluble enough, refused to make any after-match comment and was thought to resent the fact that the introduction of 'Rhondda forwards' into the pack enabled Wales to employ working-class stamina to achieve unfair victory.[34] Irish opinion had supported the IB at first, but soon turned against the 'amateur faddists' of England and Scotland. The Scottish objection was that 'veiled professionalism exists in Wales', who would be better off joining the NU or forming one of their own.[35]

Recognizing that public opinion was generally in its favour, convinced of its own rightness, and delighted to see the RFU expending its energies in investigating alleged professionalism in Hull Kingston Rovers,[36] the WFU ('We have fought hard against encouraging professionalism amongst our players under more trying circumstances ... than any of the other Unions and ... with greater success than the English Union') asserted its own 'Home Rule', a fashionable slogan in Welsh political circles at the time, and restored its subscription to the testimonial fund. In a lengthy statement it demanded 'whether

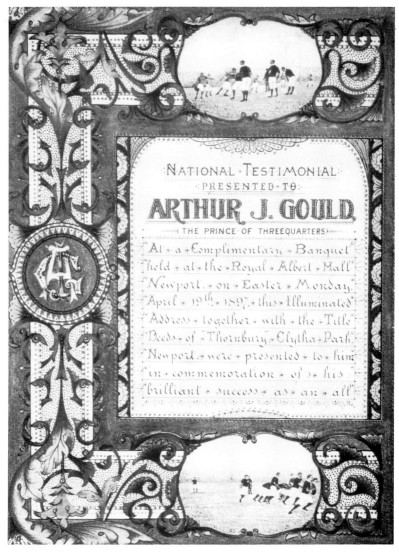

The Illuminated Address and National Testimonial presented to Arthur Gould
in 'a national banquet' at Newport on Easter Monday 1897.

any reasonable man can suggest that because £500 has been subscribed by the admirers of an International football player . . . he is therefore to be called a professional'.[37] On Easter Monday 1897, at a gathering in Newport described as 'a national banquet', Gould was presented with the deeds of his house. The breach with the RFU was fairly amicably resolved, but Scotland refused to play Wales in both 1897 and 1898. The perceived ultra-puritanism of the Scots caused a hardness of feeling in Wales towards the SRU, reciprocated with interest, until well into the next century.

III

Arthur Joseph Gould was, in truth, an amateur and a gentleman, but there were rugby players in Wales who did not fit that exacting description. It was not the links established with northern clubs from the mid-1880s that smeared Welsh rugby with the trail of finance; the emergence of rugby as a mass spectator sport with its rivalries and inducements to hire players from one club to another brought that about. The apparently similar social structure of the game in South Wales and the north of England led to a brisk traffic between the two, and in the 1890s the Welsh ports and valleys became a magnet for northern agents seeking to lure players 'north'.

Evan and David James of Swansea were in and out of the news throughout the decade, defying the transfer laws which were expressly aimed at curbing players' excessive mobility with the agility with which they nonplussed their opponents on the field. They were especially vulnerable to the persuasions of northern agents. Evidence given before a RFU committee set up to inquire into the circumstances in which the brothers had agreed to play for the Lancashire club Broughton Rangers in 1892 smacked of music-hall comedy. A Swansea policeman told of a conversation he had on his beat with a stranger who was inquiring about the Jameses, their prospects and intentions 'only a few days before', and of their mysterious disappearance north. Another Swansea witness was approached by a person with a strong northern accent looking for the brothers and claiming to be their long-lost cousin from Gloucester who, when confronted, admitted he indended making the brothers an offer to come north. Declared professional by the RFU in March 1893, reinstated at the behest of the WFU in January 1896 'the curly-headed marmosets' went back to Broughton once and for all in 1899 for £200 down, £2 a week and jobs as warehousemen. They took the whole family with them, including their grandmother.[38]

Throughout the 1890s and into the next decade the South Wales and northern papers carried regular stories of sightings of such extra-terrestrial beings as 'Welshmen in Leeds' and 'Welshmen in Bradford'. In Wales itself, the news that Castleford NU club intended putting its faith in 'Welsh mutton' for their backs and 'English beef' for their forwards, like the recurrent headline 'Northern Football Poachers at work', caused frequent bouts of indignation.[39] Irritated by the occasional mass defection, as when six Llanelli players joined Rochdale in 1896 for £50 down, £3 a week and work for three years, some followers adopted a vigilante approach against northern mar-

Evan James (kneeling, centre) with copper ladlers at White Rock Works, Swansea.

The James brothers, of Swansea, Broughton Rangers, and Wales.

(by permission of Swansea RFC)

auders. In November 1896 a Swinton agent was the object of a hostile demonstration at Llwynypia in the Rhondda Valley: discovered at a local hotel he was unceremoniously ejected and frogmarched to the station, 'hooted all the way', where he caught the next train out. Nor was such behaviour confined to the upland districts. In 1899 a scout from Wigan who had made overtures to players from the seaside club of Penarth was pulled from his cab, dragged down the landing stage, thrown into the water and rolled in the sand. In the course of this activity he lost a sovereign and went to complain to the Cardiff police. They advised him to return to Penarth to find either the coin or the culprits, but he decided against it. [40]

By 1900 it was not international success alone that led one peevish critic to complain that Wales had 'got upon the national nerves in Rugby football'. [41] It was the miasma of monetary reward in which its affairs seemed, to outsiders, to be conducted. An accusation increasingly levelled was that of dishonesty in signing for a northern club, receiving a fee, and then not only failing to turn up but continuing to enjoy amateur status in Wales, even as reserve to the national XV. Players thus accused argued that they had signed to be rid of importunate poachers and had no intention of going north. *Athletic News's* 'Old Ebor' condemned 'the immorality of those who take cash on behalf of a contract they have no intention of fulfilling . . . Welshmen have been the chief offenders hitherto . . . It is due to our Taffy friends to make this admission'.[42]

Examples abound from this period of players who did go north and stayed; who went north, became disillusioned with their conditions of work and returned to Wales; some who were readmitted to amateur rugby; some, again, who returned in order to persuade others to join them up north. Fred Miller, an international from Mountain Ash who had initially denied that he was 'leaving his native hills for the salubrious ozone of the Humber' joined Hull in 1901 and was soon back seeking more recruits. One player he was believed to have signed was the strapping Mountain Ash collier W.T. Osborne. The ever-vigilant Scottish Union informed the WFU in 1902 that they would not play Wales if Osborne was in the side since they believed he had signed northern papers. Osborne made a full statement of his amateur status and went on to win six caps before joining Huddersfield NU in 1903.[43] That year Scotland demanded that Newport drop one of their players in any fixtures involving Scottish clubs because he had signed NU forms in 1901, although he had never left Newport and was reinstated. Such actions foundered on the reluctance of leading clubs to lose their Welsh fixtures, and the matter dropped when the IB ruled that it was a matter for each union' clubs to decide for themselves.[44]

Although the Welsh and English Unions had agreed to a common set of tightened regulations on professionalism in April 1900, and though the WFU had in 1901 further tried to check abuses by refusing transfer permission from one club to another after 1 December to prevent continued moving around, it was commonly believed that financial inducements still lubricated the cogs of Welsh club rugby. The stimulus was the intensely competitive nature of, particularly, the Glamorgan League established in 1894, and the availability of money generated by large crowds of spectators. The WFU recognized its existence; one of its own executive members admitted in September 1901 that 'professionalism is rampant in the Rhondda Valley' and thought it high time the union conducted an inquiry 'into the whole business' since 'the thing [illegal payment] had become 'so glaring that something must be done'.[45]

In fact, something was already being done. In April 1901 the WFU made it an offence even to sign NU forms, and in October it instituted an inquiry into *sub rosa* payments as a result of which the Aberaman club, in the Cynon (Aberdare) Valley, was expelled from the union because of proven allegations that two of its committeemen had offered six shillings a week to certain players from neighbouring Mountain Ash. Although the evidence of account-books and ticket-rolls produced by the club seemed to corroborate their protestations that proceeds averaged a paltry £2 a match or less, the union concluded that in reality gates were much higher. Aberaman were reformed as Cynon Stars and re-admitted to the union, provided they changed their committee and their ticket sellers.[46]

Such public washing of dirty linen did nothing to mollify 'Old Ebor's' mordant view of the essentially 'shamateur' nature of rugby in Wales which

> is our great remaining stronghold of purity, guilelessness and self-abrogation in amateur Rugby Football . . . there is no part of his Majesty's dominions in which the amateur principle of Rugby football is so studiously upheld and fought for . . . as the Principality of Wales—unless it be the Palatinate of Durham where the local priests of amateurism wear phylacteries.[47]

IV

As in Durham and much of the north of England, it was the working-class nature of the game in Wales, its genuine grass-roots popularity, that discomfited the other unions. English sides of the time were of a pronounced public-school and professional composition—65 per cent of those who played international rugby for England between 1902 and 1911 came from social classes I and II, while 'up to the present [March 1902] . . . the representatives of Ireland have been members of a few strictly limited professions or collegiate students and in a club it was almost impossible for anyone without the hallmark of the schools to get a place'. This writer was glad to say, however, that 'this silly exclusiveness is being gradually broken down. The Welsh colliers and tinplaters have demonstrated that they can be gentlemen in sport which . . . knows no aristocracy except in regard to skill'.[48]

It was again the Scots, the most persistent critics of the Welsh, whose national sides were least contaminated by working men. Every member of the Scotland XV that played Wales in 1901 had a public-school education.[49] After his team had lost to Wales at Inverleith in 1905 a disgruntled Scotsman urged the other unions

> to put a stop to the discreditable conduct that is becoming a feature of Welsh international football. I do not refere merely to the technical unfair play, e.g. [handling in the scrum, late-tackling etc.] but to downright caddish tricks [which] are unheard of in the Irish and English matches where gentlemanly play is the rule . . . Ask the pack what goes on in the scrums and loose scrummages and they can tell things which will astonish the football public.

This letter was given wide coverage and provoked considerable response. A WFU member attributed it to 'hysteria'; a more measured correspondent to the *Irish Independent* wanted to know 'is it caddishness for a collier to play better football than a college man?' and condemned 'the cursed canker of class, the desire to make a Rugby a ''respectable'' game, a football minuet . . . It is snobbery [which] spelt disaster for England at Cardiff [25-0]. The Welsh players are drawn from the people—bone of their bone and flesh of their flesh. Therein lies their caddishness . . . They play to win: so do we all and if we could be as tricky as they are on the field, we would'.[50]

Whether or not the lukewarm nature of Welsh-Scottish

relations in these years was a legacy of the Gould controversy, they were not helped by the apparently obtuse, certainly—to the Welsh—irksome rulings of Scottish referee Crawford Findlay, who controlled several Welsh international matches and who was reckoned to have cost them the Triple Crown in 1904, especially, when he refereed two of their three games and disallowed several perfectly legitimate—in Cymric eyes— Welsh tries. Against England he penalized the Welsh scrum-half R.M. Owen so often for not putting the ball into the scrum straight that eventually Owen, in desperation, handed the ball to his opponent to do so even on the Welsh 'put in'. When Findlay was then invited to referee the game with Ireland, the Welsh rugby public was aghast that he had accepted it. 'It is futile to waste words on Mr. Crawford Findlay', fumed Wales's leading sports critic, 'he must be pachydermatous'. [51] It was not so much Findlay's integrity that was in doubt as his ability, not least his ability to appreciate the social structure of the Welsh game. In 1903 at a post-match dinner, he had expressed to the Welsh centre-threequarter R.T. Gabe, a schoolteacher, his surprise 'that Wales selected miners, steelworkers and policemen for their international teams and suggested that these players should join the Northern Union'. [52]

It took a protracted correspondence between the SRU and RFU to prevent Scotland breaking off relations even with England in 1909 because the Scottish Union believed that the recently announced accounts of the 1905-06 All Blacks' tour in Britain showed that the New Zealanders had been paid excessively generous expenses. The Scots, 'sound to the core of their amateur heart', were accusing their English equivalents of conniving at professionalism and giving aid and sustenance to it in Australasia. It was their suspicions concerning the professional nature of the game in the Antipodes that precluded any Scottish support for, or participation in, the proposed 1908 British team to Australia and New Zealand which eventually went as an Anglo-Welsh combination. The Scots were not alone in their doubts about the amateurism of the game in New Zealand. The RFU's Rowland Hill told the assembled tourists before they embarked, 'speaking, as he is usually wont to do, with a suspicion of emotion in his voice', that 'the object of the trip was to kill professionalism in the Antipodes before it assumed any great dimensions'.[53]

In Wales the attitude to expenses was rather different. The great majority of the Welsh players, it was thought, took 'a serious view of the game, and the public has no wish to inconvenience or harass them in the way of limiting reasonable expenses, and there is wide appreciation of the sacrifices for the game made by our artisan players'.[54] In many parts of South Wales there is no doubt that the term 'reasonable expenses' was interpreted generously, so that they virtually constituted broken-time payment. Writing in 1905, the former Welsh international W.M. McCutcheon, who had left Swansea for Oldham before the NU existed, strongly implied that his old club had been doing this for the last 20 years. He reckoned it was only the down payment that tempted players north, since their weekly salary might not exceed that already paid them in amateur Wales.[55]

Such exposures by 'defectors', roundly condemned in the Welsh press, were rarely made from purely disinterested motives. The Welsh Union that year was even more exercised by the reality of a flurry of club-to-club moves that indicated possibly monetary inducements. The same WFU meeting which decided to play the Wales v. New Zealand match at Cardiff Arms Park on 16 December 1905—what turned out to be the most historic rugby game ever played—also refused transfers to several players, who lived at suspiciously long distances from the club they sought to join. A trio who applied to Aberdare, for instance, lived in Swansea and Llanelli in west Wales, nor was it a coincidence that Aberdare had a Glamorgan League cup final pending. The Welsh Union's presumption was that inducements had been offered. Each player was called before the WFU and the balance-sheets of the club in question threatened with scrutiny. In the event the players were exonerated, but all Aberdare transfers were postponed until further inquiries were instituted.[56] Further allegations of professionalism in Aberdare would in 1907 present Welsh rugby with its most serious crisis since the Gould affair of ten years earlier.

V

The belief that an element of tacit professionalism within the amateur rugby game in Wales would be sufficient to prevent a thorough-going professional version from being established was rudely shattered on New Year's Day 1908 when the first-ever NU international to take place in Wales was played in front of a crowd estimated at between 15,000 and 20,000. The venue was Aberdare, an appropriate location since it was from there that a bombshell had been lobbed into the WFU camp, exposing the 'shamateur' nature of rugby union in Wales and unambig-uously confirming the darkest suspicions of its critics from outside.

In May 1907 the *South Wales Daily News* carried a sensation-al notice: 'Northern Union club at Aberdare—all players desir-ous of joining the new club which is in contact with the NU should send their names immediately to E.H. Rees', at an Aber-dare address. Rees was not lying low, nor, apparently, lying at all: 'the fact is that professionalism is rampant in Wales and the majority of clubs, big as well as small, pay players. I can prove it to the hilt'.[57]

Rees made three allegations. One concerned paying players: he cited Dai 'Tarw' ('Bull') Jones, the former international who had been Aberdare's captain for the previous two season and received 10s. a week wages. He now sought a transfer back to his old club of Treherbert, and although Aberdare were still prepared to pay him 7s.6d a match, and although he still worked as a collier in Aberdare, the fact that he now sought to transfer to Treherbert suggested that the Rhondda club's wage account 'must have been a heavy one'. A second allegation was that teams had been lured to Aberdare by the promise of gener-ous expenses: ('How the expense of bringing Merthyr players to Aberdare could amount to £7. 5s is beyond explanation unless wages were paid'). Rees's third confession was the most offensive, that Treorchy had been paid £15 to 'throw' the last game of the 1904-05 season so that Aberdare would win the match, and, thereby, the Glamorgan League championship.

We can only speculate as to Rees's motives for choosing to blow the whistle when he did. Whatever personal grudge he harboured, his evidence was corroborated by witnesses from Merthyr who likewise sought the open professionalization of their club in order to establish a viable Welsh professional organization. What is known is that E.H. Rees was an Aberdarian by birth and a hairdresser by occupation. More relevantly, he had for some years been connected with association football. He had been responsible for building up the Aberdare XI into one of the strongest in South Wales, but ground difficulties and

The formidable Dai 'Tarw' Jones, a hero of the Welsh victory of 1905 and villain of the bribery scandal of 1907.

(by permission of the BBC)

a disastrous 1905-06 season had forced its disbandment. Rees had then been appointed joint-secretary of Aberdare's rugby club, and as the season progressed the secretaryship had devolved solely on to his shoulders.[58]

There were, however, deeper issues involved than the ambitions and frustrations of an Aberdare barber, just as there were larger historical forces at work in the Cynon Valley that since the late nineteenth century had made it an arena and a focus of debate over monetary rewards in sport. Aberdare had played a distinctive role in the recent history of South Wales, a distinctiveness shaped by geographical circumstance and industrial development, and given political articulation. Some twenty miles north of Cardiff the river Cynon meets the Taff: upstream what were once mining communities hug the hillsides of both valleys, the Taff going north, the Cynon north west. Both began their industrial history as iron valleys but from the mid-nineteenth century Aberdare, like the adjacent Rhondda Valleys, turned to coal. The aggressive industrial politics of the coalfield asserted themselves in the six-month lock-out of 1898; they would flare up again in the Aberdare Miners' Strike of 1910, which was eclipsed by the Cambrian Combine dispute and the Tonypandy riots in the Rhondda, but which experienced its own episodes of violence and brutality. Aberdare had long had powerful radical associations. It was one of the last active centres of Welsh Chartism, and the first Welsh Co-op had been established at Cwmbach in 1860; Aberdare, with Merthyr, was the parliamentary seat of Henry Richard whose great Liberal victory of 1868 announced the end of the landed Tory hegemony in South Wales, and of Keir Hardie as the first independent Labour member in 1900. Aberdare produced maverick figures like the revolver-toting revolutionary socialist and miner's agent C.B. Stanton.[59] It produced maverick sportsmen too.

One of the Cynon Valley's more distinctive features is its physical broadness, well-reflected in Aberdare's spacious Central Park. This is attributed to the softer rocks of the Lower Coal Series which predominate along the northern crop of the South Wales coalfield.[60] It was perhaps this broader, more open appearance that nurtured the distinctive local fondness for cycling. The Aberdare Workmen's Bicycle Club had been established in 1894 from which emerged a chain of champions who dominated world cycling in the last years of the nineteenth century: the Linton brothers, Jimmy Michael and George Burge, who raced widely in Britain, France and North America. Arthur Linton's parents had moved from Somerset to Aberaman, near Aberdare, when he was three, so that Linton became a naturalized Welshman and 'always was proud to be called a Cymro'. At twelve years of age he had gone underground at the Treaman colliery, and saved steadily for a machine of his own. In the meantime he built up his strength and speed on a stationary training cycle at the Swan Hotel, Aberaman, and was winning races all over South Wales and beyond on one of the first machines with pneumatic tyres, a Raleigh. He died at the age of 28 in 1896, ostensibly of typhoid but by general reckoning from over-exertion in the Bordeaux-Paris race, in which he had cut the time by three hours. His great rival was the French champion, Huret, who wheeled the bicycle Linton had last ridden at his funeral, an event which attracted a massive turnout of admirers, representatives from cycling clubs all over England and Wales, and wreaths from D.A. Thomas, MP, and the Dunlop Pneumatic Tyre Co.[61] Arthur Linton's brother Tom set up five world records at the Crystal Palace in one day in October 1896, while Jimmy Michael, 'the diminutive Aberdarian' who raced regularly at the Paris Vélodrome, became the first world professional motor-paced champion at Cologne.[62] When another renowned Aberdare cyclist, Tom Jones, was sued for alimony in 1906 he was referred to as 'the champion cyclist of Wales ... for the past 16 years' which suggests that the apparently infinite variety of distances and measurements possible in the sport invested the designation of 'champion' with a certain elasticity.[63] Cycle-racing, nevertheless, made high demands on effort and, on account of its technology, on expenditure. The expense involved in it signified rising living standards and an expectation of proportionate rewards. Its professional exponents, necessarily young unmarried men, attracted enviable adulation and material enhancement.

Aberdare's population rose from 40,000 in 1891 to 52,000 by

1911, and the majority of its immigrants were young single men. This coloured the nature of local recreation. Foot-racing (pedestrianism) was popular, for cash prizes; Aberaman produced several professional Powderhall runners; prize-fighting for money was by the turn of the century mutating into a professional sport.[64] The pressure towards the equalization of rewards in rugby, too, mounted, especially in the face of a growing challenge from semi-professional soccer.

When in 1896 Cardiff was chosen to host its first soccer inter-national—played on the Cardiff Arms Park, on a Monday, a Cardiff v. Newport rugby derby having priority on the Saturday —the aim was a missionary one since 'the dribbling code is to many Cardiffians a novelty'. The Welsh XI were drawn from leading clubs of North Wales and the north of England, and attempts were made to remedy their obvious unfamiliarity with South Wales by taking them to see Cardiff and Newport docks and other places of interest.[65]

In the industrial valleys north of those rugby strongholds, however, soccer was making rapid headway.[66] Its membership drawn from south-east Wales, there had been a South Wales League in existence since 1890: Aberdare and Mountain Ash were founder members. Various First-division English sides paid promotional visits to South Wales during the decade: in April 1899 Aberdare had the temerity to beat Sheffield United 2-1, though a year later they had their come-uppance in a 1-7 thrashing by proselytizing Notts County. In terms of South Wales soccer Aberdare were the 'pioneers of professionalism', though they were not alone by 1900 when, at the October meeting of the South Wales and Monmouthshire FA its chair-man Jack Sandiford, a northcountryman, successfully pro-posed the adoption of a professionalism that was already 'not only rife but rampant'. Aberdare were pioneers in other ways as well. The first South Welshman to play in the Football League came from that district, Aberaman's Hugh Jones, in 1902. The South Wales League's first international player was also from Aberdare, Bill 'Barber' Jones, capped from West Ham in 1901 and 1902.

The Cynon Valley was the pre-eminent soccer area in South Wales. In 1903 Aberaman and Aberdare headed the South Wales

League. Later that year Aberaman became the first South Wales team to enter the English FA Cup; that year too they became the first South Wales club to reach the final of the Welsh cup. The continual rain which fell relentlessly throughout the season proved to be too heavy a financial cross for a wage-paying club like Aberaman. In May 1903 a representative from Aberdare pleaded for assistance for both his own club and for neighbouring Aberaman. Aberdare, he reckoned, 'had incurred debts of £200 for the cost of professionals ... and were £100 out'. Aberaman wound up, and Aberdare survived to savour future success. For his part, E.H. Rees turned his attention from professional soccer to the promotion of professional rugby, in Aberdare.

Aberdare had been admitted to the WFU in September 1903. Its status had been closely investigated as to whether it was an association or a rugby club since both games were played on the same ground. In the event the union was satisfied 'that the two forms of sport were absolutely distinct in every way'. Aberdare's captain was Dai 'Tarw' Jones, a 1905 Welsh hero against New Zealand, a 1907 villain—or scapegoat—when the WFU investigated the Aberdare club in the wake of Rees' headline-making, appalling frankness.

They were headlines which demanded attention. 'Rugby deceit: a formidable document', recognized the main organ of Liberal South Wales which printed E.H. Rees's statement in full. 'Wages, payments and allowances: striking array of instances'. While Rees himself went north to negotiate with NU officials, the WFU's Ack Llewelyn, who represented the Mid-Glamorgan district which included the valleys and must have had some inkling of past transactions, attributed the whole affair to the silly season 'when they were generally entertained by the Press to fairy yarns about sea serpents and the like'. This year it was 'the Aberdare bubble'.[67]

The WFU, however, faced with an elephant on its doorstep, realized it would not go away of its own accord. It instigated an inquiry and conducted it to nobody's satisfaction: it was slow to get going, it allowed sufficient time for the submission of account books for discrepancies to be rectified and alternative accounts to be substituted, it was held behind closed doors with bald and meaningless summaries issued to the press, and it adjourned during the summer. This fumbling response was not a little due to the indisposition of the union's president, H.S. Lyne, who on his recovery brought matters to a speedy conclusion in September. The upshot was a lengthy statement issued by the WFU to the effect that

> Mr. Rees's allegations that 'Professionalism is rampant in Welsh clubs' has [sic] not proved . . . the cases . . . in which money has been paid to players merely for playing football are rare . . . As regards what is known as the Treorchy v. Aberdare 'squared' match . . . it is only too clear that this disgraceful proceeding actually did take place . . . the most disgraceful one that has even taken place in connection with Welsh football.

The union's findings resulted in the suspending of the entire committees of both clubs, eight players banned for life, and another six temporarily suspended. And to allay any suspicions of negligence on the WFU's part, 'your Committee desire to add that as regards any irregularities which have taken place, there was not the slightest evidence to show that any Member of your Committee was or ought to have been aware of such'. [68]

While Aberdare's professionals looked for a new ground to play on, events moved even faster at Ebbw Vale, further to the east in Monmoushire (Gwent). The driving force here was W.M. Evans, one of Ebbw Vale's secretaries in 1906-07, who was anxious to get his club into the Northern Union 'because it is the more honest way of doing business. We have all been thoroughly disgusted with the method of conducting football in South Wales' where 'so-called amateurism' was a farce. Professionalism was 'rampant' in the Monmouthshire League and payment, apparently, had been going on in Ebbw Vale for years. Bandwaggoning Jack Games of Abercarn claimed he could prove by documentary evidence, though he did not, 'that half the players in Wales were paid for their services'. Rumour had it that there were eight clubs in Monmouthshire that were distinctly professional; there was a pre-echo of 'a thunderclap from the west' as clubs in the Swansea area were reckoned to be on the verge of declaring themselves professional. Not all these ambitions were realized, but many were. Professional rugby made significant progress in South Wales in 1907-08. By the beginning of the 1908-09 season there were six professional sides in the Welsh rugby union heartland, at Ebbw Vale, Merthyr, Aberdare, Treherbert, Mid-Rhondda and Barry.[69]

VI

It was no accident that there was an upsurge of interest in establishing professional rugby openly, as opposed to merely operating it covertly, in South Wales at this time. To be fully understood it has to be seen in the context of what was happening in sport and beyond, in England as well as in Wales, in the first decade of the twentieth century.

These were years that saw an assertion of player-power in professional soccer. The Professional Footballers' Association (PFA), formed to defend players' interests regarding wages and transfers, held its inaugural meeting at Manchester in December 1907. Collective action in the trade-union world was seen as feasible in the wake of the Trade Disputes Act of 1906. In 1908 the PFA indicated it would be bringing a number of court cases over wage arrears under the Workmen's Compensation Act of 1906, and formed a Players' Union which in 1909 threatened to join the General Federation of Trade Unions. The FA and League authorities ordered all players to resign from it under threat of expulsion, to which the players' own response, backed by Arthur Henderson, was a strike threat. Both sides eventually made concessions to end the deadlock, but just as it is difficult to isolate the players' assertiveness from the wider rank-and-file militancy of the period, so it is difficult to believe that amateur rugby's sheltered enclaves were untouched by the gusts of disaffection that swirled around them outside.[70] In 1907 the RFU itself set up a committee to investigate veiled professionalism; in 1908 there was a move to expel the Leicester club because of financial impropriety; Coventry was suspended for three months in 1909, Torquay, Plymouth and Newton Abbot in 1912.[71]

The language of strike and lock-out now intruded into the

vocabulary of sporting journalism. Several Neath rugby players went 'on strike' over a personal slight in 1907, a gesture, which the press was unsure whether to designate a 'strike' or 'lockout'. Early in 1909 when some of Newport's second team threatened to strike, it is interesting to note that one of their grounds for dissatisfaction was that 'they are cutting down on expenses to the lowest limit'.[72] Such behaviour seemed to provide further evidence that Welsh rugby was in decline. There was concern at the deterioration in standards of play and behaviour, at the onset of cynicism at the expense of 'the recreative and educative side of Rugby Football'. One critic felt that commercial considerations were becoming paramount, 'and that the play-to-the whistle man who stoops to the most contemptible trickery if it can benefit his side and glories in deceiving the referee is in a large majority'. In October 1908 the WFU issued a circular urging 'cleaner football' and asking players to be sportsmen.[73]

In retrospect it can be seen that for Welsh rugby the years between 1906 and 1914 constitute not so much a landslip of declining standards as a plateau where the consistency of earlier success was maintained but where innovation was now the victim of intense club rivalry and constant familiarity, and where unpredictability was somehow lost sight of in the wheels and cogs of smoothly-running machinery. Complacency, that makes for less than zealous practice of moves, and tradition, as a standard to be maintained and emulated, can inhibit and burden. The WFU responded to the situation by a variety of proposals intended to revitalize the game's juices, from fostering junior rugby to advocating a league of the top clubs.[74] At root, however, action was necessary to preserve the organic link which distinguished the Welsh game from others, namely the relationship between the game and its popular following. This was where the other football codes, Northern Union and Association, constituted a threat.

It was a threat which rugby union in Wales, irrespective of periodic bouts of self-doubt and concern about standards of play, was able to withstand. Its 30-year head start and its remarkable run of international success since 1900 (six Triple Crowns 1900-11) had established it as the national game. As a vehicle for promoting national unity and social consensus it was increasingly taken up by editorialists, politicians, cartoonists and entertainers, an argument to be developed in my final section. But in any case South Wales, with its relatively limited though densely concentrated demographic and geographical base, could not accommodate three winter football games. A number of factors dictated the inability of the NU to maintain its position: the failure to build up an administrative base, the sheer distance separating South Wales from the north of England, the paucity of professional clubs and their poor playing records. Ebbw Vale achieved the dubious distinction of becoming the first NU side to be beaten by a non-league team, Beverley, in the 1909 Challenge Cup competition, though they could also boast the longest spell of any Welsh club in the NU, from September 1907 to April 1912, by which time attendances had dropped to below a thousand. Nor did NU agents ever relax their efforts to attract good players direct to the north, by-passing the professional South Wales clubs: 18 Welsh rugby union internationals went north between 1907 and 1913.[75]

Attendances fell drastically in the face of stern competition from soccer, whose firm grip on Merthyr may serve as an example. In January 1908, in the NU's early days there, 500 spectators saw visiting star-studded Swansea play amateur rugby at Penydarren Park, while three to four thousand were at College Field to watch Huddersfield NU. But the novelty wore off. After finishing eighth in the Northern RL Championship in 1908-09, by the end of 1910 Merthyr were right at the bottom of it and able to fulfil away fixtures only if they were forwarded their rail fare. In January 1911 the club was wound up, while later that year Merthyr AFC, itself only three years old, entered the Southern League and, immediately after the war, the Football League itself.[76] While amateur rugby survived, but only just, in Merthyr, it actually revived in Ebbw Vale as further expansion in coal and steel in the Monmouthshire valleys attracted new waves of immigrants from rugby-playing industrial west Wales to thrust clubs like Pontypool and Abertillery into the first rank. Ebbw Vale would always be a target for RL's organizers whenever a campaign was mounted to re-establish professional rugby in South Wales.

VII

Rugby Union retained its hold in Wales, irrespective of the jibes of socially superior practitioners from outside and in defiance of rival codes within. The reason for this enduring appeal, finally, remains to be considered.

It has become the national game more through geographical and industrial factors than any ethnic or cultural affinity. This had implications which have been missed by some perceptive writers on the team. Dunning and Sheard, for instance, argue that rugby league failed to develop in South Wales because, although there was a 'separate' working class (whose cultural separation they exaggerate), it did not express itself though NU football as did the comparably 'separate' northern working class 'because the crucial condition for such a development was absent, namely a middle class able and willing to sue the game for purposes of social control'.[77] In actual fact this is precisely what Wales *did* have. It is not true that 'middle class Welshmen were apparently apathetic towards the administration of the game', because all the major clubs from Newport to Llanelli were founded and run by industrialists, solicitors, businessmen and shopkeepers. The WFU itself was guided by men like Sir John Llewellyn, Bart., H.S. Lyne and W.E. Rees, all three privately educated in England, Conservative in politics, Anglican in religion, and thereby temperamentally and culturally quite removed from the players whose rugby activities they supervised.[78] What Dunning and Sheard miss is that the industrial revolution's final volcanic spasm that brought about the dramatic economic development of South Wales in the second half of the nineteenth century created a different social configuration from that in the north of England whose cotton-, metallurgical- and coal-based managerial class was more securely established and self-sufficient to assert its regional independence and challenge the southern gentry of the RFU.

The situation in Wales was altogether different. Politically and educationally as well as economically, the Welsh nation was 're-born' from 1868 onwards, and the leaders of this new Wales sought to promote Welsh aspirations and ambitions within the British political system and Empire. As one of those leaders, Tom Ellis MP, put it in 1892 when addressing the British Empire Club in London, 'The more Wales has the power of initiative and decision in her own affairs the more closely will she be bound to the very texture of the imperial fabric'.[79] The Bishop of Llandaff in his 1906 St David's Day sermon, in Welsh, stressed 'how a Welshman's love of country was consistent with his pride in the great Empire of which his country formed a part . . . Welshmen should be given the right to serve the Empire and to be a blessing to the World'.[80] A WFU that cut itself off from the international amateur rugby fraternity by countenancing professionalism could not play the required role, since Wales would thereby be reduced to a region playing the regional representatives of the north of England. As the Cardiff and Wales outside-half, Percy Bush, reasoned at the height of the Aberdare rumpus, 'If open professionalism came in the Welsh Union would find the Scottish, English and Irish Unions would have nothing more to do with them'. It would also lose its greatest source of income 'and the public would lose the always attractive International games'.[81]

That public was an important consideration. In Wales rugby was the game of the masses and classes, of a democracy, which increasingly provided a focus for national pride and expression. 'What could have brought such a multitude together in Wales but an International match?' mused 'Morien' on the occasion of the Wales v. Scotland game of 1902, a match the Mayor of Cardiff also attended not because he professed to be an expert on rugby but in order 'to give countenance to the national complexion it took'.[82] Eight years and four Triple Crowns later the *Western Mail* showed St. David and the ubiquitous Dame Wales gleefully surveying the sturdy tree trunk of Welsh nationalism and the stout branches that sprouted from it: education, literature, music, language, science—and football.[83]

Given the specific character and needs of South Wales at the beginning of this century, what was required was not a game that proletarianized itself through professionalism, but one which could embrace the spectrum of the whole community. The game had embedded itself sufficiently deeply in popular culture and national consciousness alike by now for there to be give-and-take on both sides. Working men were never excluded, and they deferred to the discipline and obligations imposed by the game and its formalities. Equally, the game's administrators were quite prepared to tolerate the over-generous payment of expenses to working-class players. What they would *not* consent to was the professionalizing and therefore proletarianizing of the game which would mean its forfeiting its middle-class support, and replacing a classless with a class-specific image. With few exceptions rugby in Scotland, Ireland and, in its different ways, in the north and south of England, was socially exclusive. In Wales, where it was cast in a symbolic unifying role, it was socially *inclusive,* 'a game democratic and amateur . . . a unique thing to be cherished, and therefore the concern of thinking men who value the complex influences making for higher levels of citizenship'. [84]

NOTES

[1] A. Budd, *Rugby Football* (London, 1899), p. 2.
[2] F.M.L. Thompson, 'Social Control in Victorian Britain' *Economic History Review* xxxiv (May 1981), 189-208, quotations at 207.
[3] A. Metcalf, 'Organised Sport in the Mining Communities of South Northumberland 1800-89', *Victorian Studies* 25 (Summer 1982), 469-95.
[4] W.F. Mandle, 'Games People Played: Cricket and Football in England and Victoria in the Late Nineteenth Century', *Historical Studies* (April 1973), 528-9; K.A.P. Sandiford, 'Amateurs and Professionals in Victorian County Cricket', *Albion* 15 (Spring 1983), 32-51.
[5] P. Lovesey, *The Official Centenary History of the AAA* (London, 1979), p. 22.
[6] K.A.P. Sandiford, 'Cricket and the Victorian Society', *Journal of Social History* 17 (Winter 1983), 313.
[7] P.J. Doyle, 'Some Problems for the Regional Historian of Rugby League', *Journal of Local Studies* 1 (Summer 1980), 9.
[8] E. Dunning and K. Sheard, *Barbarians, Gentlemen and Players* (Oxford, 1979), p. 195.

⁹D. Smith and G. Williams, *Fields of Praise: the Official History of the Welsh Rugby Union 1881-1981* (Cardiff, 1980), pp. 2-4; T. Delaney, *The Roots of Rugby League* (Keighley, 1984), p. 7.

¹⁰M. Shearman, *Athletics and Football* (London, 1887), pp. 330-1, quoted by Dunning and Sheard, op. cit., p. 155.

¹¹T. Mason, *Association Football and English Society 1863-1915* (Brighton, 1980), pp. 70-78.

¹²D.J. Smith, 'The Growth of Working Class Sport in Lancashire 1880-1914' (unpublished MA thesis, University of Lancaster, 1976), p. 41; Mason, op. cit., pp. 69-70; Dunning and Sheard, op. cit., pp. 207-8.

¹³Smith thesis, pp. 41-2; P.M. Young, *A History of British Football* (London, 1973 ed.), pp. 170-180.

¹⁴A recent treatment is C. Andrew, '1883 Cup Final: Patricians v. Plebeians', *History Today* 33 (May 1983), 21-4.

¹⁵U.A. Titley and R. McWhirter, *Centenary History of the Rugby Football Union* (Twickenham, 1970), p. 186; T. Godwin, *The International Rugby Championship 1883-1983* (London, 1984), p. 31.

¹⁶Delaney, op. cit., pp. 8, 12.

¹⁷Quoted in B. Dobbs, *Edwardians at Play* (London, 1973), p. 90.

¹⁸H.H. Almond, 'Football as a Moral Agent', *Nineteenth Century*, Dec. 1983, 911.

¹⁹E. Ensor, 'The Football Madness', *Contemporary Review*, Nov. 1898, 754, 760.

²⁰This paragraph is based on Delaney, op. cit., *passim*; Titley and McWhirter , op. cit., pp. 111-14.

²¹The RFU's first official historian revealing remarks at this point 'Evidently the Communists were not the first to think of the idea of cells'. O.L. Owen, *History of the Rugby Football Union* (Twickenham, 1955), p. 96.

²²Delaney, op. cit., p. 64.

²³Idem, p. 70; K. Macklin, *The History of Rugby League Football* (London, 1974 ed.) p. 20.

²⁴The phrase is used by Titley and McWhirter, op. cit., p. 111.

²⁵To adopt Tony Mason's words in *Victorian Studies* 25 (Winter 1982), 259.

²⁶A.J. Gould's career is treated more fully in Smith and Williams, op. cit., pp. 65-95. See also A. Richards, *A Touch of Glory* (London, 1980), pp. 71-86.

²⁷Welsh Football Union Minutes (hereafter *WFU*), 26 March 1896. The WFU did not officially change its name to the Welsh Rugby Union until 1934. I am grateful to the WRU for allowing me to quote from their Minute Books.

²⁸*WFU* 22 Feb. 1897.

²⁹The IB's statement and the WFU's reply were printed in full in the *South Wales Daily News* (hereafter *SWDN*) 24 Feb. and 1 March 1897.

³⁰Delaney, op. cit., p. 40; *SWDN* 30 July 1897; E. Midwinter, *W.G. Grace: His Life and Times* (London, 1981), p. 125. Cf. *The Morning Leader*, 'I suppose if Dr Grace wished to play Rugger the Union could not expel him because he received that £10,000 last year?' quoted in *SWDN* 28 Jan. 1897.

³¹Titley and McWhirter, op. cit., p. 116.

³²*SWDN* 8 Feb. 1897.

[33] *SWDN* 8 Feb. 28 and 29 Jan. 1897.

[34] *SWDN* 11 Jan. 1897. On the meaning and significance of 'the Rhondda forward' concept see Smith and Williams, op. cit., pp. 103-8.

[35] *SWDN* 18 and 28 Feb., 28 Jan. 1897.

[36] Ibid., 3 Feb. 1897.

[37] The WFU's statement of 17 Feb. was published in the *SWDN* 1 March 1897.

[38] On the James brothers see Smith and Williams, op. cit., pp. 72-7, 118-9; Richards, op. cit., pp. 59-70; Delaney, op. cit., 46-7, 102.

[39] *SWDN* 13 Nov. 1896, 5 Jan. 1899.

[40] *SWDN* 5 Jan. 1897 (Rochdale). 11 Nov. 1896 (Swinton), 23 Jan. 1899 (Wigan).

[41] *SWDN* 27 Jan. 1900.

[42] *SWDN* 4 Sept. 1900.

[43] *SWDN* 30 Jan. 1900; 29 Jan. 1902; 30 Jan. 1902.

[44] *SWDN* 1 Dec. 1903; 1 Jan. 1904.

[45] *SWDN* 30 Sept. 1901.

[46] *SWDN* 24 Oct. 1901.

[47] Quoted in *SWDN* 17 Sept. 1907.

[48] Dunning and Sheard, op. cit., p. 237; *SWDN* 8 March 1902.

[49] *SWDN* 9 Feb. 1901.

[50] *SWDN* 7 Feb. 1905; 11 Feb. 1905.

[51] *SWDN* 14 March 1904.

[52] Smith and Williams, op. cit. p. 124.

[53] *SWDN* 14 Jan. 1909; 6 April 1908.

[54] *SWDN* 12 Sept. 1910.

[55] *SWDN* 8 Nov. 1905.

[56] *WFU* 4 Oct. 1905.

[57] *SWDN* 25 May 1907.

[58] *SWDN* 17 July, 27 May 1907.

[59] K.O. Morgan, *Wales in British Politics 1868-1922* (Cardiff, 1963), p. 206.

[60] G. Melvyn Howe, 'The South Wales Coalfield' in E.G. Bowen (ed.), *Wales* (London, 1957), pp. 357-8, 382-3. I owe this reference to Dr. Roy Lewis.

[61] *Aberdare Times*, 1 Aug. 1896; *Western Mail* (hereafter *WM*) 25 July 1896; W.J. Edwards, *From the Valley I Came* (London, 1956), pp. 12-13.

[62] *SWDN* 20 Oct. 1896 (Tom Linton): *WM* 7 June 1895, 25 July 1895, *Aberdare Leader* 3 Dec. 1904 (Jimmy Michael).

[63] *SWDN* 15 Nov. 1906.

[64] Martin Barclay, 'Class and Community: Aberdare 1880-1920' (unpub. University of Wales MA thesis, Cardiff, 1985), whose section on popular culture was kindly made available to me at draft stage.

[65] *WM* 16 and 17 March 1896.

[66] This section draws heavily on B. Lile and D. Farmer, 'The Early Development of Association Football in South Wales 1890-1906', *Transactions of the Hon. Soc. of Cymmrodorion*, 1984, 193-215, which the authors generously allowed me to see in typescript.

[67] *SWDN* 13 June, 30 and 31 May, 22 June 1907. See also W.J. Edwards, op. cit., pp. 12-13.

[68] *WFU* 18 June, 3 Sept. 1907; *SWDN* 9 Sept. 1907.

[69] Delaney, op. cit., pp. 111-2; *SWDN* 17, 27, 31 July, 7 Sept. 1907.

[70] B. Dabscheck, ' '' Defensive Manchester'': A History of the Professional Footballers' Association', in R. Cashman and M. McKernan (eds.), *Sport in History* (St. Lucia, Queensland, 1979), 227-257. A similar scandal in soccer had virtually destroyed Manchester City FC the previous year. The key involvement of the famous Billy Meredith aroused great interest in the affair in Wales. See J. Harding *Football Wizard: the Story of Billy Meredith* (Derby, 1985), pp. 93-115.

[71] Delaney, op. cit., pp. 113-5.

[72] *SWDN* 30 Dec. 1907; 8 Jan. 1909.

[73] *SWDN* 12 March, 29 Oct., 9 Nov. 1908; 24 Oct., 14 Nov. 1910.

[74] Smith and Williams, op. cit., pp. 180-6.

[75] Information derived from a series of articles by G. Morris, 'Rugby League in Wales', *Open Rugby*, nos. 36-9 (Oct. 1981-Jan. 1982), kindly made available to me by Robert Gate.

[76] R. Gethin, 'The Story of Merthyr Rugby 1876-1976' in *Merthyr RFC Centenary Brochure* (Merthyr, 1976), pp. 8-11.

[77] Dunning and Sheard, op. cit., p. 222.

[78] Smith and Williams, op. cit., pp. 23-8, 309-11.

[79] Quoted in D. Smith (ed.), *A People and a Proletariat* (London, 1980), p. 222.

[80] *SWDN* 2 March 1906.

[81] *SWDN* 27 April 1907.

[82] *SWDN* 2 and 4 Feb. 1902.

[83] *WM* 1 March 1910. See p. 82 above.

[84] *Welsh Outlook* Feb. 1914. See also Dai Smith, *Wales! Wales!* (London, 1984), pp. 34-5.

CHAPTER 8

FROM GRAND SLAM TO GREAT SLUMP: ECONOMY, SOCIETY AND RUGBY FOOTBALL IN WALES DURING THE DEPRESSION*

'Whatever indicator we turn to . . . the 1880s and the quarter century that followed them appear as a watershed'.[1] Those words, written *à propos* the modernising process that turned peasants into Frenchmen between 1870 and 1914, are equally applicable to the history of modern Wales. Dr Kenneth O. Morgan's acclaimed volume in the Oxford History of Wales takes 1880 as the year from which 'the rebirth of a nation' can be traced. Dr Morgan convincingly reaffirms—his indicators being political self-confidence, massive industrial and urban growth, and cultural vitality—that the years from 1880 to 1914 in the history of Wales have a unity of their own. Within that period, it is the Edwardian era from 1905 to 1914 that, with a Gibbonian flourish, he portrays as 'Wales's Antonine Age . . . when the economic prosperity, national awareness and political creativity of the Welsh people were most effectively deployed'.[2] As a further indicator of this 'buoyant national confidence', Dr Morgan does not hesitate to invoke the famous victory registered by the Welsh rugby team, captained by Gwyn Nicolls, over the (otherwise) all-conquering New Zealand All Blacks at the Cardiff Arms Park on 16 December 1905, their only defeat in thirty-two games played the length and breadth of Britain. This epic victory was recorded within a mere ten days of Lloyd George becoming the first Welshman to attain high office since the reign of Charles II, when he was appointed President of the Board of Trade in Campbell-Bannerman's Liberal cabinet. Only two months before that—albeit a cheap vote-catching device in intention—Cardiff, the funnel of the greatest coal export region in the world, had been formally granted city status by letters patent of the great seal. The rebirth of the Welsh nation had been signed by Lloyd George, sealed by the king of England, and delivered by Gwyn Nicholls.

Rightly dismissive of the highly dubious Darwinian and biological arguments that were drummed up in pseudo-intellectual confirmation of that victory, Dr Morgan is surely also right in his readiness to defy a myopic academic convention which relegates sporting endeavour to somewhere vaguely beneath the contempt of the serious historian, and to accord recognition to the fact that sport, far from being untouched by the upheaval in the political and economic structure of Wales, as of Europe, in the late-nineteenth century, in fact evolved closely in step with those wider changes. An attempt has been made to account for the way in which rugby football, a game which had been made to account for the way in which rugby football, a game which had been the élite preserve of public schoolboys, became within the last quarter of the nineteenth century the collective winter passion of most of south Wales,[3] and it confirms how Dr Morgan's Edwardian high noon of prosperity, optimism and confidence—when, because of 'the international impact of the Welsh . . . the eyes of the world . . . were increasingly focussed upon gallant little Wales'[4]—what Dr Morgan himself calls 'a kind of golden age' was mirrored, even articulated, in the exploits of the national XV. Between 1900 and 1911 the mythical Triple Crown was won six times; the 'Welsh style' of thrillingly fluent three-quarter play, built on a platform of mobile and skilful forwards and engineered by endless inventiveness at half-back, was universally regarded[5] as the finest exposition of the game yet seen (Gwyn Nicholls's coaching manual was in French translation by 1914);[6] and rugby football, along with coal, hymns[7] and Lloyd George, signalled the full blown arrival of Wales into the modern world.

Undeniably, rugby football had accompanied the take-off of the economy into self-sustained growth.[8] Indeed, historians of organised sport, rare breed as they are,[9] seem more comfortable in tracing its rise as a facet of modernisation, linking it with economic progress. What actually happens to a sport when the 'modernising' indicators stick, and even move back, is apparently a less attractive field of inquiry. The purpose of this paper is to provide some empirical evidence of what happens to a spectator sport that had become an integral part of a popular culture when it experiences the impact not of economic growth but of economic recession: more precisely, to examine what happened to Welsh rugby football, locked as it was into the socio-economic matrix of Welsh society, during the inter-war years of industrial depression. For if the first decade of the twentieth century saw Edwardian Wales's 'high noon' and Welsh rugby's 'Golden Era', the second saw the Great War and the dividing line (it would soon become clear) between one hundred and fifty years of industrial growth and thirty years of economic stagnation. The third decade, which saw south Wales brought to its knees by British capitalism in crisis, were 'the locust years' in every respect.

In rugby terms, the contrast between the pre-war and post-war periods is striking. Between 1900 and 1911 Wales won thirty-five out of forty-three games, dominating the inter-national championship in the process. In the immediate post-war period, when miners returned to the pits and steelworkers to the plants, there was a brief economic boom which was paralleled by short-lived and misleading rugby success, as Wales shared the championship in 1920 and won it outright in 1922.[10] But between 1923 and 1930 only nine games were won out of thirty-two. Whereas in a sequence of twenty-five games between 1901 and 1912 the only side to win in Wales were the 1906 Springboks, from 1923 to 1930 England won every game against Wales except for a draw at Cardiff in 1926, and in 1924 won at Swansea for the first time since 1895. Scotland won every game against Wales between 1920 and 1927, except for a draw at Inverleith in 1922, and in 1923 won at Cardiff for the first time since 1890. In the mid-'twenties the Irish beat Wales in three successive seasons, for the first time ever, and in doing so won at Swansea for the first time since 1889. Since their inception in 1908 Wales's matches with France, even in an indifferent season, were commonly regarded as the annual con-solation prize; in 1928 even France won. On the field, the mantle of technical innovation passed to England, who won the Triple Crown four times between 1921 and 1928. Off the field, too, selectorial myopia, administrative inadequacies and

financial constraints can, with hindsight, be plainly identified,[11] but they were only symptoms of a deeper malaise that
was undermining the old confidence and, with it, the infrastructure of Welsh rugby at grass-roots club and spectator level.

In economic terms the basic data are familiar enough.[12] The
slump disembowelled whole areas of south Wales. Nearly half a
million moved out, a fifth of the entire population. Only in
1961 did the population of Wales return to the level of 1921.
The coal industry was undermined by the loss of foreign
markets, competition from other fuels, and the lessening
demand for coal. South Wales was the loser as her customers
adopted protectionist policies and war reparations were made
in coal. Thus, the Italian market for the two and half million
tons of coal exported from south Wales to Italy in 1913 was
immediately lost to Germany. The British Admiralty changed
to oil firing just after the war and other navies and merchant
services followed suit. In 1914 90 per cent of the world's
mercantile marine was powered by coal; by 1939, less than 50
per cent.[13] At home, the decision to return to the pre-war gold
standard crippled exports, while greater industrial efficiency
meant, ironically, that the amount of electricity produced by a
ton of coal doubled between the wars, while the amount of coal
required to produce a ton of steel was reduced by a half in the
same period. The output of coal from south Wales fell from its
1913 peak of nearly 57 million tons to 35 million by 1939;
exports plummeted from 35 million to 19½ million. Mechanization coming on top of lessening demand reduced the labour
force even further.[14]

While there had been 265,000 miners employed in south
Wales in 1920, by 1933 their numbers had shrunk to 138,000,
with a consequent drop in the wages bill from £65 million to
£14 million. The result sent poverty accelerating on a downward spiral through south Wales.[15] Because such a large
proportion of its population—56 per cent in 1930—was engaged
in the mining and metallurgical industries, Wales suffered
more acutely than other regions in proportion. Unemployment
in Wales reached 13.4 per cent by December 1925, 23.3 per cent
by December 1927, 27.2 per cent by July 1930— and in so far as
these statistics relate to the insured population and omit cate-

gories that did not come within the purview of the Industrial Insurance Acts, they are under-estimates. Also, they serve only to obscure the real situation in some areas; by the early 'thirties unemployment rates stood at 43 per cent in the Rhondda, 59 per cent in Merthyr, 76 per cent in Pontypridd. As money coming in to Wales dwindled to a trickle, and as the numbers of people going out rose to a flood (the Rhondda lost 20 per cent of its population between 1921 and 1931, while a thousand people left Merthyr every year on average between 1921 and 1937),[16] the social fabric and cultural vitality of south Wales began to crumble. Its institutions, politically, industrially and socially, were savaged.

Both religion and recreation were mauled. The Rhondda suffered a 70 per cent reduction in chapel membership between 1921 and 1935. There were nine chapels in Cwmavon in 1930 without a minister; the total debt of the nonconformist churches of south Wales in 1937 was near half a million pounds.[17] The monopoly that the great mixed and male choirs of the Rhondda and Dowlais had exerted on the choral competitions of the National Eisteddfod was broken by Ystalyfera and Morriston from the less economically hard-hit Swansea Valley.[18]

Many rugby clubs, especially in east Wales, were not merely less in evidence, but in danger of actual extinction. In the season 1926-27 the Welsh Rugby Union, whose own takings halved during the decade, was inundated by requests from clubs like Ebbw Vale, Cross Keys, Blaenavon, Pontypool, Pontypridd and Skewen for financial assistance.[19] Their pleas were both poignant and persistent: 'We are forced to appeal to you to again kindly consider granting us financial assistance to enable us to carry on', wrote the Cross Keys club to the Union late in 1926; 'please ask your Committee to be good enough to give the matter their serious consideration to see if something cannot be done for us'.[20] In May 1927 the secretary of the Glamorgan League wrote from Treorchy to the WRU appealing for a cup competition to be launched to revive interest and gates, since 'the season 1926-7 has been disastrous for all clubs'.[21] The evidence was all around. Treherbert RFC had been in financial trouble since 1924; by 1928 the rent charged by the Great

Western Railway, which owned the club's playing-field, was consistently higher than the gate-takings. In March of that year the GWR announced that 'the club was in a state of hopeless insolvency [and] could be forced into disbandment . . . local distress has seriously affected the club's recipts'. In December 1929 Treherbert RFC was forced to disband.[22] That year, in the Llynfi valley in mid-Glamorgan, Nantyffyllon RFC also disbanded. Around the same time, Pencoed RFC was decimated when nine of the first XV left in one particular fortnight for the midlands and London.[23]

In the valleys of Monmouthshire the outlook was no less gloomy. Machen had already had to withdraw from the WRU in 1926.[24] Cwmbran, or Pontnewydd RFC as it was then called, collapsed in 1927.[25] By the end of the decade Pontpool was hovering near bankruptcy with an overdraft of £2,000. The closing of the works at Tredegar between 1924 and 1926 led to the closure of Tredegar RFC itself in 1929.[26] That year steel-making ceased at Ebbw Vale, putting 10,000 out of work. Disaster stared the local rugby club in the face. Within a year, even with admission reduced to 4d., a gate of £4 was handsome. By 1932 the receipts seldom reached £1, despite a catchment area of 40,000, and the club resorted to public subscriptions.[27]

Nor were the coastal clubs unaffected. The ports, dependent on their hinterland as they were, lay stranded like beached whales. Cardiff and its environs had a 25.3 per cent unemployment figure by 1930, despite a diversified labour force in port services and distribution trades. Penarth RFC fell into a £1,000 debt which was eventually brought within manageable limits by the tireless efforts of its renowned secretary J. Lot ('leave it to Lot') Thorne in organising countless bazaars, raffles and—this being Penarth—fêtes. Rugby at Barry had already come to a halt in 1923; Pembroke Dock Quins RFC was reduced to five members by 1927; Haverfordwest RFC struggled and went under between 1926 and 1929.[28]

The picture was not wholly uniform throughout south Wales. While Welsh tin plate suffered in common with other metal-based industries, demand was generally buoyant for much of the 1930s. For the fifteen steel works arcing from Margam to Llanelli that produced steel bars for domestic industry, the situation was worrying but less bleak than that further east. Swansea docks handled oil exports from the Skewen refinery. The peak year for anthracite mining was not reached until 1934. The relative prosperity of west Wales must go some way towards explaining the cultural vitality—literary, musical and sporting—of inter-war Swansea. In 1935 when Swansea, spearheaded by the Gowerton half-backs W.T.H. Davies and Haydn Tanner, became only the second British side ever to beat the All Blacks (the first had been Wales in the historic match of 1905), unemployment was a modest 13.8 per cent in the Amman Valley, but 40 per cent in the Rhondda and Cynon Valley and 51 per cent in Merthyr.

The buoyant, bustling pre-war world of spectacular industrial and urban expansion, of immigration, investment and innovation, in sport as in society, was turned upside down as far as south Wales rugby was concerned. From the 1890s, when the thousands tumbling into south Wales began to win for it rugby renown, the other football unions had looked on enviously and muttered darkly about Englishmen, working and playing in Wales, achieving honours in the scarlet jersey.[29] In the inter-war period that process was sharply reversed. The Welsh full back against France in 1930, though born in Cross Keys, played for Torquay. The Torquay Corporation found employment for a number of Monmouthshire players in the late 1920s, including Welsh internationals Gwyn Richards (Cardiff) and Bobby Delahay (Bridgend), who captained the south coast club from 1929 to 1937. Significantly, and certainly in striking contrast to the experience of any Welsh club of this period, the ten years or so from 1926 were among the most successful the Torquay club has ever known.[30] Weston-super-Mare RFC was another club that actively sought to attract unemployed Welshmen to its ranks. In 1929 Aberavon complained to the WRU about a notice in the local Labour Exchange 'inviting prominent footballers, more particularly centre threequarters and forwards, to get in touch with Weston RFC where, provided they fulfilled all requirements, they would be given permanent employment by the Weston UDC'. The surveyor and engineer of the UDC also happened to be the chairman of the local rugby club. In the 1930s, one of the most memorable phases in the history of the club, when there were as many as twelve Welshmen playing, its strong Cymric connection earned it the name of 'Weston Welsh'. The tendency of the Welshmen to go home to Wales at holiday times could prove embarrassing for Weston when they were visited by first-class touring sides. One Good Friday a strong UAU side came down and put fifty points across a hitherto unbeaten Weston side because all the Welshmen who were the backbone of the side had gone home for Easter.[31]

It was in the 1930s too that Oxford received its biggest influx of Welshmen since the foundation of Jesus College, only this time they arrived not to become students but college servants, or car workers. Where choirs disappeared in Wales they reappeared in England; the Oxford Gleemen were a familiar aspect of the south midlands musical landscape.[32] The personal manager at the Bournville chocolate factory in Birmingham was known, in Blaina anyway, as 'the Prince of Wales'.[33] The midlands received an injection of rugby activism from the thousands of immigrant Welshmen, as the inter-war rise of the Coventry and Moseley clubs testify; politics and trade unionism were similarly affected. The emigration haemorrhage— characterised by Gwyn Thomas as 'a Black Death on wheels'[34] —reached its *reductio ad absurdum* in January 1933 when a Welsh-speaking Welshman from Pontarddulais found himself in the backrow of the pack at Twickenham, playing for England! This was 'Gwalia Deserta' with a vengeance.

If the fact that sixteen of the thirty players on view in the final Welsh rugby trial of 1934 were playing their rugby in England tells the same story from one angle, then the fact that half the players on the field in the 1939 Rugby League Cup Final were Welshmen tells it from another. The professional rugby ranks were bursting with Welshmen lured north in the 'twenties and 'thirties. The process had begun as soon as the Northern Union (as the Rugby League was officially known until 1922) broke away in 1893, but it was in the inter-war period that the road to Tonypandy was widened, extended and signposted 'Wigan Pier'. About 150 Welsh internationals, capped in the amateur game, went north in the first hundred years of the WRU's existence. Sixty-nine of them went up in the two inter-war decades: the equivalent, in other words, of more than four full international XVs. But we can never know the whole story: how many hundreds of ordinary, unemployed club players were lured north by a persuasive agent offering anything from £300 to £500 down, £4 for a win, £3 draw or lose, *and* the promise of a job. It would soon become apparent that some of these acquisitions, like Jim Sullivan and Gus Risman, were far from ordinary.*

The extent of the loss was brought home to Welsh audiences in the flesh when a rugby league international was staged at Pontypridd during the angry summer of 1926. The game, between Wales and England, drew 22,000 spectators, the biggest crowd ever to watch a professional rugby game in Wales before or since. Rugby league sides were established at Pontypridd, Cardiff and Ebbw Vale. But the alluring prizes of the north of England itself continued to draw the ablest players who were so minded away from Wales, and this factor, allied to the distance involved in fulfilling fixtures in Yorkshire and Lancashire and low attendances at home, condemned the professional game (occasional showpiece international matches apart) to a lingering death in Wales itself.[35]

Falling attendances posed problems to the amateur game too. Only 15,000, the lowest figure of the century in Wales, turned up to watch France at St Helen's in 1927, partly because neither Wales nor France was a great drawing card at that time, partly because the 2s. (10p.) admission to the field was regarded as excessive. Only 30,000 turned up to watch even England in 1932, despite the attendance of 'the sporting' prince of Wales.[36] In

A Note on Wales and the Rugby League. Since its foundation in 1895 the RL (or Northern Unions it was officially known until 1922) has been a magnetic attraction to Welsh RU players: of the 237 home countries RU internationals who have changed codes between 1895 and 1990 seven have been Irish, 14 Scottish, 50 English, and 156 Welsh. Between 1919 and 1939 70 Welsh internationals turned professional, compared with five English, five Scottish and one Irish. The RL historian Robert Gate estimates that the proportion of uncapped to capped Welsh players is at least twelve to one. This means that not only between four and five full Welsh international XVs but *around 900 players overall* took the road from Wales to Wigan pier in the years between the wars. For the careers of Welshmen in the Rugby League, see the two volumes of Robert Gate, *Gone North* (Sowerby Bridge, 1986, 1988).

January 1933 the gates of Neath's ground at The Gnoll were rushed by a crowd of three to four hundred, protesting against the 1s. admission charge for the game with Aberavon. For the next game, against Bath, admission was reduced to 7d. (3p.).[37]

Welsh soccer, too, was no less immune to the decreased spending power of the community. The Welsh soccer XI enjoyed strident success in the 'thirties, but it was composed of Welshmen playing outside Wales. It was via the Irish club Glenavon and Wolves that Merthyr's Bryn Jones joined Arsenal for a record £14,000 in 1938.[38] The early 'twenties had augured well for Welsh club soccer. With the arrival of Merthyr and Aberdare Athletic in the Third Division (South) in 1920 and 1921 respectively, there were five south Wales sides in the Football League. Cardiff City was promoted to Division One in 1920, reached the Cup Final in 1925, and won it in 1927—in circumstances of savage irony, for the winning Cardiff goal was scored by a Scot, Ferguson, whose shot spun out of the grasp of the luckless Arsenal goalkeeper Dan Lewis, who came from Maerdy. That was the highpoint of Cardiff's achievement. In 1929 they went down to the Second Division and in 1931 were relegated lower again, when their attendances were down to 2,000, until by 1934 they were propping up the whole English League. Newport County dropped out of the League in 1931 and had to be re-elected in 1932.

As in the case or rugby, the fortunes of the ports reflected the grimmer conditions in the valleys they served. Most Rhondda soccer clubs—Treherbert, Ton Pentre, Maerdy, Porth, Mid-Rhondda—were forced to withdraw from the Southern and Welsh Leagues in the 1920s. Some were in a terminal condition. Cwmparc AFC dissolved in August 1926. Mid-Rhondda AFC, whose main support came from Clydach Vale where the miners had been idle since 1926, collapsed in March 1928.[39] Aberdare Athletic had had to apply for re-election to the League in 1923 and 1928; their third attempt in 1930 failed, and Thames United were elected instead. By that time, when visiting teams were leaving Penydarren Park with less than £1 as their share of the gate, the League authorities finally lost patience with Merthyr's plangent pleas for special consideration. Led by chairman T. Wilson Beech, Merthyr continued to make its annual pilgrimage to the Football league into the 'thirties, but to no avail. With two-thirds of the town's work force unemployed, Merthyr was in the poignant position of having thousands of spectators to watch the team train, but empty terraces on the Saturday because the admission charge was an unaffordable 9d. (4p.). When, in 1932, Merthyr announced that the unemployed—62.3 per cent of the population, 73 per cent in Dowlais—would be admitted for 2d., Southern League attendances rocketed from 500 to 4,000. That year there were five Merthyr products in the Welsh XI, including Dai Astley of Aston Villa, Charlie Jones of Arsenal and Dai Richards of Wolves.[40] But valley soccer was as chilled by the economic blizzard as was valley rugby.

One much-canvassed alternative to emigration or unemployment was to join the swelling—indeed already swollen—ranks of the Glamorgan Constabulary. The white gloved, Prussian-helmeted Capt. Lionel Lindsay has become something of an ogre in the demonology of Welsh labour history. Chief constable of Glamorgan since 1891, Lindsay had succeeded his father *via* the inspectorate of *gendarmerie* in Egypt, so that he was prone to confuse coal-blackened faces with the dusky skins of the toiling fellaheen of the Nile Valley.[41] Since his experience at the Cambrian Collieries in 1910, he had seen to it that he was not short of policemen—in 1922 the Home Office actually advised him that he had more than he needed—and he ensured that a good proportion of them were burly rugby forwards. Thanks to unwitting collusion between Lindsay and the Welsh selectors, there were more policemen than miners in the Welsh international teams of the inter-war years. There were six in the Welsh pack of 1926. Cardiff had an average of ten policemen in its first XV every year between 1923 and 1939; in 1925-26 it had twelve, in 1934-35, eleven.[42] The contemporary press made much use of headlines like 'arresting facts about the Welsh team', and cartoonists never tired of portraying puny international opponents dangling helplessly four feet above the ground in the brawny grasp of immense police-uniformed Welsh forwards.

There was, indeed, much affection for bulky and genial personalities like P.Cs. Tom Arthur, Ned Jenkins and Archie

February 2nd, 1927.

Dear Constable Jenkins,

        Will you let me join the many friends you
will have congratulating you on being selected to play
for Wales next Saturday. I am proposing to give myself
the pleasure of seeing you in action, and I hope that
the best side will win, and the spectators will witness
a fine display of the great game.

                    Yours very sincerely,

                    Ramsay Macdonald

Constable E. Jenkins,
Police Station,
Port Talbot.

The leader of the Labour Party, and M.P. for Aberavon, J. Ramsay Macdonald, extends good wishes to one of his constituents, P.C. Ned Jenkins, on winning his first cap. J.R.M. cannot have been too disappointed that Scotland won, 5-0.

Skym, who brought skill as well as strength to Welsh packs of this period. There was less affection in some parts of south Wales for the institution they represented. In the strife-torn coalfield there was plenty for policemen to do. Capt. Lindsay ensured that there were plenty of them to do it. Among the six policemen in the Welsh pack of 1926 was Bryn Phillips of Aberavon. In July of the previous year, he had been one of the sixteen casualties of the 'Battle of the Rock' at Glynneath. Hywel Francis has reminded us that in the anthracite coalfield it is 1925 rather than 1926 that ought to be remembered as the critical year.[43] A total of 18,000 men were out, and strikers and strike-breakers settled their scores on the rugby field. Apparently 'one young man from Cwmtwrch, the sole supporter of a widowed mother with eight children, was so badly beaten by a police batoning around the head that he was hospitalized for a long period and never worked as a miner again. The police constable responsible was not forgotten; the next time he played rugby against one of the Swansea Valley teams he received such severe injuries he was crippled for life'.[44]

Another coalfield storm-centre was the upper Afan Valley in the following year. This was an area dominated by the two isolated single-industry colliery communities of Cymmer and Glyncorrwg. In 1926 it lapsed into a sort of guerilla warfare, certainly a condition that can be described as neither orthodox political activity nor criminality in the normal sense. There was large-scale imprisonment and fines; the injured included twelve policemen, forty-four men and three women.[45] This background makes quite plausible the otherwise startling discovery that a referee took the field in Glyncorrwg at this period with a revolver strapped to his waist.[46]

The Garw district in 1929 was yet another flashpoint for social and political tensions, arising by now from the attack on the South Wales Miners Federation by the Spencer 'Non-Political' Union. In 1921 there had been 198,000 men organised in the S.W.M.F.; by 1929 the number had slumped to under 60,000, and the intrusion of non-unionists into mines in the Garw Valley provoked a strike affecting three pits and 2,500 men in the Ogwr, Llynfi and Garw Valleys. The strike had the support of chapels, clubs and many other institutions in the locality; it also required the attendance of large numbers of police.[47] In October 1929 a 'truce match' was arranged between Blaengarw RFC and the Glamorgan Police, but on the grounds of short notice (though there was also considerable hostility in the community because of police protection for the non-unionists) the police declined the fixture. Neighbouring Pontycymmer RFC stepped in to take their place, but before the kick-off, 'when press representatives applied for names of the teams the officials and players resolutely refused to supply this information on the grounds that the strike situation had not been described as they would have liked it described. ''We don't want anything to do with the press . . . Out you go'' several of the players and officials answered in chorus'. The reporter covering the incident viewed this 'extraordinary attitude' with some puzzlement. Needless to say, he was covering it for the *Western Mail.*[48]

Clearly this is an example of popular direct action taken in accordance with deeply-held communal notions of moral legality. Historians like N.Z. Davis on religious riot in sixteenth-century France, E.P. Thompson on eighteenth-century English food riots, and D.J.V. Jones, G.A. Williams and David Smith on popular disturbances in nineteenth- and twentieth-century Wales have followed the trail blazed by George Rudé in *The Crowd in the French Revolution* so that we have come to see the patronisingly-dismissed 'mob' as neither irresponsible nor wanton but acting according to a constant and traditional view of social norms and obligations.[49] The crowd, on this reading, is prompted to act as it does by political and moral conditions which legitimize its behaviour, a behaviour that has its own inner logic and sense of legitimacy. We can see this type of morally legitimate direct popular action at work in the Rhondda in 1925, when Penygraig were playing at home to a star-studded Llanelli XV and 1,000 unemployed miners, unable to find the requisite entrance money, scrambled over the gates and fences to watch the game peaceably from the popular bank. The match proceeded without interruption.[50]

We should beware, though, of reducing the inter-war period, on or off the field, to a simple left-right dichotomy. The fact that a Rhondda side could entertain (and beat 11-0) the Llanelli of Albert Jenkins and company reminds us that Penygraig was itself going through a very successful period. Between 1925 and 1927 it had an unbeaten ground record, though in this case maybe the exception proves the rule: by the end of the decade Penygraig was in desperate financial straits. Another Rhondda club, Treorchy, won the Glamorgan League in 1929, under the captaincy of popular P.C. Gus Broughton, an indication that not all policemen were bogeymen. It is worth remembering too that industrial stoppage could provide the incentive to organised recreation, instead of acting as a brake on it. Vardre RFC in the Swansea Valley was formed during the miners' three-month lock-out of 1921:[51] so was the Cwmbach Male Choir.[52] Tylorstown's rugby pitch at Penrhys Park, overlooking the Rhondda Fach, was excavated out of the hillside during a thirteen-week recreation scheme in 1932.[53] Rhondda football pitches are notorious for their perilous locations. Before moving to the Welfare Park in the mid-1920s, Penygraig played on top of Dinas mountain, where there was no question of charging spectators, only whether they should be recompensed.[54] The late Gwyn Thomas remembered his native Cymmer, at the confluence of the two Rhonddas, as 'the least level pitch in Christendom. Those who survived it got a diploma from Darwin. It was the only rugby field where the players were allowed to dip their bits of lemon in adrenalin while sitting in an oxygen tent at half-time. The Trebanog and Cymmer boys mastered the slope. They were only defeated but once and then the victors were found to have two Sherpas on the wing from Tibet'.[55]

The fact that the Llanelli club was star-studded, and wealthy, confirms too, as does the founding of the West Wales League in Swansea in 1929—the sort of initiative that was unthinkable in harder-hit east Wales—that not all of south Wales was in the grip of economic paralysis. In the west, where anthracite and tinplate dominated the industrial scene, unemployment stood at little more than three per cent in 1923 and 8.3 per cent in 1930. While Abertillery, which was 'almost totally derelict with unemployment approaching 85 per cent',[56] was threatened with extinction in 1931 because it could not afford its £3 ground rent, Llanelli was making a profit of £300 a season. After some notable losses, such as capped players like Fowler, Bryn Williams, Bryn Evans and Edgar Morgan in the immediate post-war period, Llanelli retained that remarkable galaxy of talent (Albert Jenkins, Dai John, Ernie Finch, Frank Evans, Ivor Jones and Archie Skym) that made it the champion-ship side of the era. In 1928 Llanelli supplied seven players to the Welsh XV. [57]

At the official level, the W.R.U., itself struggling to stay afloat in the dislocated economic world in which it found itself, clung bravely to the ideal of sport as the bringer of peace and happiness, even as a sort of social educator. The founder of the Welsh Secondary Schools Union, a Rhondda headmaster, was 'determined to cultivate the right type of manhood in sport. If a boy played the game on the field, he would play the game in every affair of life'. [58] The sharpening of social conflict in the south Wales of the 1920s was viewed uneasily by the WRU's T.D. Schofield. 'Men who play football are sportsmen, and spoprtsmen are good citizens. If we could make every one in this country play football we would not have this trouble we are passing through now', declared Schofield, echoing Lucien Romier's assurance that a football team for every thousand inhabitants would solve the social problem. [59] From that stand-point, the provision of sporting facilities by the Ebbw Vale Steel Company in the early 'twenties 'to afford employees . . . an opportunity for indulging in all healthy games, social inter-course, mutual helpfulness and general recreation', is directly paralleled by the serious interest taken by several large industrial concerns in France, like Peugeot, Michelin and Renault, in acquiring extensive playing fields adjacent to their factories in the 1920s. [60]

Certainly, outside observers, especially in England and Scotland, of the Welsh rugby scene attributed Wales's dismal international showing in the 'twenties to the travails of that wider society with which Welsh rugby, uniquely in Britain and apparently to its detriment, was too closely involved. The pseudonymous 'Oval', writing in the *Rugby Football Annual* for 1927, accounted for the Welsh XV's failure of that year as 'not untypical of modern South Wales where discipline and belief in anything is at a discount'.[61] Such comment, fatuous as it was, was nevertheless irksome to a WRU which took especial care to sniff around the scent of any unwelcome political activism in rugby circles. In 1926 Pontypridd RFC, faced by liabilities of £200 and a rival rugby league side, appealed to the WRU for financial help. The WRU, in turn, was anxious to establish the social prominence of the club's leading members, especially since one of the (four) policemen in the team, P.C. Gwilym Jenkins, had reported the club secretary, Mr Berriman, to his superior for 'a most disgusting speech' at a miners' meeting during the strike. The WRU's investigators reported back that 'it was gratifying that the President [of the Pontypridd club] was Major Griffiths, vice-president W.G. Brown, agent of the Great Western Collieries, Chairman was Tom Bryant of the County Court Offices, and vice-chairman Mr Lane a retired gentleman, while the remainder of the committee were well-meaning townspeople among whom there is an electrical engineer, mechanical engineer, builder and contractor, builder and undertaker, and an insurance superintendent, the others being ordinary working men'. As for the secretary, who, it transpired, was not even at the meeting referred to by P.C. Jenkins, 'Mr Berriman had in fact been instrumental in rescuing the club from an even worse financial mess, and while he certainly holds Labour views . . . he is a most respected person in Pontypridd [and] a member of the Pontypridd section of the Miners' Federation; that is all. He is not an A.J. Cook'. This satisfied the WRU, and money was duly allocated.[62]

There is noticeably little evidence that players or supporters ever swallowed the ideological sauce with which some aspiring social engineers garnished their sport. Most, after all, played or watched rugby, as they did any other game, for its own sake rather than from any desire to further social harmony and good citizenship.[63] The fact remains that much rhetoric was expended in the late 'twenties in the cause of amateur rugby football as 'the game of the masses and classes' in the editorial columns of the south Wales press, by prominent figures in the WRU, by advocates of schoolboy rugby (it cannot be a coincidence that several schools, like Cardiff High School, Cowbridge Grammar School, and Rydal School, swung over to rugby in the 'twenties) and by social philanthropists like Geoffrey Crawshay.[64] A few exceptions like the Cambridge student, Rowe Harding, and schoolteachers like Arthur Cornish apart, Welsh teams of the mid-'twenties had a resolutely working-class appearance. Their dismal playing record was not unconnected with selectorial errors,[65] though the selectors were themselves victims of their disjointed times. But by the end of the decade, coincident with a slight economic revival, it appeared that an amalgam of manual workers and college boys was bringing better results. In 1931 Wales won the international championship for the first time since 1922, and in 1933 won at Twickenham (which opened in 1910) for the first time ever. The social complexion of the Welsh team had changed in the meantime. Consider the side of 1926: at full back was D.B. Evans, a colliery foreman, at three-quarter George Andrews, a ship's painter, Albert Stock, an electrician, Cornish and Harding, at half back Bobby Jones, a civil engineer, and Bobby Delahay, a carpenter; while the pack comprised six policemen, a miner, and a fitter's labourer.[66] Then consider the side that laid the Twickenham bogey in 1933: everyone of the backs—Vivian Jenkins, Boon, Davey, Wooller, A.H. Jones, Bowcott and Turnbull—were products of secondary school and college rugby, while even at forward, and captaining the side, was a graduate of University College, Swansea, the formidable Watcyn Thomas.

This social admixture also characterised the Welsh team that beat New Zealand in 1935. Apart from Vivian Jenkins (Llandovery and Oxford), Wooller (Rydal and Cambridge), Idwal Rees (Swansea G.S. and Cambridge), Rees-Jones (Ipswich and Oxford), Davey (Ystalyfera G.S. and Swansea), Cliff Jones (Llandovery and Cambridge) and Haydn Tanner (Gowerton G.S. and Swansea) behind, there was a Llandoverian (A.M. Rees) and Caerphilly grammar schoolboy (Eddie Watkins) in the pack alongside tinplate workers, a miner and a colliery blacksmith.[67] The heroic Welsh victory of 13-12, achieved through three superb tries and clinched by fourteen men with a last-gasp score, was hailed as a triumph for social cohesion. 'Wales is proud of this victory', applauded the *Western Mail*; 'she is particularly proud of the fact that Welsh peers and labourers—with all the intervening stratas of society—were united in cheering the Welsh team. It was a victory for Wales in a sense that probably is impossible in any other sphere'.[68]

That victory was more significant than even the self-gratifying editorial of the *Western Mail* could conceive. Though any direct correlation between the two spheres is difficult to identify, was there perhaps a symbolic affinity between a revival on the rugby field and the resurgence of morale in south Wales societ at large? The historians of the South Wales Miners Federation, 'The Fed', have recently portrayed the years between 1933 and 1935 as a period of revitalised political activity that resulted in a wresting back of lost initiatives, particularly in the control of coalfield society.[60] It appears that this stemmed from a mobilising of concern, political and extra-political, at the permanence of mass unemployment—over 20 per cent of the more than 50,000 unemployed south Wales miners had been out of work for over four years, 75 per cent for over a year, by 1934—at government inertia, and at the destructive social effect of the Means Test. In 1934 and 1935 the valleys of east Glamorgan witnessed tidal waves of mass demonstrations. Magistrates, ministers and unemployed miners marched side by side with shop assistants, Salvationists and the chamber of commerce cheek by jowl with Communists. On 27 January 1935, 300,000 marched at different places all over south Wales: 50,000 in a two-and-a-half mile procession at Mountain Ash, 20,000 at Pontypool, 60,000 marched twelve abreast in the Rhondda; there were meetings at Blackwood, Briton Ferry, Neath, even in Barry. The demonstrations were peaceful and orderly, though the next day Merthyr was the focus of a spasm of urgent violence reminiscent of 1831 when the local unemployment office was ransacked, and the government responded by scrapping its proposed new and punitive scale of unemployment benefit. This was the only time in the 1930s when extra-parliamentary pressure caused the government to back down. Parallel with this assertion of popular defiance was the reinvigoration of the Miners' Federation itself, in its numerical revival (from its all-time low of 59,000 in 1928 it was back up to 77,000 by 1934 and to 112,000 by 1936) and in its concerted campaign against 'scab' unionism. The victory of stay-down strikers (the imprisonment of several club stalwarts after the Taff-Merthyr fracas in October 1935, on top of its endemic indebtedness forced Nelson RFC into closure in 1937)[70] marked a turning-point in the coalfield's inter-war history. The retiring Feder-ation president, James Griffiths, reviewed the events of 1935 as revealing 'a new spirit of revolt amongst our people'. In the general election of that year, ten of the thirteen Labour-held coalfield seats were held by prominent Federation men. The new determination was diffused through the blood stream. In 1936 the Non-political Union was finally defeated and in 1937 a new wages agreement was reached, the first real increase since 1915.

The year 1935, then, was when south Wales announced it would not go gentle into anyone's good night. We can see why the *Western Mail* hailed the Welsh defeat of the 1935 All Blacks as 'a victory that is probably impossible in any other sphere'. Here was a successful mixing of classes on the field that seemed unattainable off it. Rugby football apparently was the vehicle of civic tranquillity, the means whereby individuals could com-municate and establish personal and social bonds that trans-cended the boundaries of class. The idea of recovery from the mid-'thirties cannot be pushed too far, of course. While the clouds of industrial depression began to lift in some depressed areas, thanks to armament and ordnance factories, unemploy-ment was in 1937 still at 56 per cent in Ferndale, 40 per cent in Pontypridd and 45.6 per cent in Merthyr. The proportion of the unemployed that could be classed as long-term still stood at 63 per cent in the Rhondda. In rugby terms, the cramping pains of the depression still twinged sharply. Rugby clubs were still buckling: Aberaman, Taibach and Cwmtwrch, as well as Nelson, went to the wall between 1934 and 1937. Star players still went north—including three internationals, W.T.H. Davies, Arthur Bassett and Sid Williams, within a few months of each other in 1939—in sufficient strength and depth of talent to enable Wales to win the Rugby League international champ-ionship in three successive seasons in the late 'thirties. But there were also glimmers of a more purposeful and confident future. Something had been salvaged from the débris of the locust years to be refashioned to suit new conditions. Welsh rugby shared this new optimism, institutionally and on the field. Only a drawn match with England denied Wales the Triple Crown in 1936, though Wales won the championship outright the next year, and shared it again in 1939.

The post-1945 economic boom brought a new prosperity, a return to high employment and a substantial rate of capital investment. Thanks to new growth points like Bridgend, a rash of government-sponsored factories, the diversification of Welsh industry and investment in the new Steel Company of Wales, the *South Wales Industrial Review* could by 1950 talk of 'a second Industrial Revolution which had transformed the economic and employment pattern in South Wales'.[71] Welsh rugby again articulated that transformation. Its infrastructure was strengthened as club facilities were improved and extended, and new progressive initiatives—like the foundation of the Welsh Youth Rugby Union in 1949—were taken in the organisation of the game in Wales.[72] With the glut of talent fore and aft, typically represented by white-collar sons of manual workers, Wales, inspired by players like Bleddyn Williams, Ken Jones, Billy Cleaver and Cliff Morgan, won the Triple Crown and championship outright in 1950 for the first time since 1911, and again in 1952.

Catalytic agents of a different sort, and a newer generation of even more amazingly gifted players, made the second golden era of Welsh rugby possible between 1969 and 1979. Increased social and geographical mobility, rising aspirations, a new affluence, a scatter of new industries, a quickening of the political tempo across a broad spectrum of affairs, a surge of Welsh awareness that took different forms and required various kinds of legislative, administrative and institutional expression[73] these galvanising factors, which were in many ways reminiscent of those that saw the 'rebirth of a nation' between 1880 and 1914 and Welsh rugby's first golden era, in aggregate terms provided the context within which the second golden era could etch itself on the public consciousness in the 1970s.[74]

The 1980s, however, constantly bring to mind uncomfortable echoes of a different period. Whatever indicators we turn to, the feeling persists that we have been here before. Given Welsh rugby's barometric inclination to register all too accurately the prevailing economic climate, it looks as if we are in for another lean time, on and off the field. [75]

(Postscript: It is not pleasant to record successful prophecy).

NOTES

* *This* article is the revised text of a lecture orginally given at a Llafur/Wales T.U.C./W.E.A. History Weekend Conference at the Polytechnic of Wales, Treforest, in April 1981. The conference theme was 'Wales out of Work'.

[1] Eugen Weber, *Peasants into Frenchmen: the modernization of rural France, 1870-1914* (London, 1977), p. 40.

[2] Kenneth O. Morgan, *Rebirth of a Nation: Wales 1880-1980* (Oxford and Cardiff, 1981), p. 123.

[3] David Smith and Gareth Williams, *Fields of Praise: the Official History of the Welsh Rugby Union, 1881-1981* (Cardiff 1980).

[4] Morgan, op. cit., pp. 123-24.

[5] Though not in New Zealand.

[6] Theodore Zeldin, *France 1848-1945: Taste and Corruption* (Oxford, 1980), p. 338.

[7] It was in 1905, inspired by Evan Roberts's revival, that Dowlais-born John Hughes (1873-1932), by then working as a clerk at the Great Western Colliery, Pontypridd, composed what has become the favourite battle-hymn of Welsh rugby crowds, 'Cwm Rhondda'. Huw Williams, *Tonau a'u Hawduron* [Hymn-tunes and their composers] (Caernarfon, 1967), p. 194.

[8] The Welsh Rugby Union was founded in 1881, the year when 'brash new Cardiff raised its merchant palace of a Coal Exchange' according to Gwyn A. Williams, *Marxism Today*, December 1981, p. 16, *The Welsh in their History* (London, 1982) p. 184. It opened for business in 1886.

[9] Rare maybe, (at least in 1981, when this was written; for more recent developments see chapter 1) but also good, e.g. Tony Mason, *Association Football and English Society, 1863-1915* (London, 1980); Richard Holt, *Sport and Society in Modern France* (London, 1981); James Walvin, *The People's Game: a social history of English football* (London, 1975). By far the most perceptive account of the development of rugby football in England remains the sociological study of Eric Dunning and Kenneth Sheard, *Barbarians, Gentlemen and Players* (Oxford, 1979), though on rugby in Wales they can be quite wrong.

[10] W.E. Minchinton, 'The Evolution of the Regional Economy' in G. Manners (ed.), *South Wales in the Sixties* (Oxford, 1964), p. 21; Smith and Williams, op. cit., pp. 204-6.

[11] Ibid., pp. 201-38.

[12] Unless stated otherwise, the figures for industrial production, unemployment rates, etc., which I have assembled to provide the framework for this article are derived from Morgan, op. cit., especially pp. 210-40, which I have quarried ruthlessly.

[13] M.J. Daunton, *Coal Metropolis: Cardiff, 1870-1914* (Leicester, 1977), p. 226.

[14] Minchinton, loc. cit. Another mine of information for the economic history of south Wales in this period is Colin Baber and Dennis Thomas, 'The Glamorgan Economy, 1914-45', in A.H. John and Glanmor Williams (eds.), *Glamorgan County History, vol, v, Industrial Glamorgan* (Cardiff, 1980), pp. 519-79.

[15] David Smith, 'Leaders and Led' in K.S. Hopkins (ed.), *Rhondda Past and Future* (Rhondda, 1974), p. 50.

[16] J.W. England in Graham Humphreys, *Industrial Britain: South Wales* (Newton Abbot, 1972), p. 29. Moreover 'between 1921 and 1937, 50% of the total number leaving [Glamorgan] were in the 15-29 age group'. Baber and Thomas, op. cit., p. 541.

[17] Morgan, op. cit., p. 229; Hywel Francis and David Smith, *The Fed: a history of the South Wales Miners in the Twentieth Century* (London, 1980), p. 50, n. 111; D. Ben Rees, *Chapels in the Valley* (Wirral, 1975), ch. 4.

[18] A valuable source for the music scene, eisteddfodic and otherwise, in Wales between the wars is the bilingual *Y Cerddor* [The Musician], published at bi-monthly, sometimes monthly intervals: 1920-1932 (Wrexham), 1932-1939 (Cardiff).

[19] W(elsh) R(ugby) U(nion) minutes, 12 May 1927.

[20] Ibid., 20 December 1926.

[21] Ibid., 19 May 1927.

[22] *Western Mail*, 27 March 1928, 11 December 1929.

[23] *Welsh Rugby* [*Magazine*], January 1969, p. 35.

[24] Ibid., December 1965, p. 9.

[25] Denis Gane (ed.), *Cwmbran R.F.C.: One Hundred Years of Rugby* (Cwmbran, 180), p. 29. See pp. 232-3 below.

[26] *Merthyr Express*, 31 August, 1929.

[27] *Western Mail*, 8 January 1932; *Welsh Rugby*, April 1972, pp. 11-12.

[28] John Musselwhite, *The Butcher Boys of Donkey Island: an historical profile of Penarth R.F.C.* (Penarth, 1980), pp. 56-64, photo p. 75; *Welsh Rugby*, July 1975, pp. 33-35 (Haverfordwest); ibid., May 1973, p. 19 (Pembroke Dock) In Barry, 'things began to go badly wrong from the 1921-22 season'. M.G. Bassett, *Games of Interchanging Praise* (Barry, 1988) p. 32.

[29] Gwyn Nicholls, like several others of that totemic team of 1905, was not Welsh-born. Nicholls came from Gloucestershire, H.B. Winfield from Nottingham, A.F. Harding from Lincolnshire. The implications of massive immigration into late-nineteenth-century Wales for the rapid growth, cos-

mopolitanism, and self-confident innovativeness of Welsh rugby are discussed in Smith and Williams, op. cit., pp. 28-119 *passim*.

[30] *Torquay Athletic R.F.C., 1875-1975* (Torquay, 1975), pp. 29-39.

[31] W.R.U. minutes, 24 January 1929; *Weston-Super-Mare R.F.C., 1875-1975* (Weston, 1975), pp. 44-50. The U.A.U. were the Universities Athletic Union.

[32] Morgan, op. cit., p. 231.

[33] Barbara M. Evans, *Blaina Rugby Football Club, 1875-1976* (Risca, 1976), p. 52.

[34] Gwyn Thomas, *The Subsidence Factor* (University College, Cardiff, 1979 Gwyn Jones Lecture), p. 15.

[35] On rugby league in south Wales in this period, see Smith and Williams, op. cit., pp. 225-27, 294-97.

[36] *Western Mail*, 18 January 1932.

[37] *Western Mail*, 16 January 1933; *Neath Guardian*, 20 January 1933.

[38] Geraint H. Jenkins, *Cewri'r Beldroed yng Nghymru* [Giants of Welsh Soccer] (Llandybie, 1977), pp. 49-52.

[39] *Rhondda Gazette*, 14 August 1926 (Cwmparc A.F.C.); 7 April 1928 (Mid-Rhondda A.F.C.).

[40] Peter Corrigan, *100 Years of Welsh Soccer* (Cardiff, 1976), ch. 7.

[41] R. Page Arnot, *South Wales Miners* (London, 1967), p. 182; David Smith, 'The Struggle against Company Unionism in the South Wales Coalfield, 1926-1939', *Welsh History Review*, , vol. 6, no. 3 (June 1973), p. 370. Lindsay's concept of 'sedition' was a flexible one, see Deian Hopkin, 'Patriots and Pacifists in Wales, 1914-1918: the case of Capt. Lionel Lindsay and the Rev. T.E. Nicholas', *Llafur*, 1, No. 3 (May 1974), 27-41.

[42] D.E. Davies, *Cardiff Rugby Club, History and Statistics, 1876-1975* (Cardiff, 1975), pp. 197-98.

[43] Hywel Francis, 'The Anthracite Strike and the disturbances of 1925', *Llafur*, 1, No. 2 (May 1973), 15-28.

[44] Ibid., p. 19.

[45] Francis and Smith, op. cit., pp. 60-62.

[46] Tony Lewis, *The Mules: a history of Kenfig Hill R.F.C.* (Pyle, 1973), p. 24.

[47] Francis and Smith, op. cit., pp. 135-36.

[48] *Western Mail*, 31 October 1929.

[49] For these and other examples of the moral legitimacy of popular direct action in pre-industrial and industrial society, see N.Z. Davis 'The Rites of Violence: Religious Riot in Sixteenth Century France', *Past and Present*, 59 (May 1973), 51-91; John Walter and Keith Wrightson, 'Dearth and the Social Order in Early Modern England', ibid., 71 (May 1976), 22-43, especially 32; E.P. Thompson, 'The Moral Economy of the English Crowd in the Eighteenth Century', ibid., 50 (February 1971), 76-136; D.J.V. Jones, *Before Rebecca* (London, 1974), especially pp. 182-205; G.A. Williams in Glanmor Williams (ed.), *Merthyr Politics* (Cardiff, 1966), pp. 12-20; D. Smith, 'Tonypandy 1910: Definitions of Community', *Past and Present*, 87 (May 1980), 158-84; G. Rudé, *The Crowd in the French Revolution* (London, 1959), *The Crowd in History* (New York, 1974), and *Ideology and Popular Protest* (London, 1980).

⁵⁰ *Western Mail*, 5 October 1926.

⁵¹ Stanley Owen, *Vardre United R.F.C., 1921-1971* (Clydach, 1971), pp. 9-10.

⁵² Francis and Smith, op. cit., photograph and caption between pp. 332-33.

⁵³ *Tylorstown Rugby Football Club 1903-1978* (Tylorstown, 1978), p. 11.

⁵⁴ *South Wales Echo*, 23 January 1933; *Penygraig R.F.C.: 100 Years of Valley Rugby, 1877-1977* (Penygraig, 1977), p. 15.

⁵⁵ Gwyn Thomas, *A Welsh Eye* (London, 1964), p. 12.

⁵⁶ Francis and Smith, op. cit., p. 248.

⁵⁷ On the fortunes, playing and otherwise, of Llanelli in the twenties, see Smith and Williams, op. cit., pp. 234-238, and Gareth Hughes, *The Scarlets* (Llanelli, 1986), pp. 99-145.

⁵⁸ *Western Mail*, 19 April 1926. The Rhondda headmaster was R.D. Chalke of Porth Secondary School. For the ideals that inspired the founding of the Welsh Secondary Schools Rugby Union, see *South Wales News*, 10 June 1923.

⁵⁹ *Western Mail*, 30 September 1926. For Schofield, see Smith and Williams, op. cit., pp. 215-16; W.A.D. Lawrie, *The History of Bridgend Rugby Football Club: the First 100 Years* (Bridgend, 1979), pp. 10-12. Romier quoted in E. Weber, 'Gymnastics and Sports in fin-de-siècle France', *American Historical Review*, 76 (February 1971), 29.

⁶⁰ Arthur Gray-Jones, *A History of Ebbw Vale* (Risca, 1976), p. 192; Holt, *Sport and Society in Modern France*, p. 203. For factory sport and company recreation in England, see S.G. Jones, *Workers at Play* (London, 1986), pp. 69-71.

⁶¹ *Rugby Football Annual, 1927-1928* (London, 1927), p. 53.

⁶² W.R.U. minutes, 2 September 1926.

⁶³ Cf., 'Then [1905] and later, most of the Welsh were content to have it that way. They rejoiced in their rugby skills, made no protest, and asked few questions', Morgan, op. cit., p. 134.

⁶⁴ *Western Mail*, 20 January 1930 (editorial), 14 October 1929 (for the view expressed by W.R.U. President, Horace Lyne). For Captain Crawshay (1892-1954), see *Western Mail*, 9 November 1954, *The Times*, 9 November 1954, 20 November 1954.

⁶⁵ Smith and Williams, op. cit., pp. 201-95 *passim*. For the acerbic views of a contemporary player, see Rowe Harding, *Rugby Reminiscences and Opinions* (London, 1929).

⁶⁶ Information obtained from match programme, *Wales v. England, Cardiff Arms Park, 16 January 1926*.

⁶⁷ Match programme, *Wales v. New Zealand, Cardiff Arms Park, 21 December 1935*.

⁶⁸ *Western Mail*, 23 December 1935.

⁶⁹ It will be readily apparent how much I have relied for this paragraph on Francis and Smith, op. cit., pp. 244.

⁷⁰ *Welsh Rugby*, September 1969, p. 43.

⁷¹ Morgan, op. cit., p. 309. See also Brinley Thomas, *The Welsh Economy* (Cardiff, 1972) pp. 30-50.

[72] These aspects are discussed more fully in Smith and Williams, op. cit., pp. 314-16, 329-33.

[73] Morgan, op. cit., ch. 13, 'Nationalism and Devolution'.

[74] These interconnections are followed through in Smith and Williams, op. cit., pp. 373-76, 415-18, 435-40.

[75] In September 1982, the Welsh jobless figure stood at over 185,611 or 17.4 per cent of the working population, the highest level since 1938. As Welsh rugby stumbled into its second century, it was symbolic that the worst unemployment blackspot should be Lampeter (24.2 per cent), where rugby was first played in Wales over a hundred years before. See *Western Mail* 23 September 1982; D.T.W. Price, *A History of St David's College Lampeter, vol. 1: to 1898* (Cardiff, 1977), pp. 152-53.

ENWOGION O FRI

1
GEORGE NEPIA (1905-86)

Mae'n go anghyffredin i unrhyw chwaraewr gael ei ystyried y gorau yn y byd yn ei safle pan fo'n 19 oed. Dyna a ddigwyddodd i George Nepia, y Maori o Seland Newydd. Mae'r wlad honno wedi cynhyrchu nifer o gefnwyr enwog dros y blynyddoedd, ceidwaid eu llinell a fedrai gicio gôl o unrhyw bellter ac o unrhyw gyfeiriad; gwŷr fel Bob Scott a Don Clarke. Ond chwaraeodd George Nepia, hefyd, fel unig gefnwr carfan na chafodd mo'i churo, sef Crysau Duon 1924 ym Mhrydain. Fe chwaraeodd Nepia ym mhob gêm ar y daith, 30 gêm o'r bron, yn aml ddwywaith yr wythnos, dros bedwar mis. Gwisgodd Nepia'r crys du gyda'r rhedynen wen 46 gwaith i gyd a 38 o'r troeon hynny yn gyfres ddi-fwlch, record sy'n debyg o sefyll am byth.

Ganed George Nepia yn Wairoa ar 25 Ebrill 1905. Blwyddyn arbennig oedd honno ym mherthynas Seland Newydd â Chymru, oherwydd buddugoliaeth Cymru o un cais i ddim ar Barc yr Arfau oedd unig golled y Crysau Duon ar eu taith 32 gêm ym Mhrydain yn 1905. Byddai Nepia ymhlith y Crysau Duon nesaf i ymweld â Chymru a melys fyddai'r dial am yr hyn a ystyrid yn anghyfiawnder yn 1905. Tybiai pob Selandwr gwerth ei halen fod cais digon teg wedi ei wrthod gan y dyfarnwr y diwrnod hwnnw; dyna a ddysgodd George Nepia o'r crud. Un o amcanion ei fywyd fyddai unioni'r cam â wnaed yng Nghaerdydd yn 1905; ac fe wnaeth.

Ni chafodd George Nepia blentyndod esmwyth. Trigai ei rieni ar wahân i'w gilydd ac yn ôl arfer y Maoris, magwyd George a phedwar cefnder gan eu mam-gu. Aeth i ysgol Wairoa ond pwysicach nag unrhyw addysg ffurfiol a gafodd yno oedd y cae y tu ôl i'r ysgol lle y chwaraeai ddydd a nos. Yno, hefyd, y gwyliai'r tîm lleol. Roedd y crwt, Nepia, yn edmygydd mawr o gefnwr o'r enw Kingi Waniata, yn arbennig ar ôl iddo'i weld mewn un gêm bwysig yn cicio pedair gôl adlam mewn deng munud.

Pan oedd yn wyth oed, aeth George i fyw gyda'i dad yn Nuhaka, i'r dwyrain o Wairoa. Cosbid ef yn aml yn ysgol y Maoris yno am gyrraedd yn hwyr ar ôl helpu ar y fferm ond nid oedd pall ar ei awydd i gicio pêl rygbi. Roedd y Rhyfel Mawr wedi cychwyn pan chwaraeodd George ei gêm gyntaf o bwys, ar yr asgell dros ysgol Nuhaka. Mae'n syn meddwl, o gofio'i ddewrder anhygoel yn ddiweddarach, fod George yn gymeriad ofnus y pryd hwnnw. Treuliodd y gêm gyntaf honno ar encilion y chwarae, yn cadw o ffordd y bêl a'i wrthwynebydd, nes i'w dad ddod i'r cae a rhoi bonclust iddo am fod mor ddiniwed. Mewn gêm arall ychydig wedi hynny, hyrddiwyd George yn bendramwnwgl i'r ddaear ac ar ôl iddo ddod ato'i hun, er bod pob asgwrn yn ei gorff yn gwingo, penderfynodd fynd yn syth yn ôl i ganol y chwarae a thaclo fel corwynt. Cyn bo hir, roedd George Nepia yn un o'r taclwyr mwyaf cadarn ac effeithiol a welwyd erioed.

Y gŵr a ddysgodd iddo dechneg taclo ('cadw dy lygaid ar agor') a phob agwedd arall ar chwarae, oedd ei hyfforddwr yng Ngholeg Amaethyddol Maori Hawke's Bay, lle'r aeth yn 1921. Gan Elder Moses (henadur gyda'r Mormoniaid oedd pob athro yno) y dysgodd George sut i roi tro ar y bêl wrth ei chicio, i wneud iddi hedfan yn bellach a chreu cryn anhawster i'r sawl a fyddai'n ceisio'i dal. Erbyn ei drydedd flwyddyn yn y coleg, gallai gicio'r bêl i ddisgyn ar hances drigain metr i ffwrdd, ffrwyth oriau, onid misoedd a blynyddoedd o ymarfer dygn, dyfal.

Roedd George yn awr yn chwarae fel canolwr dros dalaith Hawke's Bay mewn pencampwriaeth genedlaethol. Yn 1923 fe'i dewiswyd i deithio gyda Maoris y wlad i Awstralia ond gwrthododd ei brifathro ei ganiatâd oherwydd, yn ei farn ef, roedd George, a bwysai 82 kilo a hanner ac a fesurai 1.75 metr o daldra, yn rhy ifanc am nad oedd ond deunaw oed.

Y flwyddyn ganlynol, 1924, roedd disgwyl mawr ledled dwy ynys Seland Newydd am y dewis ar gyfer y daith fawr i Brydain. Chwaraeodd George ei gêm gyntaf oll fel cefnwr yn un o'r profion cynnar. Ceid ef allan o'i safle'n aml am nad oedd yn gyfarwydd â chwarae yn y canol ond carlamai'n ôl i achub ac er gwaethaf cael ei daclo, llwyddai i ddanfon y bêl ddeugain metr yn ôl i lawr y cae. Cadwodd ei le trwy'r profion ac enillodd le yn y tîm.

Mae gorchestion Crysau Duon diguro 1924, yr Anorchfygedigion (yr 'Invincibles') yn hen hanes erbyn hyn. Ymadawsant â Wellington ar 29 Gorffennaf, a chyrraedd yn ôl yno ar 17 Mawrth 1925. Gydag olwyr athrylithgar fel Mark Nicholls a Bert Cooke (a hanai o Lanelli) a chewri deallus fel y ddau frawd Brownlie yn y pac, enillasant bob un o'u 30 gêm, gan sgorio 721 o bwyntiau a 175 cais. Er mai cael a chael oedd hi ar y Strade (8-3), yr uchafbwynt oedd curo Cymru 19-0 yn Abertawe, lle'r enillodd Nepia fanllefau o gymeradwyaeth gan y dorf o 50,000 am ei ffordd ddi-feth o blicio'r bêl o flaenau traed pac Cymru ar ruthr a chicio am yr ystlys mewn un symudiad. Sleifiai o ochr i ochr y tu ôl i'w dîm fel panther mewn caets. Ef yn aml oedd yr unig un a safai rhwng y Cymry a'r llinell gais ond symudai â sicrwydd cath a thaclodd yn arwrol; dial melys am 'gamwedd' 1905.

Os bu Nepia yn ffefryn yng Nghymru, cafodd ei eilunaddoli ar ôl cyrraedd adref, yn arbennig gan genedl y Maoris. Yn un o'r derbyniadau croeso'n ôl, cyfarfu Nepia â'i ddarpar wraig a phriodasant ym Mai 1926. Dim on 21 oed yr oedd, a chanddo flynyddoedd o rygbi o'i flaen. Roedd disgwyl mawr i'w weld eilwaith ym Mhrydain y flwyddyn honno ond trwy falais rhywrai neu'i gilydd, hysbyswyd y pwyllgor dewis na fynnai Nepia deithio. Celwydd noeth oedd hyn ond cafodd gyfle i wynebu nifer o'r chwaraewyr y byddai wedi cwrdd â nhw yn 1926 bedair blynedd yn ddiweddarach, pan ymwelodd y Llewod Prydeinig â Seland Newydd. Nepia oedd cefnwr y Crysau Duon yn y pedair gêm brawf a chapten tîm y Maoris yn ogystal.

Gydol ei yrfa, roedd George Nepia yn ysbrydoliaeth i rygbi'r Maoris. Bu'n gapten arnynt ar sawl taith i Awstralia, yn ogystal ag yn erbyn y Llewod ond oherwydd lliw ei groen nid ystyriwyd ef, na'r un Maori arall, ar gyfer taith y Crysau Duon i Dde Affrica yn 1927. Teimlodd yr anghyfiawnder yma i'r byw a bu erioed yn feirniad hallt o agwedd sarhaus gwlad y Springbok.

Bu'n gapten y Maoris yn Awstralia yn 1935, pan enillwyd naw o'r un gêm ar ddeg a sgoriodd cyfanswm o 256 o bwyntiau, sef cyfartaledd o 23 y gêm. Yna, a'r dirwasgiad economaidd byd eang yn gwthio'i fferm i ddyledion cynyddol, yn 1935 derbyniodd £500 i ymuno â chlwb rygbi proffesiynol Streatham and Mitcham yn Llundain. Ymhen y flwyddyn aeth y clwb i drafferthion ariannol gan fethu talu cyflogau ei chwaraewyr, a symudodd Nepia i Halifax. Erbyn haf 1937, roedd yn ôl yn Seland Newydd. Chwaraeodd rygbi proffesiynol am rai misoedd gyda thîm yn Auckland a chynrychiolai'r Maoris yn erbyn y Kangaroos (tîm proffesiynol Awstralia). Yn 1938, rhoes ei esgidiau i gadw am y tro olaf. Bu farw ar 27 Awst 1986, ond deil cyfaredd arbennig i berthyn i'r enw George Nepia, y Maori o gefnwr digymar.

2
BLEDDYN WILLIAMS

Cyfrifir Bleddyn Williams y canolwr mwyaf clasurol a chaboledig erioed i chwarae dros Gymru ac un o'r anfarwolion yn holl hanes rygbi. Mae hyn yn syndod ar un olwg oherwydd dioddefodd wahanol anafiadau nad oeddynt byth yn ddifrifol ond a oedd eto'n ddigon i gwtogi ar nifer ei ymddangosiadau yn y crys coch i ddwy ar hugain, allan o tua deugain posibl, cyn iddo ymddeol yn 1955.

Ganed Bleddyn Llewellyn Williams yn Ffynnon-taf ar 22 Chwefror 1923. Deuai ei fam o Went ond un o Fro Morgannwg oedd ei dad, trimiwr glo yn nociau Caerdydd. Roedd Bleddyn yn un o deulu niferus o frodyr a phob un ohonynt â gallu uwch na'r cyffredin ar y maes rygbi. O'r wyth brawd, bu Bleddyn a Lloyd yn gapteniaid yn eu tro ar Gaerdydd a Chymru a rhyngddynt fe wisgodd y chwech arall, Gwyn, Vaughan, Brinley, Cennydd, Elwyn a Tony, ddu a glas clwb Caerdydd dros gyfnod yn ymestyn o 1934 hyd 1973, record nad yw'r un teulu arall yn debyg o'i churo.

Ar ôl addysg gynnar yn ysgol Ffynnon-taf a datblygu digon dan ddylanwad ei athro chwaraeon, Del Harries, i ennill cap bechgyn Cymru dan bymtheg oed, enillodd Bleddyn ysgoloriaeth i ysgol breswyl Rydal Mount, ym Mae Colwyn yng ngogledd Cymru. Yr un a oedd yn gyfrifol am y trobwynt yma yn ei fywyd oedd cyn-ddisgybl o Rydal, Wilfred Wooller, a oedd y pryd hwnnw yn chwarae dros Gaerdydd a Chymru. Roedd Wooller wedi sylwi ar addewid Bleddyn wrth ei weld yn chwarae dros ysgolion Caerdydd ac awgrymodd i'w gynbrifathro yn Rydal, y Parchedig A.J. Costain, y byddai dawn rygbi Bleddyn Williams yn gaffaeliad i'r ysgol. Rhwng 1937 a 1941, felly, bu'r crwt o Gwm Taf ymhlith disgyblion Rydal, yn perffeithio'i sgiliau rygbi dan lygad craff y Parchedig Costain a'r athro chwaraeon, Donald Boumphrey. Fel maswr y chwaraeai y pryd hwnnw ond pan ymunodd â'r Llu Awyr yn ystod dyddiau blin yr Ail Ryfel Byd yn 1941, rhaid oedd iddo symud i'r canol, gan mai'r enwog W.T.H. (Willie) Davies a lenwai safle'r maswr yn yr Awyrlu y pryd hwnnw. Roedd Willie Davies, Abertawe a Chymru gynt, wedi troi at rygbi'r Gynghrair er 1939, ond yn ystod y rhyfel llaciwyd y rheolau i ganiatáu cyd-chwarae rhwng amaturiaid a chwaraewyr proffesiynol, a manteisiodd Bleddyn ar gwmni cewri gêm y gynghrair fel Gus Risman ac Alan Edwards i chwarae rygbi gorau ei fywyd, rygbi agored, ymosodol a chyflym.

Yn ystod y rhyfel tyrrodd cefnogwyr i weld gemau rhyngwladol y lluoedd arfog a sgoriodd Bleddyn dri chais yn erbyn Lloegr yng Nghaerloyw yn 1943. Pan ddaeth heddwch ymunodd â Chlwb Caerdydd, a chyfrannu at y cyfnod mwyaf llwyddiannus yn hanes y clwb. Diolch i ddisgleirdeb sêr fel Haydn Tanner, Jack Matthews, Billy Cleaver a Bleddyn ei hun, enillwyd 140 gêm o 166 mewn pedwar tymor (1945-1949). Sgoriodd Bleddyn 30 cais yn y tymor cyntaf wedi'r rhyfel ac yn 1947-8, pan enillodd clwb Parc yr Arfau 39 gêm o 41, sefydlodd Bleddyn record a saif hyd heddiw o 41 cais mewn tymor.

Ar y cae rhyngwladol, enillodd ei gap cyntaf yn erbyn Lloegr yn Ionawr 1947 fel maswr. Cafodd brynhawn anesmwyth oherwydd anaf i'w goes yn y munudau cyntaf, ac o hynny ymlaen fel canolwr chwith yr ymddangosodd dros ei wlad. Un cydnerth, cyhyrog ydoedd, gyda morddwydydd fel dau foncyff. Roedd yn gryf a thrwm a chyfrannai hyn at ei gadernid fel taclwr. Roedd sglein ar bopeth a wnâi. Fel y gweddai i gynfaswr, gallai gicio'n effeithiol â'i ddwy droed ac roedd yn feistr ar y gic fach bwt ymlaen ar gyfer ei asgellwyr. Ond yr hyn a'i anfarwolodd oedd ei allu i ochrgamu, math o ledgamu a olygai

Bleddyn Williams.

drosglwyddo pwysau'r corff o'r naill goes i'r llall yn sydyn i newid cyfeiriad. Yn aml gwelid amddiffynnydd yn cael ei adael yn hurt a chegrwth yng nghanol y cae ar ôl i Bleddyn ei ddrysu â chlasur o jinc. Wrth ymosod, tuedda rhai canolwyr golli cyswllt â'u hasgellwyr ond ni ellid byth gyhuddo Bleddyn Williams o hyn. Roedd yn gwbl anhunanol a chanddo'r gallu i amseru ei bàs i'w asgellwr i'r hanner eiliad ceinaf, fel bod hwnnw'n derbyn y bêl gyda lle i symud a chyfle i sgorio.

Cyfrannodd Bleddyn a chlwb Caerdydd yn sylweddol at lwyddiannau'r tîm Cymreig. Roedd gan y du a glas un ar ddeg o'u haelodau ym mhymtheg Cymru yn 1948. Er mai Iwerddon a gipiodd y Goron Driphlyg y flwyddyn honno, sgoriodd Bleddyn gais gwych odiaeth yn eu herbyn yn Belfast, fel y gwnaethai yn erbyn Yr Alban fis ynghynt. Câi hwyl arbennig yn erbyn y Sgotiaid. Rhedodd yn gelfydd trwyddynt i sgorio yn y fuddugoliaeth ysgubol yn Murrayfield o 22 pwynt i 8 yn 1947 ac ochrgamodd yn drydanol heibio i dri gwrthwynebydd ar ei ffordd i'r lein eto yng Nghaeredin yn 1949. Yn 1953, ar yr un cae, pan oedd yn gapten Cymru, sgoriodd ddau gais arbennig, er derbyn y bêl y ddau dro dros ugain metr o'r llinell, pan orfu Cymru 12-0.

Ni chollodd Cymru yn ystod y pum gwaith y bu Bleddyn yn gapten arni ond oherwydd mân anafiadau prin oedd ei gyfraniad i'r ddwy Goron Driphlyg a enillodd Cymru yn 1950 a 1952 dan arweiniad John Gwilliam. Roedd Prydain gyfan yn ddiolchgar bod Bleddyn wedi adfer ei ffitrwydd erbyn haf 1950, pan aeth i Awstralia a Seland Newydd fel is-gapten y Llewod. Er colli'r gyfres yn erbyn y Crysau Duon, cafodd Bleddyn daith dra llwyddiannus, gan arwain y Llewod mewn tair gêm brawf. Barn y Springboks ar sail yr hyn a welsant yng ngwledydd Prydain yn 1951-2 oedd mai ef oedd y canolwr gorau yn y byd. Er i Gymru golli 6-3 iddynt trwy gicio ymaith y meddiant rhagorol a enillwyd gan Roy John yn y leiniau, sgoriodd Bleddyn gais campus yn y munudau olaf ar ôl sisyrnu'n ddeheuig â'i gydganolwr Malcolm Thomas.

Blwyddyn fawr Bleddyn Williams oedd 1953, pan oedd y Crysau Duon ar eu pedwaredd daith ym Mhrydain. Dim ond dwy gêm a gollwyd ganddynt ac ar Barc yr Arfau y bu'r ddwy, unwaith yn erbyn Caerdydd (a Cliff Morgan ar ei uchelfannau) ac yna ym mis Rhagfyr yn erbyn Cymru. Bleddyn oedd y capten

buddugol y ddau dro. Os oedd Cymru yn ffodus i ennill y gêm
ryngwladol, 13-8 a Clem Thomas yn trawsgicio'n dyngedfennol
i Ken Jones groesi wrth y pyst, nid oedd unrhyw gwestiwn nad
arweiniad ysbrydoledig Bleddyn, ar ôl cynllunio manwl ac
astudiaeth drwyadl o gryfderau a gwendidau'r gwrthwynebwyr
oedd yn bennaf cyfrifol am fuddugoliaeth Caerdydd o 8 pwynt i
3 ar 21 Tachwedd 1953.

Gwisgodd Bleddyn y crys coch am y tro olaf yn erbyn Lloegr
yn Ionawr 1955 a chwaraeodd ei gêm olaf dros Gaerdydd yn
erbyn Llanelli ar Galan Mai yr un flwyddyn. Erbyn hyn, roedd
wedi sgorio 185 cais dros ei glwb, saith dros ei wlad a thri ar ddeg
dros y Llewod. Ond yn fwy na hynny, trwy ei chwarae clasurol a
gorffenedig gosododd safon o berffeithrwydd nad oes yr un
canolwr arall yn unman eto wedi llwyddo i ddod o fewn
cyrraedd iddi.

3

LUCIEN MIAS

Yn 1959, enillodd Ffrainc bencampwriaeth y pum gwlad (sef
gwledydd Prydain a Ffrainc) am y tro cyntaf yn ei hanes. Er y
flwyddyn honno, dim ond Cymru sydd wedi cipio'r bencampwriaeth fwy o weithiau. Ffrainc, erbyn heddiw, yw'r cryfaf
ymhlith pwerau rygbi Ewrop. Mae'n syn cofio, felly, mai dim
ond yn niwedd y pumdegau y peidiodd â bod yn gymdoges
dlawd rygbi. Os gellir priodoli'r chwyldro a ddigwyddodd yn
hanes rygbi Ffrainc i un dyn yn arbennig, Lucien Mias yw'r dyn
hwnnw.

Ym mlynyddoedd olaf y ganrif ddiwethaf y daeth rygbi i
Ffrainc, pan daenwyd gwybodaeth am y gêm gan wŷr busnes a
myfyrwyr o Brydain. Bu clybiau fel Rosslyn Park ac Abertawe
yn teithio yno yn nawdegau'r ganrif ond dim ond yn 1906 y
chwaraeodd y Ffrancwyr eu gêm bencampwriaeth gyntaf yn
erbyn Lloegr (a cholli 35-8). Yn 1908 y bu'r ornest gyntaf â
Chymru a chollodd Ffrainc y gêm honno, yng Nghaerdydd, 36-
4. Am yr ugain mlynedd nesaf, dyma'r fath o grasfa y gallai
Ffrainc ei disgwyl gan wledydd Prydain. Hyd yn oed ym
mlynyddoedd llwm y dauddegau, a Chymru'n colli'n rheolaidd

i'r tair gwlad Brydeinig arall, roedd y fuddugoliaeth arferol dros Ffrainc yn wobr gysur. Mae'n wir i'r Ffrancwyr guro Cymru am y tro cyntaf erioed (8-3) yn Paris yn 1928, ond buan y daethant yn gocyn hitio unwaith eto. Fe'u chwalwyd yn Abertawe yn 1931 o 35 pwynt i 3.

Erbyn hyn, roedd poblogrwydd y bêl hirgron yn Ffrainc wedi cynyddu'n ddirfawr a'r sêl drosti yn arbennig o frwd yn y de-orllewin; yn rhy frwd, oherwydd am weddill y tridegau ni chyfarfu yr un o dimau Prydain â Ffrainc. Esgymunwyd hi o'r bencampwriaeth oherwydd llygredd ac annisgyblaeth y gêm yn Ffrainc, lle'r oedd y rheolau amatur yn cael eu tramgwyddo a'r chwarae'n aml yn frwnt ac yn orgorfforol. Adferwyd y berthynas ar ôl yr Ail Ryfel Byd a buan y gwelwyd bod y Ffranc-wyr (a gurodd Cymru deirgwaith rhwng 1947 a 1951) bellach yn bygwth herio meistrolaeth draddodiadol gwledydd Prydain. Yn 1951, curodd Ffrainc nid yn unig Gymru (8-3) ond hefyd Yr Alban (14-12) a Lloegr (11-3) am y tro cyntaf erioed yn Twicken-ham. Un o aelodau pymtheg Ffrainc y tymor hwnnw oedd hwrdd o ail reng, dros ddau fetr o daldra a 15 stôn 3 phwys (96.59 kilo) o bwysau. Ei enw oedd Lucien Mias.

Ganed Lucien Mias yn Sant-Germain de Calberte yn nhalaith Lozere yn ne Ffrainc ar 28 Medi 1930. Cydiodd mewn pêl rygbi am y tro cyntaf yn ei ysgol uwchradd yn Narbonne yn ddeuddeg oed a daliodd i chwarae'r gêm wrth gael ei hyfforddi i fod yn athro mewn coleg addysg. Fel nifer o chwaraewyr rhyngwladol Ffrainc yn y pumdegau a'r chwedegau roedd ei hoffter o bêl-fasged yn fodd iddo ddysgu symud yn gyflym, sut i drin a thrafod y bêl a sut i basio'n uchel ond yn gywir. O'u haddasu i'r bêl hirgron roedd y medrau yma o fantais fawr ar y cae rygbi ac enillodd Mias ei gap cyntaf yn erbyn Lloegr yn 1951. Am y tri thymor nesaf roedd yn aelod sefydlog o'r tîm cenedlaethol, gan ennill 15 cap rhwng 1951 a 1954. Yna trodd oddi wrth ddysgu at feddygaeth a thra daliai i chwarae dros ei glwb, Mazamet, ciliodd o'r llwyfan cenedlaethol i ganolbwyntio ar ei efrydiau meddygol. Ond ni fedrai ddileu o'i gof y gosfa (25-3) a roddodd De Affrica i Ffrainc yn Paris yn 1952 a chyfraniad blaenwyr y Springboks i'r fuddugoliaeth honno. Yr oedd gwers yno i'w dysgu.

Lucien Mias yn arwain trwy esiampl.

Am y pedair blynedd nesaf (1954-58) canolbwyntiodd Mias ar sut i ffrwyno brwdfrydedd, harnesio gwylltineb a gwella arddull y gêm Ffrengig. Fe'i trwythodd ei hun yn nhacteg a thechneg y chwarae. Fel ernes o'i ymroddiad, collodd dair stôn (19 kilo) o bwysau. Pan ddychwelodd i dîm Ffrainc yn 1958, cafodd gyfle i roddi ei syniadau ar waith ar lefel genedlaethol. Y canlyniad oedd ysgwyd y gêm i'w seiliau. Diolch i Mias, 'le Dr. Pack', fel yr adwaenid ef, trowyd syniadau am y gêm wyneb i waered. Lle gynt roedd y Ffrancwyr yn bymtheg unigolyn yn hytrach na thîm unedig ac yn chwarae'n fyrbwyll, yn esgeulus ac yn brin o grebwyll tactegol, gwelwyd nawr ôl meddwl dwfn, rhagbaratoi manwl a'r medr yn y sgiliau newydd a bwysleisid gymaint gan Mias yn chwyldroi eu chwarae. Gwelwyd y blaenwyr, mulod ufudd y gêm Brydeinig, yn cychwyn ac yn gorffen ymosodiadau, yn rhedeg ac yn trafod y bêl fel olwyr. Dan arweiniad Mias, dyfeisiwyd toreth o gynlluniau cyfrwys, fel 'pilio' o'r leiniau a 'chorddi' o reng ôl y sgrym, pryd y câi'r bêl ei throsglwyddo o law i law fel cadwyn yn datod nes y deuai bwlch i glamp o flaenasgellwr cyflym fel Celaya neu Moncla fwrw drwyddo. Amcan y symudiadau hyn oedd tynnu i mewn gymaint o wrthwynebwyr ag oedd yn bosibl yn agos i'r chwarae gosod, cyn rhyddhau'r bêl i olwyr ysgafndroed fel y brodyr Boniface, Jackie Bouquet, Dupuy a Rancoule. Dull arall a feddai Mias i ddrysu'r gelyn oedd i neidwyr yr ail reng, fel Bernard Mommejat neu Mias ei hun, newid lle byth a hefyd yn y leiniau.

Gwelwyd dwyn ffrwyth y meddwl hir a dwys yma am bosibiliadau technegol y gêm ar brynhawn o Fawrth 1958, pan enillodd Ffrainc ei buddugoliaeth gyntaf ar Barc yr Arfau o 16 pwynt i 6. Am y pedair blynedd nesaf, roedd Ffrainc ar ben y bencampwriaeth a dim ond dwywaith yn ystod y chwedegau yr enillodd Cymru yn eu herbyn. Rhwng 1959 a 1971 roedd y Stade Colombes yn Paris yn fynwent i obeithion disgleiriaf y crysau coch a deil i fod yn anodd tu hwnt ennill yn y Parc des Princes.

1958 oedd blwyddyn y chwyldro yn rygbi Ffrainc. Yr haf hwnnw, teithiodd y tîm cenedlaethol i Dde Affrica. Doedd neb wedi ennill cyfres brawf yno y ganrif hon. Anafwyd y capten dewisedig, Michael Celaya, yn gynnar ar y daith ac ymddiriedwyd yr arweinyddiaeth i Lucien Mias. Ni siomwyd *la France*.

Llwyddwyd i gadw'r sgôr yn gyfartal (3-3) yn y gêm brawf gyntaf, ac yn yr ail llyncodd Mias, yn ôl y sôn, hanner potel o rym cyn mynd i'r cae. Fflangellwyd tîm Ffrainc gan ei dafod o'r eiliad gyntaf, nes ennill buddugoliaeth hanesyddol o 9 pwynt i 5.

Dychwelodd y Ffrancwyr i Ewrop i ennill y bencampwriaeth yn ddi-dor tan 1962. Chwaraeodd Mias ei gêm ryngwladol olaf, ei bumed ar hugain, yn erbyn Cymru yn Paris yn 1959 ac arwain Ffrainc i ennill 11-3. Nid gwobr gysur fyddai curo'r Ffrancwyr o hyn ymlaen ond sialens fywaf y bencampwriaeth a chryn her i brif wledydd rygbi'r byd. Chwyldro yn wir, diolch i Lucien Mias.

4
LEWIS JONES

Ym mhumdegau'r ganrif hon cyfrifid B. Lewis Jones, gan ddilynwyr y bêl hirgron yn Ne Cymru a Gogledd Lloegr o leiaf, yn wythfed rhyfeddod y byd. Roedd sawl Cymro o'i flaen wedi cyrraedd y brig ym myd rygbi proffesiynol y cynghrair, fel Jim Sullivan o Gaerdydd, Emlyn Jenkins o'r Rhondda a Gus Risman o'r Barri. Mae rhai hefyd a enillodd fri yng ngogledd Lloegr ar ôl gyrfaoedd lawn mor nodedig yn y gêm amatur. Ymhlith y rhain gallwn nodi'r ddau faswr W.T.H. Davies (Abertawe, Cymru a Bradford) a David Watkins (Casnewydd, Cymru a Salford). Ond o ran y clod a enillodd, y campau sgorio a gyflawnodd ac ias gynhyrfus ei chwarae yn y ddwy gêm, mae Lewis Jones yn rhagori arnynt i gyd.

Ganed Benjamin Lewis Jones ar 11 Ebrill 1931 yng Ngorseinon a chafodd ei addysg yn yr ysgol leol. Roedd rygbi, pêl-droed a chriced yng ngwaed y teulu o Lime Street a rhannai Lewis y diddordebau hyn â'i frodyr Cliff ac Alun; chwaraeodd y tri ohonynt dros Lanelli a'r triawd yn gricedwyr medrus, hefyd. Yn Ysgol Ramadeg Tre-gŵyr y daeth doniau Lewis Jones i'w blodau. Roedd yr ysgol honno eisoes wedi esgor ar chwaraewyr rhyngwladol adnabyddus fel Gwyn Francis, Rowe Harding a'r ddau gefnder, Willie Davies a Haydn Tanner a ysbrydolodd Abertawe i'w buddugoliaeth dros y Crysau Duon yn 1935 pan oeddynt yn fechgyn ysgol. Yr athro chwaraeon yn Nhre-gŵyr oedd W.E. Bowen a gwnaeth ef yn siŵr fod Lewis yn ymarfer yn gyson i sicrhau meistrolaeth lwyr ar y medrau sylfaenol, ond gofalodd hefyd na fyddai dim pylu min yr awydd ymosodol oedd yn ail natur iddo a'i hoffter o agor symudiadau o'r sefyllfaoedd mwyaf annisgwyl. O'r cychwyn, roedd rhyw wefr yn nhraed aflonydd Lewis Jones; gallai droi, gwyrdroi ac ymlwybro drwy wal o amddiffynwyr. Wrth redeg, gallai amrywio ei gyflymdra yn y fath fodd ag i ddrysu'r gwrthwynebydd mwyaf penderfynol. Gallai gicio fel mul ac, o gymryd ychydig gamau yn unig yn ôl, ergydio'r bêl bellter maith. Fel y gellid disgwyl gan gricedwr profiadol, dilynai'r bêl â llygad barcud ac roedd ei ddwylo wrth faesu'r bêl yn hollol ddiogel.

Doedd dim syndod, felly, mai fel cefnwr yr enillodd ei gap dros ysgolion Cymru yn erbyn Ffrainc yn 1948, ddiwrnod cyn ei ben blwydd yn 17 oed, yng Nghastell-nedd, dan gapteniaeth Carwyn James o'r Gwendraeth. Yn syth ar ôl gadael ysgol yr haf hwnnw, ymunodd â chlwb Gorseinon a sgorio 88 pwynt cyn y Nadolig. Derbyniodd wahoddiad i chwarae rygbi dosbarth cyntaf gyda Chastell-nedd a sgoriodd 33 pwynt yn ei dair gêm gyntaf drostynt. Gyda'i igam-ogamu hudolus a'i gicio nerthol a chywir roedd Lewis Jones yn prysur droi'n beiriant sgorio.

Yn ystod 1949-51 bu'n gwasanaethu gyda'r Llynges yn ne-orllewin Lloegr ac yno, wrth chwarae dros Devonport Services, ffurfiodd bartneriaeth dra effeithiol gyda chanolwr cydnerth o Fachen yng Ngwent, Malcolm Thomas. Yn 1950, sgoriodd Lewis holl bwyntiau'r Llynges ym mhencampwriaeth y lluoedd arfog a chafodd ei ddewis fel cefnwr ar gyfer ei gêm gyntaf dros Gymru yn Twickenham. Wyth munud cyn yr egwyl yn y gêm honno, maeswyd y bêl gan y cefnwr newydd deunaw oed ar y llinell hanner-ffordd. Yn lle cicio'n saff am yr ystlys fel y disgwyliai pawb iddo wneud, yn reddfol naturiol cychwynnodd Lewis Jones ar hynt droellog ar draws y cae, cyn ymsythu a dawnsio trwy'r canol i'r cyfeiriad arall. Roedd Malcolm Thomas yn ffyddlon wrth ei ysgwydd i barhau'r symudiad a chroesodd y prop Cliff Davies yn y gornel. Curwyd Lloegr 11-5, Yr Alban 12-0 ac yn Belfast rhoes Lewis Jones bas deheuig uchel i Malcolm Thomas groesi am y cais a sicrhaodd fuddugoliaeth 6-3 a'r Goron Driphlyg gyntaf i Gymru er 39 mlynedd. Aeth tîm John Gwilliam ymlaen i ennill y gamp lawn, gyda Lewis yn awdur traean (17) o holl bwyntiau Cymru (50) y tymor hwnnw. Er, yn rhyfedd, nad oedd Lewis yn ddewis gwreiddiol ar gyfer taith Llewod 1950 i Seland Newydd ac Awstralia, ymunodd â'r garfan yn ddiweddarach a phrin ei fod wedi disgyn o'r awyren nag y ciciodd saith gôl mewn saith cynnig yn ei gêm gyntaf yn Brisbane a gorffen y daith â chyfanswm o 92 pwynt mewn un gêm ar ddeg. Yn ei gêm brawf yn erbyn y Crysau Duon roedd yn nodweddiadol iddo, ar ei lein ei hun, ryng-gipio pas oddi wrth ei faswr Jackie Kyle i Bleddyn Williams, a rhedeg ar hyd hanner y cae cyn trosglwyddo'r bêl i Ken Jones fynd fel ewig am y cais.

Dychwelodd i Gymru a chwarae ei gêm ryngwladol orau yn Abertawe yn 1951 pan chwalwyd y Saeson 23-5. Tro'r Cymry i gael eu chwalu oedd hi y mis canlynol yn Murrayfield (19-0) a beiwyd Lewis Jones yn annheg am y trychineb. Er colli ei le yn nhîm Cymru, bu chwarae criced yr haf hwnnw dros y llynges yn Lord's a thros dîm Cernyw mewn cystadleuaeth arall yn beth cysur iddo. Erbyn diwedd y flwyddyn roedd yn ôl yn nhîm Cymru i wynebu'r Springboks, ac yn 1952 helpodd y cochion i'w hail Goron Driphlyg mewn tair blynedd.

Yna, yn Nhachwedd 1952 cyhoeddwyd y newydd bod Lewis Jones, a oedd erbyn hyn yn chwarae dros Lanelli ac yn gymaint o eilun ar y Strade ag y bu Albert Jenkins yn y 1920au, wedi ymuno â chlwb proffesiynol Leeds am £6,000. Dim ond 21 oed ydoedd a byddai 12 tymor o'i flaen yng Nghynghrair y Gogledd. Yn y cyfnod hwnnw, torrodd bob record gwerth ei thorri. Yn 1956-57, sgoriodd 505 o bwyntiau. Ef oedd y cyntaf erioed i gyrraedd 500 mewn un tymor. Saif ei record (197 gôl, 37 cais) hyd heddiw.

Dewiswyd ef fel canolwr ar gyfer taith 1954 tîm cynghrair Prydain i Awstralia, dan gapteniaeth Cymro arall, Dickie Williams (Hunslet), ac yn yr ail gêm brawf yn Brisbane, ar yr union faes lle y cafodd y fath lwyddiant gyda'r Llewod yn 1950, creodd record newydd trwy gicio wyth gôl adlam. Erbyn diwedd y daith gallai Lewis Jones hawlio cyfanswm o 278 o bwyntiau.

Dal i ddenu'r tyrfaoedd a wnâi. Bu'n aelod allweddol o dri ar ddeg Leeds a gurodd Barrow 9-7 am Gwpan y Cynghrair yn

Wembley yn 1957 a choronwyd ei yrfa pan benodwyd ef, yn 30 oed, yn gapten ar Leeds, ac arweiniodd y clwb i'w bencampwriaeth gyntaf yn 1960. Croesodd Lewis ei hun am gais arbennig yn y gêm dyngedfennol yn Stadiwm Odsal, Bradford, o flaen 60,000, a phan chwythodd y bîb olaf a Warrington wedi'u trechu 11-4 codwyd Lewis ar ysgwyddau ei dîm a'i gadeirio o'r cae.

Yn 1964 gorffennodd gwrs i'w hyfforddi'n athro a rhoes y gorau i chwarae. O fewn blwyddyn, denwyd ef i Awstralia gan swydd dysgu a'r cyfle i hyfforddi clwb Westworthville ger Sydney. Yno y bu tan 1972 cyn dychwelyd i Leeds, lle mae'n dal i fyw ar ôl ymddeol o fod yn athro mathemateg. Roedd yn un o'r chwaraewyr mwyaf naturiol ddawnus erioed i gyffwrdd â phêl rygbi.

5

MICHAEL GIBSON

Gan Michael Gibson o Iwerddon y mae'r record am ennill mwy o gapiau rhyngwladol na'r un chwaraewr arall o Brydain. Gwisgodd y crys gwyrdd â'r siamroc 69 o weithiau rhwng 1964 a 1979, mewn amryw o safleoedd. Ymddangosodd 40 gwaith fel canolwr, 25 gwaith fel maswr a phedair gwaith fel asgellwr. Ar ben hynny chwaraeodd mewn deuddeg gêm brawf dros y Llewod, wyth gwaith fel canolwr a phedair gwaith fel maswr. Deil yn gydradd â'i ffrind mawr a'i gyd-Wyddel, Willie John McBride, y record o deithio bum gwaith gyda'r Llewod, sef tair gwaith i Seland Newydd a dwy waith i Dde Affrica.

Eithr nid ar bwys nifer ei gapiau na'r pwyntiau a sgoriodd y mae ystyried Mike Gibson yn un o gewri'r gêm ond oherwydd y cyfrifir ef yn un o'r chwaraewyr canol cae mwyaf diwylliedig a fu erioed. Crefftwr a pherffeithydd ydoedd, pêl-droediwr cyflawn ym mhob ystyr. Roedd ganddo nid yn unig y gallu tactegol i weld pob gêm yn ei chrynswth ond hefyd ymwybyddiaeth o'r chwaraewyr o'i gwmpas. Pur anaml y gwelid Mike Gibson yn 'marw' gyda'r bêl; yn hytrach, gwnâi hi yn gyfleus i gyd-chwaraewyr a oedd mewn safle well. Roedd yn hynod amryddawn, fel rheolwr, ciciwr, taclwr, gwarchodwr a chyn-

Michael Gibson.

heilydd, a cheid ymroddiad llwyr ganddo hyd eiliad olaf pob gêm. Roedd gallu naturiol ganddo, wrth gwrs, ond deilliai ei feistrolaeth lwyr ar bob agwedd o'r chwarae rhwng y mewnwr a'r cefnwr o ymarfer dyfal a diwyd. Cysegrai oriau bwygilydd i berffeithio'i sgiliau a sicrhau ffitrwydd trylwyr. Ei feirniad llymaf oedd ef ei hun; yn wir, os oedd yn ddiffygiol mewn rhyw-beth, hunanhyder oedd hwnnw. Oddi ar y cae, roedd yn swil a diymhongar; ar y cae roedd yn gwrtais a boneddigaidd. Ni welwyd ef erioed yn chwarae'n annheg. Roedd yn ei elfen gyda'r chwaraewyr gorau (cyfle na ddaeth yn aml i'w ran dros Iwerddon) yn annog, cynorthwyo a dod â'r gorau o'i gyd-chwar-aewyr yn ddeallus a heb dynnu sylw. O ganlyniad, ffurfiodd gyda Barry John a John Dawes driawd canol y cae digymar gyda Llewod 1971 yn Seland Newydd.

Ganed Cameron Michael Henderson Gibson yn Belfast ar 3 Rhagfyr 1942 a magwyd ynddo ddiddordeb mewn chwaraeon o'i febyd. Yn ei ddyddiau cynnar yn yr ysgol bu'n fewnwr, ond wedi mynd ymlaen i ysgol foned Coleg Campbell, Belfast, blagurodd fel maswr ac yn y safle hwnnw y chwaraeodd dros dîm cyntaf yr ysgol. Aeth ymlaen wedyn i Goleg y Frenhines, Caergrawnt, i astudio'r gyfraith, ac yng ngêm yr hen brifysgolion yn 1963 y daeth i amlygrwydd am y tro cyntaf, gan sgorio cais ym muddugoliaeth Caergrawnt o 19 pwynt i 11 yn erbyn Rhydychen. Ymhen deufis dewiswyd ef i chwarae dros Iwerddon ac enillodd ei gap cyntaf yn Twickenham, gan gyfrannu'n odidog at gêm agored a chyffrous a enillwyd gan Iwerddon 18-5. Roedd ei yrfa ryngwladol wedi'i lansio o ddifri.

Enillodd dri 'glas' dros Gaergrawnt yn y gêm flynyddol yn erbyn Rhydychen. Yn 1965 fe oedd y capten a sbardun y symudiad a arweiniodd at gais Caergrawnt mewn gêm gyfartal (5-5), sgôr nad oedd Gibson yn anfodlon arni gan mai capten Rhydychen y flwyddyn honno oedd hen gyfaill iddo o Goleg Campbell, Fred Craig. Erbyn haf 1966 roedd wedi chwarae dair ar ddeg o weithiau dros Iwerddon fel maswr a dewiswyd ef ar gyfer taith y Llewod i Seland Newydd. Gorfu iddo golli rhan gyntaf y daith yn Awstralia oherwydd ei arholiadau terfynol yng Nghaergrawnt ond wedi iddo gyrraedd gwlad y Crysau Duon buan y daliodd lygaid y cyhoedd gyda llithrigrwydd ei chwarae ymosodol a sicrwydd ei amddiffyn. Er iddyn nhw

golli'r gemau prawf oherwydd anallu'r blaenwyr i ennill digon
o'r bêl, bu'r profiad o chwarae fel canolwr tu fâs i David
Watkins o Gymru yn werthfawr iddo. Ymwelodd â Seland
Newydd dair gwaith wedyn yn y saithdegau, gyda Llewod John
Dawes (1971) a Phil Bennett (1977) a chyda charfan Iwerddon
yn 1976.

Gwnaeth Gibson iawn am fethu ymweld ag Awstralia yn
1966 trwy fynd yno gyda thîm Iwerddon yn 1967 a chyfrannu at
fuddugoliaeth hanesyddol (11-5), y gyntaf mewn gêm brawf gan
unrhyw dîm o ynysoedd Prydain yn hemisffer y de. Yn 1968
roedd ar ei hynt unwaith eto, i Dde Affrica gyda Llewod Tom
Kiernan, a bu'n faswr yn y pedair gêm brawf ar ôl i Barry John
dorri pont ei ysgwydd. Ond dyna derfyn ei yrfa fel maswr.

Torrodd asgwrn ei foch cyn gêm gyntaf pencampwriaeth
1968-69 a chymerodd Barry McGann ei le ym mhymtheg
Iwerddon i wynebu Ffrainc. Enillodd y Gwyddelod yn dda (17-
9), cadwodd McGann ei le a daeth Gibson yn ôl i'r tîm fel
canolwr. 1969 hefyd oedd y flwyddyn a welodd Gerald Davies
yn symud o'r canol i'r asgell; byddai'r Crysau Duon cyn bo hir
yn teimlo effeithiau'r newidiadau yma. Yn Seland Newydd yn
1971 darganfu Mike Gibson awch newydd at y gêm a'r rhyddid
i'w fynegi, wrth benelin Barry John a John Dawes. Cyffesodd
Barry John ag edmygedd fod Gibson, â'i chwarae cytbwys,
deallus, yn estyniad ohono ef ei hun. Roedd fel pe bai'n pasio,
meddai, i faswr ychwanegol. Ym marn capten y Crysau Duon,
Brian Lochore, Mike Gibson ynghyd â Mervyn Davies yng
nghefn y lein oedd yn bennaf gyfrifol am lwyddiant y Llewod
yng nghyfres y gemau prawf a enillwyd 2-1 gyda un yn gyfartal;
y tro cyntaf erioed i'r Llewod ennill cyfres yn yr ugeinfed ganrif.
Er y byddai Gibson yn teithio ddwy waith eto gyda'r Llewod, bu
hyfforddwyr y timau hynny mor annoeth ag anwybyddu ei
brofiad enfawr ar gyfer y profion.

Daliodd ei ddoniau disglair i befrio dros ei glwb N.I.F.C.
(North of Ireland Football Club) ac ym mhymtheg cenedlaethol
Iwerddon. Roedd y Goron Driphlyg o fewn eu cyrraedd yn 1972
am y tro cyntaf er 1949, ond a hithau'n gyfnod arbennig o gyth-
ryblus yn y Weriniaeth y pryd hwnnw, gwrthododd Cymru,
deiliad y Goron, deithio i Ddulyn i'w hamddiffyn. Gwobr
gysur, felly, oedd y gampwriaeth a ddaeth i ran Iwerddon yn

1974 a hwnnw'n brofiad melys odiaeth i Mike Gibson yn arbennig. Yn 1978 torrodd record capiau'r byd (63) Willie John McBride. Erbyn hynny roedd Gibson yn chwarae ar yr asgell ond dychwelodd i'r canol ar gyfer ei gêm gartre olaf, yn erbyn Crysau Duon Graham Mourie, yn Nhachwedd 1978 (collodd Iwerddon 6-10). Yna, cyhoeddodd ei ymddeoliad.

Ond ymhen pum mis roedd yn ôl yn y crys gwyrdd, yn 36 oed ac ar yr asgell, yn helpu Iwerddon i guro'r Awstraliaid ar eu tomen eu hunain yn haf 1979, pan enillwyd y gemau prawf 27-13 a 9-3. Roedd y ddwy fuddugoliaeth yma yn goron haeddiannol ar yrfa Michael Gibson, y pencampwr urddasol, teg a thawel o dalaith Ulster.

6

GARETH EDWARDS

Dros y blynyddoedd mae Cymru wedi cynhyrchu mewnwyr hynod ddawnus fel Dici Owen (35 cap, 1901-1912) a Haydn Tanner (25 cap, 1935-1949), ond ni fu erioed neb mwy disglair ei ddoniau nag mor enwog â Gareth Edwards. Er bod J.P.R. Williams yn berchen ar fwy o gapiau (55), chwaraeodd Gareth yn ddi-dor dros Gymru o'i gap cyntaf yn 1967 tan ei olaf yn 1978. Yn ystod y 53 o weithiau y gwisgodd y crys coch, sgoriodd 88 o bwyntiau, yn cynnwys ugain cais (record gydradd â Gerald Davies), dwy gôl adlam, un gôl gosb a dau drosiad.

Ganed Gareth Owen Edwards ar 12 Gorffennaf 1947, yn fab i löwr yng Ngwauncaegurwen, Cwm Tawe, a daeth ei ddawn yn amlwg yn gynnar, mewn sawl math o athletau a chwaraeon. Aeth o ysgol y Waun i Ysgol Dechnegol Pontardawe, lle y llywiwyd ei yrfa gan ei athro ymarfer corff Bill Samuel o Gwmgors. Sylweddolodd 'Bil Sam' yn fuan fod addewid anghyffredin yn y llanc esgyrniog (y pryd hwnnw) a mynnodd ei fod yn ymarfer yn gyson i ddatblygu ei gyneddfau naturiol. Ac yntau'n gryf a chyflym o'r cychwyn, prin bod yr un gamp na fedrai Gareth Edwards roi cynnig arni, yn arbennig mewn athletau. Yn 1963 a 1964 roedd yn bencampwr ysgolion Cymru ar y 220 llath, y ras dros y clwydi, y naid hir a thaflu'r ddisgen. Gallasai'n hawdd fod wedi troi at yrfa bêl-droed. Roedd rheolwr

Abertawe'n pwyso arno i ymuno â'r tîm pan oedd Gareth yn bymtheg oed. Byddai wedi cytuno oni bai bod ei rieni'n benderfynol iddo gael mwy o addysg.

Carreg filltir yn ei hanes oedd cael cynnig ysgoloriaeth yn 1964 i un o ysgolion bonedd drutaf Lloegr, Millfield, yng Ngwlad-yr-haf. Millfield a benderfynodd mai rygbi ac nid athletau fyddai bywyd Gareth o hyn ymlaen. Rhedodd dros ysgolion Lloegr pan oedd yno ond cafodd ei gap rygbi dros ysgolion Cymru yn 1965. Yn 1966 aeth Gareth i Goleg Addysg Caerdydd, ac oddi yno yr enillodd ei gap hŷn cyntaf yn Paris yn 1967, yn 19 oed. Er mai colli a wnaeth Cymru roedd lle Gareth yn y tîm cenedlaethol yn sefydlog o'r diwrnod hwnnw ymlaen.

Y pryd hwnnw, ei ddull o basio o fôn y sgrym oedd ei daflu ei hun ar ei hyd ond ar ôl sylwi ar dechneg Ken Catchpole o Awstralia (ar daith ym Mhrydain 1966-67) o droelli'r bêl wrth ei phasio, penderfynodd Gareth ei efelychu. Fe berffeithiodd y pas drwy'r haf yn Ne Affrica gyda Llewod 1968 a thrwy'r gaeaf dilynol gan roi sylw arbennig i basio oddi ar ei law chwith, y wannaf o'r ddwy. Erbyn tymor Coron Driphlyg 1969, roedd Gareth wedi ychwanegu pas anferth o hir at arfogaeth ei fedrau, ac yn Paris y flwyddyn honno (cyfartal 8-8) sgoriodd gais nodweddiadol o'i benderfyniad ffyrnig pan daranodd i lawr y llwybr cul ar hyd yr ystlys, yn chwalu a gwyro heibio i hanner dwsin o wrthwynebwyr cyn ei hyrddio'i hun dros y llinell.

Roedd Gareth eisoes wedi arwain Cymru, y tro cyntaf yn 20 oed yn erbyn yr Alban (enillwyd 5-0) yn 1968, a'r ail dro yng ngêm y goron (30-9) yn erbyn Lloegr yn 1969, ond y farn gyffredinol, er nad barn Gareth ei hun, oedd bod cyfrifoldebau capteniaeth yn amharu ar ei gêm naturiol. Dan arweiniad syber John Dawes dros Gymru a'r Llewod yn 1971, cyflawnodd Gareth wyrthiau mewn partneriaeth â'i gymar o glwb Caerdydd, Barry John. Sgoriodd glamp o gais yn Murrayfield (19-18), dau arall yn erbyn y Gwyddelod (23-9) a rhedodd fel ewig hanner hyd y Stade Colombes ar ôl i J.P.R. Williams ryng-gipio a gwrthymosod o'i linell ei hun yn Paris (9-5). Yn Seland Newydd y flwyddyn honno cafodd y gorau ar ei elyn mawr, Sid Going, mewnwr di-ildio'r Crysau Duon; yn y drydedd gêm brawf (enillwyd gan y Llewod 13-3) Gareth a osododd sylfaen cais yr un i Gerald Davies a Barry John, i sicrhau 13 pwynt i'r Llewod mewn

Cymru v. Awstralia, 1975. Gareth yn rheoli, Steve Fenwick (12) yn cynorthwyo, a Grav (13) yn camsefyll!

deunaw munud. Petai angen profi'n bellach fod Gareth ymhlith y gorau o'r goreuon, cafwyd hynny gyda'r cais diangof a sgoriodd ar Barc yr Arfau yn erbyn Yr Alban yn 1972. Torrodd yn rhydd oddi wrth sgarmes yn ddwfn yn hanner Cymru a'i heglu hi i lawr yr ochr dywyll. Ffrwydrodd drwy ddau dacl, cyrraedd y cefnwr, pyntio'n gytbwys dros ben hwnnw a chicio ymlaen dros y lein. Yna, gydag amseru perffaith, a hynny ar ôl ras wyllt o 80 metr, fe'i taflodd ei hun ar y bêl cyn iddi lithro dros yr ystlys. Cais rhyfeddol a buddugoliaeth ysgubol (35-12).

Y flwyddyn ganlynol, sgoriodd Gareth gais hanesyddol arall, dros y Barbariaid yn erbyn Crysau Duon 1973, pan chwyrnellodd am y gornel i goroni symudiad a oedd wedi sgubo fel tân gwyllt o un pen o'r cae i'r llall ar ôl i Phil Bennett danio'r ffiws y tu allan i'w linell ei hun.

Gyda Llewod Willie John McBride. yn Ne Affrica yn 1974, gwelwyd agwedd wahanol eto ar athrylith lachar y bachgen o'r Waun. Diléit Gareth nawr oedd codi'r bêl o reng ôl y sgrym, cipedrych yn gyflym o'i gwmpas ac yna gollwng cic letraws anferth a fyddai'n rowlio a thasgu'n ddieflig ar grastir y veldt i gymryd y chwarae hanner canllath o'r lle'r aeth y sgrym i lawr. Gallai gyflawni camp debyg ar feysydd lleidiog Prydain hefyd. Un tro, yn Twickenham yn 1978, gyda'r bêl yn drwm a seimllyd a'r gelyn yn gwasgu, taniodd Gareth daranfollt o gic ar hyd y llinell ystlys a'r bêl yn hedfan 70 o fetrau'n syth fel saeth cyn gwyro allan ychydig o fetrau o linell gais Lloegr. Cyfaddefodd blaenwyr Lloegr wedi'r gêm mai'r gic hon a dorrodd eu calonnau ac aeth Cymru ymlaen i ennill ei thrydedd Goron Driphlyg o'r bron.

Y gêm honno oedd hanner canfed cap Gareth ond roedd ei emosiwn, bwrlwm ei egni a'i awydd tanbaid i ennill gymaint ag erioed. Os nad oedd mor gyflym â chynt, gwae'r neb, a sgrym Cymru yn bachu'r bêl ddeg metr o linell y gelyn, a feiddiai sefyll yn llwybr Gareth ac yntau ar ei ffordd i lawr yr ochr dywyll i sgorio'i gais anochel. Dro yn ôl yng ngemau cyffrous y Goron Driphlyg yn Nulyn yn 1976 a 1978 gwelwyd blaenasgellwyr yn disgyn arno i'w gladdu dan borfa daear Iwerddon, ond dro ar ôl tro dihangodd o'u crafangau gan ennill tir trwy gicio neu redeg.

Nes ei ymddangosiad olaf, yn erbyn Ffrainc yng ngêm y gamp lawn yng Nghaerdydd yn 1978, amheuthun oedd ei weld yn arbed nerth ei flaenwyr gyda chiciau cyfrwys a chywir ac yn trawsnewid gwedd y gêm gyda fflach o ysbrydoliaeth, bylchiad sydyn, neu fagnel mawr ei gicio dihafal. Yn bendant, dyledwyr oedd Barry John (23 gêm gyda Gareth dros Gymru) a Phil Bennett (25 gêm) i bas anferth a gofal bugeiliol eu mewnwr drostynt. Yn bendant, hefyd, Gareth Edwards oedd angor tîm Cymru gydol ei ail oes aur (1969-1979), y mewnwr gorau a welodd y gêm erioed, a'r chwaraewr mwyaf gwefreiddiol yn hanes rygbi yng Nghymru.

7
BARRY JOHN

Ym myd rygbi mae Cymru'n enwocach na'r un wlad arall oherwydd ei maswyr, rhai fel Percy Bush a W.J. Trew ar ddechrau'r ganrif, Cliff Jones a Willie Davies yn y tridegau, Glyn Davies a Cliff Morgan ar ôl yr Ail Ryfel Byd, Phil Bennett yn y saithdegau a Jonathan Davies yn yr wythdegau. Dyma'r safle sydd wedi tanio dychymyg dilynwyr Cymreig y bêl hirgron. Dewiniaid oeddynt a doniau a chryfderau pob un yn ddigon gwahanol i'w gwneud hi bron yn amhosibl dewis y gorau ohonynt. Ond yn yr olyniaeth dywysogaidd yma mae un a gafodd ei ddyrchafu'n 'frenin', sef Barry John (25 cap, 1966-72), y chwaraewr rygbi cyntaf â'i enw mor gyfarwydd ag enwau'r pêl-droedwyr enwocaf a sêr y byd pop.

Nid ymdebygai i nifer o'i ragflaenwyr yn y safle. Nid dyn bach byr, bywiog, ydoedd. Roedd ymron yn ddau fetr o daldra a phwysai 74.42 kilo. Nid gwibio o gwmpas y maes fel comed oedd ei ddull o chwarae, achos meddai ar y ddawn ryfeddaf i hollti amddiffynfeydd gyda'i redeg cytbwys, twyllodrus. Daliai'r bêl o'i flaen yn hytrach na'i chofleidio'n dyn a chymaint oedd ei reddf i'w thrin yn dirion nes y rhoddai'r argraff ei bod hi'n aelod atodol o'i gorff. Hyd yn oed wrth gicio roedd cydymdeimlad rhyngddo a'r bêl, er na wastraffai yr un eiliad wrth gymryd ciciau gosod. Yn aml roedd wedi gwneud ei farc, camu'n ôl, a gyrru'r bêl yn ddi-feth rhwng y pyst cyn bod ei wrthwynebwyr wedi codi o'r ddaear. Â'r bêl yn ei ddwylo roedd yn feistr ar holl ystumiau twyllo gwrthwynebydd: ffugbasio, gwyro, symud y bêl a'r corff yn gytbwys. Gallai newid ei gyflymdra wrth redeg a rhedai'n syth yn hytrach nag ar draws ei wrthwynebwyr. Roedd yn gwbl hunanfeddiannol ar y cae, gyda'r gallu rhyfedd i beri i bawb arall gredu bod amser ganddo i gyflawni pob dim. Meddai ar ffydd ddiysgog yn ei alluoedd hynod ei hun ac ni fedrai ei bersonoliaeth radlon gelu hynny. Gyda'r ffydd yma, cyflawnodd wyrthiau.

Ganed Barry John yng Nghefneithin, yn yr hen Shir Gâr, ar 6 Ionawr 1945. Ei eilun fel crwt ysgol oedd maswr Llanelli a Chymru ar y pryd, Carwyn James, cymydog iddo yn yr un pentref a dysgodd Barry'n helaeth o wylio Carwyn yn ymarfer ar y cae y tu ôl i'w dŷ. Dysgodd yn arbennig hunanddisgyblaeth ac i ganfod manteision chwarae cynnil, cymen. Dysgodd sut i symud hanner uchaf ei gorff yn esmwyth i'r naill ochr a'r llall; yn bennaf oll, dysgodd grefft y gôl adlam. Byddai Barry John, maes o law, yn creu record trwy gicio wyth gôl adlam dros Gymru a phedair mewn un gêm dros Gaerdydd yn erbyn ei hen glwb, Llanelli (28 Tachwedd 1970).

Barry John

Tystia profiad cynnar Barry John, felly, fod amgylchedd wedi chwarae rhan bwysig yn ei ddatblygiad fel chwaraewr. Rhaid bod y galluoedd sylfaenol yn gynhenid hefyd, wrth gwrs, ond yn rhyfedd ni ddenodd galluoedd Barry John sylw dewiswyr tîm ysgolion uwchradd Cymru a bu rhaid iddo fodloni ar chwarae dros Ysgol Ramadeg y Gwendraeth a chlwb y pentre, gyda'i dri brawd, Del, Clive ac Alan. Dros wyliau'r Nadolig, 1962, gwisgodd Barry sgarlad Llanelli am y tro cyntaf, yn erbyn Moseley. Colli wnaeth tîm y Sosban ond croesodd Barry am gais pert, a'i drosi.

Rhwng 1964 a 1967 bu'n fyfyriwr yng Ngholeg y Drindod, Caerfyrddin, lle y perffeithiodd ei gicio, yn arbennig i'r ystlys, a'r gôl adlam. Cafodd gyfle i'w brofi ei hun yn erbyn maswr Cymru ar y pryd, David Watkins, yn nhreialon 1966 ac enillodd ei gap cyntaf yn erbyn Awstralia ym mis Rhagfyr. Colli wnaeth Cymru y diwrnod hwnnw (11-14) a'r gêm wedyn, yng Nghaer-edin (11-5), a bu rhaid i Barry John symud i Gaerdydd i ymuno â Gareth Edwards ac aros nes i Watkins droi at y gêm broffesiynol cyn adennill ei le yn nhîm Cymru. Hyd yn oed y pryd hwnnw, cyfnod go denau oedd hwn i Gymru a Barry John a dim ond un fuddugoliaeth o'r pum gêm yn 1967-68. Plymiodd ei lwc yn is eto pan dorrodd bont ei ysgwydd yn ystod gêm brawf gyntaf y Llewod yn Ne Affrica yn haf 1968.

Ond yn 1969 roedd ail oes aur Cymru yn gwawrio. Dechreu-odd y system hyfforddi ddwyn ffrwyth a daeth i amlygrwydd gnwd cyfoethog o dalentau cyffrous fel Gareth Edwards, Gerald Davies a J.P.R. Williams—a Barry John. Enillwyd y Goron Driphlyg trwy chwarae cyflym, ymosodol a sgoriodd Barry John gais yr un yn erbyn Yr Alban a Lloegr a gôl adlam yn erbyn Lloegr ac Iwerddon. Cafodd brofiadau chwithig gyda Chymru yn Seland Newydd yn 1969 ond cafodd ddial hefyd ymhen dwy flynedd.

Erbyn hynny, roedd Cymru yn 1971 wedi maesu efallai'r pymtheg gorau erioed i wisgo'r crys coch. Dan gapteniaeth John Dawes, cipiwyd y Goron Driphlyg a'r Gamp Lawn. Sgoriodd Cymru dri chais ar ddeg ac o'i chyfanswm o 73 o bwyntiau, Barry John oedd awdur 31 ohonynt gyda dwy gôl adlam (6) yn erbyn Lloegr; cais trosiad a gôl gosb (8) yn erbyn Yr Alban; gôl adlam, trosiad a dwy gôl gosb (11) yn erbyn Iwerddon, ac yn

Paris gôl gosb a chais gogoneddus (6) i goroni'r cwbl. Cafwyd prawf digamsyniol o'i ddewrder hefyd yn erbyn Ffrainc, oherwydd daeth trobwynt y gêm pan daclodd Barry'r cawr Benoit Dauga pan oedd hwnnw yn ei lawn ruthr bum metr o'r lein.

Yn ystod haf 1971, ar daith gyda'r Llewod (John Dawes, y Cymro cyntaf i'w harwain, a bron hanner y garfan yn Gymry) cynllwyniodd Barry John a'i hyfforddwr goleuedig, Carwyn James, gwymp y Crysau Duon ar eu tomen eu hunain. Ar bwys ei orchestion yn llywio'r Llewod i'w buddugoliaeth gyntaf erioed mewn cyfres brawf, cafodd Barry John gyhoeddusrwydd y cyfryngau poblogaidd na roddwyd i'r un chwaraewr rygbi o'r blaen. Yn y pedair gêm brawf, Barry oedd yn gyfrifol am 30 o 48 pwynt y Llewod; a chreodd record trwy sgorio 191 o bwyntiau (7 cais, 31 trosiad, 28 gôl gosb, 8 gôl adlam) mewn 17 gêm yn Awstralia a Seland Newydd. Sgoriodd gais anfarwol yn erbyn Prifysgolion Seland Newydd pan dderbyniodd y bêl ddeng metr ar hugain o'r llinell, ffugio cicio, yna ffugbasio, cyn mynd ati i wau ei batrwm arbennig ef ei hun wrth lithro a lledgamu heibio i bob aelod o'r tîm arall cyn croesi o dan y pyst. Does dim rhyfedd mai'r 'Brenin John' ydoedd o hynny ymlaen.

Ond roedd yr holl boblogrwydd yn bygwth mynd yn drech na'r gŵr ifanc, tawel o Gefneithin. Dim ond un tymor arall y gallai ei wynebu, a hyd yn oed yn hwnnw, pan fethodd Cymru gadw cyhoeddiad yn Nulyn, sgoriodd Barry John 35 pwynt yn nhair gêm y bencampwriaeth. Ym mis Ebrill 1972 ymddangosodd am y tro olaf ar y Maes Cenedlaethol, fel capten Pymtheg Barry John yn erbyn Pymtheg Carwyn James yng ngêm Jiwbili yr Urdd. Cafwyd gwledd o sgorio, gyda thîm Carwyn yn colli o 28 pwynt i 32. Yn naturiol, Barry John oedd seren y noson, gyda 14 pwynt. Gyda hynny, daeth teyrnasiad y brenin i ben.

Y llwybr nas adnabu aderyn ac na chanfu llygaid barcud oedd yr un a dramwyai Barry John ar y cae rygbi. Ond ar 7 Mai 1972 cyhoeddodd y 'brenin' fod y llwybr hwnnw wedi cyrraedd pen y dalar. Roedd yr orsedd yn wag, a'r maes chwarae yn dlotach o golli athrylith o artist a chonsuriwr o faswr.

8
GERALD DAVIES

Yn ôl yr hanes, byddai'r rhedwr enwog Guto Nyth Brân yn paratoi ar gyfer ras trwy gysgu ar domen-dail frwd fel y gallai'r gwres naturiol ei ystwytho a'i gryfhau. Mae'n annhebyg mai dyna ddull Gerald Davies o ymlacio ond serch hynny, mae'n siŵr y gellid cymhwyso iddo ef, un o'r asgellwyr gorau a welodd y byd erioed, ddisgrifiad I.D. Hooson o Guto, yn 'ysgafndroed fel sgyfarnog, yn gynt na'r gwynt a'r hebog'.

Nid o Lanwynno y deuai Thomas Gerald Reames Davies ond o Lan-saint, ger Cydweli, lle y ganed ef ar 7 Chwefror 1945. Fe'i haddysgwyd yn Ysgol Ramadeg y Frenhines Elizabeth yng Nghaerfyrddin, a chafodd brawf rhanbarth ar gyfer tîm ysgolion Cymru dan bymtheg oed pan oedd yno. Ni wnaeth fawr o argraff y pryd hwnnw ond erbyn 1963 roedd yn gapten tîm hŷn yr ysgol ac enillodd gapiau ysgol dan 19 oed yn erbyn Lloegr a Ffrainc. Er nad oedd yn dal roedd ganddo gyflymdra cynhenid a gwytnwch corfforol, a datblygwyd y nodweddion yma ymhellach yng Ngholeg Hyfforddi Loughborough lle y bu'n fyfyriwr rhwng 1963 a 1966. Yno daeth Gerald dan ddylanwad darlithydd addysg gorfforol o'r enw John Robins a oedd wedi ennill un cap ar ddeg dros Gymru ac wedi bod yn Llew Prydeinig yn y pumdegau cynnar. Astudiai Robins grefft a thacteg rygbi yn wyddonol fanwl a dysgodd i Gerald nid yn unig hanfodion hyfforddi effeithiol, ond hefyd sut i ddarllen llif a thrai gêm yn ei chrynswth.

Yn y canol y chwaraeai Gerald yn Loughborough a manteisiodd y coleg ar ei sbîd eithriadol i ennill prif gystadleuaeth saith-bob-ochr Lloegr, y Middlesex Sevens, yn 1964. Cawsai ambell gêm gyda Llanelli yn ystod ei wyliau o'r coleg ond pan adawodd â Loughborough yn athro trwyddedig a chael swydd addysg yng Nghaerdydd, ymunodd â chlwb y brifddinas yn 1966. Yno, gellid ffurfio llinell dri chwarter ddisglair iawn (Keri Jones, D. Ken Jones, Maurice Richards ac yntau), a dewiswyd y pedwar yn eu tro dros Gymru a'r Llewod.

Mae'n syn meddwl na fedrai triawd canol y cae fel Barry John, John Dawes a Gerald Davies ysbrydoli Cymru i guro Walabïaid digon cyffredin 1966 ond colli (11-14) oedd profiad Gerald pan

Gerald Davies.

(Colorsport)

enillodd ei gap cyntaf yn eu herbyn ar Barc yr Arfau. Ond cafodd glo bendigedig i'w dymor rhyngwladol cyntaf wrth sgorio dau gais pert yn 'gêm Keith Jarrett' yn Ebrill 1967, pan sgoriodd y llanc hynod hwnnw 19 pwynt ar ei ymddangosiad cyntaf a dinistrio Lloegr o 34 pwynt i 21.

Gwelwyd fflachiadau'n unig o allu Gerald ar daith y Llewod i Dde Affrica yn 1968, megis yn Boland pan ochrgamodd yn wefreiddiol i ddau gyfeiriad a rhedeg fel gwenci am hanner can metr i sgorio. Flwyddyn yn ddiweddarach, yn Seland Newydd gyda thîm Cymru, symudodd o'r canol i'r asgell, i ddyfod yn orau yn y byd yn y safle hwnnw.

Erbyn hyn, roedd Gerald yn astudio Saesneg yng Ngholeg Emmanuel, Caergrawnt. Enillodd dri 'glas' yn erbyn Rhydychen ac ef oedd capten Caergrawnt yn 1970. Yn 1971, daeth yn ôl i dîm Cymru ar ôl blwyddyn o ganolbwyntio ar ei waith coleg a sgoriodd gais ar ôl cais i ennill y Goron Driphlyg y flwyddyn honno, dau yn erbyn Lloegr (22-6), un yn Murrayfield (a throsiad cofiadwy John Taylor ar ddiwedd y gêm i sicrhau buddugoliaeth o 19-18) a dau eto yn erbyn Iwerddon (23-9). Roedd wedyn yn un o'r garfan o saith o Gymry Llundain i deithio gyda Llewod John Dawes a Carwyn James i Seland Newydd yn haf 1971. Ymunodd Gerald â'r daith yn hwyr fel y gallai sefyll ei arholiadau gradd yng Nghaergrawnt. Llwyddodd yn y rheiny a chafodd anrhydedd eto yn Seland Newydd, gan wibio fel saeth o fwa am ddau gais yn ei gêm gyntaf, yn Timaru. Sgoriodd yn yr ail a'r drydedd gêm brawf ond roedd ar ei orau gogoneddus yn erbyn Hawke's Bay pan sgoriodd bedwar cais, pob un yn dyst i'w gyflymdra ffrwydrol a'i ochr-gamu gwefreiddiol.

Wedi dychwelyd, daliodd ymlaen i sgorio dros Gymru. Ef a J.J. Williams (Pen-y-bont a Llanelli) oedd y pâr disgleiriaf o asgellwyr a welodd Cymru er Willie Llewellyn a'r Dr. Teddy Morgan ym mlynyddoedd cyntaf y ganrif. Gallasai Gerald yn deg fod wedi disgwyl cael llawer mwy o'r bêl na ddaeth i'w ran ond yng nghanol y saithdegau rhoddid gormod o bwyslais ar y canolwyr, gan afradu doniau'r asgellwyr. O leiaf cafodd Gerald ddigon o gyfle i chwyrnellu am y lein gyda Chymry Llundain, y clwb agosaf ato nid yn unig yn ddaearyddol (roedd Gerald bellach yn dysgu yn ysgol fonedd Christ's Hospital yn

Horsham, swydd Sussex) ond hefyd o ran eu hagwedd anturus a'u chwarae ymosodol.

Gwrthododd, ar dir egwyddor, ailymweld â De Affrica gyda Llewod 1974. Yr un flwyddyn, cafodd swydd gyda'r Cyngor Chwaraeon yng Nghaerdydd ac ailymunodd â chlwb Parc yr Arfau. Dyrchafwyd ef yn gapten arnynt ddwywaith, yr ail dro yng nghanmlwyddiant y clwb yn 1976-77. Mwynhâi'r cyfrifoldeb, er nad oedd yn edifar ganddo na chafodd gyfnod o gapteniaeth ar Gymru, oherwydd bod cyfle ganddo ar lefel clwb i roi stamp ei athroniaeth ef ar dîm cyfan. Er gwaetha'i siom o fethu cipio Cwpan yr Undeb dros Gaerdydd, cafwyd sawl sgôr gyffrous ganddo ar y ffordd, a llamodd am bedwar cais gwych yn erbyn Pont-y-pŵl mewn gêm gwpan ym mis Ionawr 1978.

Yn naturiol, cyfrannodd yn sylweddol at Gamp Lawn Cymru yn 1976, gan groesi ddwywaith yn y fuddugoliaeth fawr o 34 pwynt i 9 yn Nulyn. Efe, hefyd, trwy wrthymosod yn benderfynol o'i linell ddau ar hugain, a gychwynnodd y symudiad bendigedig a arweiniodd at gais Phil Bennett yn Murrayfield a'r bedwaredd Goron Driphlyg ar ddeg i Gymru yn 1977. Bu'n aelod, hefyd, o'r tîm a enillodd y bymthegfed goron yn 1978 ond bu ymron iddo golli'r cyfle i dorri record Ken Jones, Casnewydd (44 cap, 1947-57) oherwydd anaf. Bu'n rhaid iddo dynnu allan o'r tîm a dewiswyd i chwarae yn erbyn Ffrainc, ond aeth gyda Chymru ar ei thaith ddiflas i Awstralia yr haf hwnnw a sgorio pum cais yno, gan gynnwys dau yn y gemau prawf, i ddod yn gyfartal â record Gareth Edwards o ugain cais dros Gymru. Bu'n gapten yn yr ail brawf, ac yn briodol iawn sgoriodd fellten o gais i ddathlu ei gêm rygbi olaf. Yn erbyn Awstralia y daeth ei yrfa i'w therfyn, fel y cychwynnodd hi ddeuddeng mlynedd ynghynt, a gyda'r ddwy gêm brawf aeth cyfanswm ei gapiau i 46.

Rhwng 1966 a 1978, felly, chwaraeodd Gerald Davies 46 gwaith dros Gymru, un ar ddeg o weithiau fel canolwr a 35 o weithiau fel asgellwr, gan sgorio 20 cais. Sgoriodd hefyd 13 cais dros y Llewod. Roedd ei chwarae yn adlewyrchiad o'i bersonoliaeth ddiwylliedig. Mynnai bob amser osod rygbi, a'i orchestion ei hun, mewn persbectif, ac fel un a ymddiddorai mewn llenyddiaeth a'r theatr nid oedd dim a roddodd fwy o fwynhad iddo na chael ei dderbyn yn aelod o Orsedd Beirdd Ynys Prydain yn Eisteddfod Genedlaethol Caerdydd yn 1978. Byddai Guto Nyth Brân ac I.D. Hooson wedi cymeradwyo hynny. Cynghanedd bur oedd chwarae celfydd, cain Gerald Davies, bardd y Goron.

CHAPTER 10

WRITING ABOUT RUGBY

Cwmbran R.F.C.: One Hundred Years of Rugby, ed. Denis Gane, Cwmbran, 1980, pp. 116.

David Watkins: an autobiography, Cassell, 1980, pp. 234. £6.95.

Welsh Rugby: The Crowning Years 1968-80 by Clem Thomas and Geoffrey Nicholson, Collins, 1980, pp. 263. £6.95

A Touch of Glory by Alun Richards, Michael Joseph, 1980, pp. 176. £8.50.

The Illustrated History of Welsh Rugby by J.B.G. Thomas, Pelham Books, 1980, pp. 265. £10.50

Those for whom Welsh rugby is something more than a media-fest on international days know that it is only at the grass roots of the game that they can find its vitality and resilience truly affirmed. These are qualities with which the lesser clubs are well-endowed, and Cwmbran R.F.C., which is [in 1980-1] celebrating its centenary along with the W.R.U. is both representative, in possessing those qualities in abundance, and unique, by virtue of its own special history. That history, affectionately recorded in a well-produced brochure-type publication, confirms the pattern of club growth we have come to recognize as typical. The game was introduced to the locality by the sons of a Pontnewydd vicar 'who brought home a plum-shaped ball from college and taught the locals how to use it'. Only in 1961 was the club's name changed to Cwmbran. In the 1870s Pontnewydd was a village undergoing rapid industrial development in coal and tinplate. Its population of about a thousand was centred around the works, the Church, the Primitive Methodist Chapel, the School, six pubs and, from 1880, Pontnewydd Wanderers Football Club. Rivals soon appeared in the form of Croesyceiliog Wanderers, Race Mountain

Hares, Cwmbran Rovers and Upper Cwmbran Hoppers, who practised scrummaging against the *wall* of the Bush Inn, presumably from the inside late on Saturday nights.

The 1890s provide confirmation that Pontnewydd was in the mainstream of Welsh rugby development: fixtures are broken off because of regular onfield fighting, headquarters are settled on the King's Head Hotel, Pontnewydd becomes a founder member of the keenly competitive Monmouthshire League and soon wins it, becomes a feeder to bigger clubs (and the Northern Union), and produces a few capped players of its own. The post-1900 period, when the team, often overlapping with the local male choir (one of the players was a fine tenor who was later to gain fame as an opera singer appearing in London's Albert Hall) travelled in an open charabanc, is colourfully recalled by veteran Jack Hibbs, who acted as club mascot and repository of players' belongings—watch chains, several sets of false teeth, as well as Will Hiatt's glass eye.

In the twenties things got less colourful. In 1927-8 Cwmbran Colliery laid off 1300 men, the club plunged into debt and appealed to the W.R.U. for help. What it got was suspension for failure to fulfil fixtures, and the club collapsed until 1931. Even in adversity, the community knew its friends, and the club raised 'a fair sum' in a charity match for the Gresford disaster fund. Post-war rugby revived with surplus service-kit and clothing coupons. In 1947 the club, with local authority assistance, obtained a ground. The fifties saw new facilities, the appointment of an official coach, the Monmouthshire League championship won for the first time since 1899, floodlights, a youth team, an international (Graham Jones, capped from Pontypool in 1963) and the opening of £12,000 clubhouse in 1965. These are the classic indicators of the growth of second-class rugby, the lifeblood of the game in Wales. It is a proud story, and Cwmbran tell their own piece of it as well as any.

Another survivor was the product of a similar background in an adjoining valley. David Watkins went out from Blaina to the world; travelling light, he became weighted with honours. Not even the superstars of the seventies have managed two auto-biographies, but Watkins has. A ghosted *David Watkins Story* appeared in 1970. I am inclined to think that the deft style and general articulacy of this more recent production owes a fair amount to the unobtrusive editorship of David Parry-Jones who, a few years back, managed to make even the laconic Mervyn Davies sound like Ben Elton.[*] It is certainly refreshing to begin not with pre-match dressing room rituals but with the scarred landscape of the Eastern Valley, and the most intimidating front row in Welsh history, Guest, Crawshay and Homfray, industrial up-and-under specialists. Watkins was born in Club Row, near Clock Row and Shop Row, and his later affluence brought home to him a poignant if belated awareness of their significance—'history, had I but known it, was still around us, and reflected in the face of Jack Watkins', his miner father.

Some points are effectively made. Watkins determined to do well in rugby at his sec. mod. as the only way to achieve equality with successful 11-plus boys. A youth international himself, he felt that 'an unfair share of caps went to youth from West Wales since the bulk of the officials seemed to be based there'. Quite so: the Welsh Youth R.U. was founded in the Amman Valley in the late 1940s to cool the ardour of 'Red' Ammanford. His likes and dislikes are expressed in a forthright manner. He doesn't care to be known as 'Dai', which he blames on the narrow columns of Tudor James's *Sunday Mirror*; he cares less for the Barbarians 'and their weird concept of putting the game first'. In Clive Rowlands—whom he portrays as highly intelligent, self-confident, ardently patriotic and a powerful motivator—he recognised a kindred spirit: 'He never shrank from a good argument, not even with a selector'. Clive had told him before the notorious 1963 Murrayfield match, 'One way to beat these Scots is kick, kick, kick. That's what I am going to do'. As a result, Watkins touched the ball five times during the entire match, but was as delighted with the 6-0 win as the 10,000 Welshmen on the terraces who would have agreed with him: 'I see no point in not playing to win . . . sport is all about victory'. Understandably, his attitude to the ill-fated 1966 Lions tour is as venomous as his outside break. His con-

[*Mervyn Davies with David Parry-Jones, *Number Eight* (Pelham Books, 1977)]

tempt for manager Des O'Brien, who left a demoralised side for a week's sight-seeing in Fiji on the eve of the crucial Third Test, is total, though he has some sympathy for the hopelessly miscast Mike Campbell-Lamerton, whose selection as captain was the most bizarre appointment since Caligula made his horse a consul. Watkins is scathing, too, about the hypocrisy and frequent ignorance of the Welsh selectors of his day. After being dropped for the 1966 Wallabies match—a decision which filled him with 'rage, indignation, embarrassment and despair', —*three* of the Big Five told him they had voted *for* him. Given his durability and immense appetite for the game, the mind boggles at what he might have achieved in tandem with Gareth Edwards.

Ironically, David Watkins's last match in the Welsh jersey, the 34-21 defeat of England in 1967, was the precursor of the high-scoring internationals which would characterize the second Golden Era. The post-1968 period is what Clem Thomas and Geoffrey Nicholson's book sets out to analyse and describe. Clem would be on anyone's short list for inclusion in the best post-war Welsh backrow, while Geoffrey Nicholson is the most incisive sports writer in Fleet Street. Here, Clem provides an over-view of the period, Nicholson a match-by-match record. Maybe they would have played to their respective strengths better had they reversed their roles. As it stands though, the match accounts, teams, scorers, etc. are a valuable continuation of where John Billot's *History of Welsh International Rugby* (Ferndale, 1970) left off. Clem's survey is pocked by minor errors (Max Boyce did not refer to the Pontypool front row as the Viet *Cong* but Viet *Gwent*, Ireland did not win the Triple Crown in 1974, nor is Hirwaun in the West Wales coalfield) but he has a well-informed and perceptive chapter on the organisational set-up called 'Getting the coach on the road'. It is in fact very much an internalist account; the triumphs of those years are seen solely in terms of developments within the game itself, with little regard to extrinsic economic, political, social and cultural factors.

Such factors played as shaping a role in the second Golden Era as they had, in a different way, in the first. Alun Richard's *Touch of Glory* has some awareness of this, despite some

Chinese incomprehension of the circumstances attending the founding of the Union around page 50. Alun has in fact almost written an entire book about Arthur Gould and subtitled it '*100 Years of Welsh Rugby*'. There is a good precedent for this sort of thing, since Winston Churchill wrote several volumes about himself and called them *The History of the Second World War*. Churchill, though, never mentioned my father's hero, the late Glyn Davies. Alun does, often, and captures most of the other apostolic flyhalves too with affection, humour and engagement. As a personal essay by an addict, it is a highly entertaining read. It is lavishly illustrated too. There are even more pictures in J.B.G.'s pictorial history, many of them excellent. Bryn's love for the Game and his personal involvement with it over half a century shine through on every page. With its seductive visual appeal, bold print and simple text, one believes it will appeal widely to all ages.

Rugby in Focus, Colin Elsey and John Taylor, 192 pp., £14.95. David and Charles, 1986.

Rugby Wales '87, Ed. Barry John and Clem Thomas, 102 pp., £6.95. Christopher Davies, 1986.

Rugby, Gareth Edwards, 167 pp., £12.95. Partridge Press, 1986.

Rugby: Body and Soul, Bill Samuel, 155 pp., £9.95. Gomer Press, 1986.

Colin Elsey is well known as a sports photographer with the Colorsport Agency which he helped found. His *Rugby in Focus*, subtitled 'Twenty Years of Rugby Action', is an album of shots taken mainly at international venues. Some, like that of a mud-covered reptilian Fran Cotton emerging from a primeval swamp, are familiar; others, like that of NZ prop Billy Bush attacking Graham Price with boot and fist, less so. The aficionado's faith in the aesthetics of the game will be restored by the sight of that 1940s throwback, the photogenic high-fore-headed French winger Estève, frozen by the camera in the

Patrick Estève scores for France against England in Paris, 1984.

Billy Bush attacks Graham Price, 2nd Test in New Zealand, 1977.

(Colorsport)

J.J. Williams contributes to the British Lions' 26-9 defeat of the Springboks, to the obvious delight of black spectators, 3rd Test, Port Elizabeth, 1974.

The creature from the Black Lagoon, alias Fran Cotton, for the Lions in New Zealand, 1977.   *(Colorsport)*

execution of a try-scoring flourish deep in the English in-goal area, parallel to the ground and four feet above it.

My favourite shot is that of J.J. Williams leaving his Springbok pursuers floundering in his slipstream in 1974, to the jubilation of the delirious black spectators penned behind the goal-line. 'For rugby players who can convince themselves that playing in South Africa has nothing to do with supporting apartheid, or who do not care in any case, a tour of the Republic is just about perfect', notes John Taylor with the fine irony of one who experienced that perfection in person in 1968 and chose to deselect himself from the Welsh team to meet the Springboks two years later.

Elsey's photos of the peppery All Black midget Grant Batty provide vivid confirmation of Taylor's belief that a wing-threequarter cannot help having the temperament of a highly-strung racehorse: in the course of an eighty minute game the ball is in his hands so infrequently (30 seconds if he is lucky) that his frustration is bound to boil over. On the field even the mild and inoffensive Maurice Richards was transformed from a teetotal Baptist lay preacher into 'a screaming dervish cursing referee and opponents in equal measure'. My own preference is for wingers four feet off the ground and parallel to it, whenever possible deep in the English in-goal area.

In *Rugby Wales '87* John Taylor also makes the point that 'good running among the backs depends on good running forwards to give them support and confidence'. It is one of few pluses to emerge from a thin publication that is misleadingly titled, grossly over-priced, carelessly produced and, apart from a shot of R. Moriarty about to kick an opponent's head off, indifferently illustrated. Contributors who should know better take a lot of space to say what could be expressed in one sentence, while the ubiquitous J.B.G. continues to set his readers tough mental assignments. Has rubgy progressed through the years? 'I would say yes, it has, and proved a variant of economic conditions.' We must guard against complacency though, since 'horse-riding, squash and rowing are now the games of the people'. *Rugby Wales '87* threatens to be an annual affair.

Bill Samuel and Gomer Press, by contrast, have for a pound less produced not only the pick of this particular pile-up, but the rugby book of the year and maybe of the decade. In Bill Samuel's protegé Gareth Edwards' *Rugby*, Adidas boots are smoothly dismissed as 'jumped-up carpet slippers'; smoother still is the admission that 'in 1968 I already thought of [Willie John McBride] as a fine old claret, but by 1974 he was a genuine Château Latour'. Was it ever like that in Gwauncaegurwen? It certainly never was in Bill Samuel's Craig-cefn-parc. Bill—or as he would prefer, *Bil*—writes with warmth but never sentimentality of the close community of the Swansea Valley, whose protective shawl the young Gareth wrapped close around him on the occasion of his first visit to Millfield. He was so overawed that he spoke only Welsh the whole time he was there, even in front of 'Boss' Meyer ('Don't worry one bit. We teach 64 languages here and Welsh is one of them.') 'The door is ajar', Bill Samuel told Gareth—he is as quotable as the Old Testament—'As you go through it make sure that on your return your head will go through it as well'.

Bill Samuel's own career is an epic in itself. He left school at 14 to become a striker at Clydach's Graig Merthyr colliery, then worked his way to St. Luke's and a teaching diploma. En route he provides us with the best account yet written of the competitiveness, parochialism, quasi-professionalism and sheer fanaticism of West Wales rugby, where the going rate in the 1940s was thirty shillings home and away and half a ton of coal every month. There were other inducements too: 'It was quite an experience to be accosted in the toilet of the Salutation Hotel, Llanelli, by Rugby League scouts inquiring "Would you like to play for Batley?"'

Bill Samuel's account of his years teaching P.E. and scripture (body *and* soul) at Pontardawe Tech should be read by anyone with the least interest in the sociology of secondary education in Wales. The second half of the book, like the author's own career, is subordinated to the making and shaping, physically and spiritually, of Gareth Edwards. Here is the biography of Gareth that Gareth himself never wrote. But it is far more than that. Constantly compelling, deeply personal, by turns moving and hilarious, ultimately emotionally draining, it is a riveting account of Welsh rugby as a cultural force and social totality. 'Bill Samuel is unashamedly Welsh' writes his most famous pupil in an enigmatic foreword, 'and I wish him well.' Rugby is at the core of that Welshness, and rather than blinkering his vision it enhances it. In the decline of his beloved Craig-cefn-parc—industrially derelict, the 'Cop' privatised, the chapels closing, the vestry a community centre, the rugby team disbanded, the language in decline—he sees in miniature the crisis of modern Wales. Meanwhile at the Arms Park 'we see the folly of our educational system' as some spectators 'remain restless, embarrassed, lips tight . . . some singing with fervour, others mumbling, some uncomfortable, others not singing at all. Who is to blame for their ignorance? Is not *Hen Wlad Fy Nhadau* worthy of being taught in our schools?'

You do not have to be Welsh, a rugby follower, a sociologist, an educationalist or even an historian to savour and enjoy Bill Samuel's *Body and Soul*—only human. At £5.95 it is an absolute bargain. Read it.

Side-Steps, Gerald Davies and John Morgan, 157 pp., £7.95. Hodder and Stoughton, 1985.

This is a partnership to compare with the historic duos of former years, Willie Davies and Haydn Tanner, Barry John and Gareth Edwards. Gerald Davies is one of the two greatest players ever to wear the Welsh jersey: he touched the soul and ignited the imagination. A genius with a capacity for magic on the field of play, he has since shown, in his finely-chiselled autobiography and elsewhere, that he is no slouch on paper either. Few great artists have written with such probing articulacy about the springs and wells of their own deeply-pondered performances: in the often vacuous world of sports literature, where over-the-moonies are thick on the ground, literary grace is as rare as a dummy scissors at Pontypool Park. John Morgan, for his part, was last seen [as biographer of the Chicago mobster Morris (Murray) Humphreys (*No Gangster More Bold*, 1986)] pursuing a Welsh mafioso down State Street. Here his sights are less on Murray 'the Hump' than on Murrayfield. But as an opera librettist and one-time second tenor in the Orpheus, he is equally at home in Milan or Morriston: *Side-Steps* is worth reading for JM's own 'Return Journey' (not for nothing did this roaring boy follow Dylan as editor of Swansea Grammar School's magazine and holder of the cross-country cup; unlike Dylan he also captained the first XV) which takes him to Morriston RFC for a West Wales League derby with Tumble, and on to the Tabernacle in the evening for the fiftieth anniversary concert of the Morriston Orpheus Choir, where many of the afternoon's faces reappear. It is difficult to conceive of any other Welsh writer who could so deftly distill the essence of the popular culture of South Wales, and transmute it into such luminous prose.

Devotees of the Welsh rugby-as-literature school have long debated the rival claims of John Morgan and Alun Richards to be considered the Norman Mailer of Aberflyarff and beyond. Each can wield a wicked pen, each has the instincts of a bar-room brawler, each deploys a fast combination of left jabs to the ribs of pomposity, prissiness and humbug, each sees in rugby football an expression of the Welsh predicament. Though John Morgan's preference is for Covent over Madison Square Garden, it is clear that even if tough guys don't dance, they sure can write.

Side-Steps is an absorbing look at the 1984-5 season and the state of the Union generally. Gerald jinks around some of the main games and issues, while JM does the club-crawling in an attempt 'to express the social character of rugby's believers . . . even to detect a metaphor for the society's condition'. I'm not sure it always comes off, but it avoids the pretentious and is packed with insights, anecdotes and thumbnail asssments on topics as varied as professionalism, Paris and Ray Prosser. I was certainly brought up short to learn that in the *New Statesman* in 1953 John Morgan had written about the Welsh team against New Zealand 'running on to the fields of praise'. We can be sure, though, that Dylan, whose phrase it is, would have been delighted to know that Madame Patti of Craig-y-nos supported Abercrave RFC, played snooker in the village hall, drank pints, and wore a wig because she was bald.

[John Morgan died in 1988, aged 59. He is much missed.]

The International Rugby Championship 1883-1983, Terry Godwin, pp. xiv 498, £17.95. Collins Willow, 1984.

This attracive, crisply designed, large-format volume is a typically good-looking product from Collins Willow, who are among the most enterprising publishers of sports books in Britain today. It was under their imprint, and the unlikely joint auspices of the Football League and the National Dairy Council, that Simon Inglis cast a sharp, Pevsnerish eye on the architectural idioms and idiocies of *The Football Grounds of England and Wales* (1983), an enthralling survey whose sterilized title elevates self-effacement to an art form. At nearly twice the price, Terry Godwin's book is less imaginative, though just as industrious. The author has quarried newspaper and magazine files for reports, results and team line-ups of every game played in the [by 1983] 100-year existence of rugby union's annual International Championship, a tourney originally contested by the four 'home' countries alone before it acquired bite with the inclusion of France from 1910. Its meticulous, even excessive, statistical apparatus apart, this was an an undertaking that required enthusiasm and perseverance, and one's initial concern that so much effort should be directed to such an apparently unimaginative end is allayed, at least partially, by James Walvin's salutary reminder in the inaugural number of *The British Journal of Sports History,* May, 1984, that books like this, 'while often seeming uninspiring and dull, provide the raw data from which historians and sociologists can build more important structures and theories'.

The point is well taken, and it would be unusual indeed if this kind of work or this kind of author (Mr Godwin is a former rugby correspondent of *The Daily Telegraph*) came up with answers to the questions that serious historians are only now starting to ask for themselves. Thus, the statistical underpinning to France's emergence as a major rugby power in the 1950s is here amply provided, but anyone concerned to know how this came about will have to consult Richard Holt's seminal *Sport and Society in Modern France* (London, 1981). Match summaries alone cannot *explain* Ireland's two consecutive 'Triple Crowns' and three outright Championships between 1948 and 1951, but there may be clues in Terence Brown's *Ireland: a Social and Cultural History 1922-79* (Glasgow, 1981) which makes no mention of sport of any kind but sees the 1940s as 'a watershed' politically, economically and culturally in Irish history. At precisely which point a social analysis shades into reductionism is only one of the problems raised by a contextual approach; the fact remains that any socially meaningful history of steam locomotion is unlikely to be written by a train spotter, and there is a large and intelligent audience that needs to be reached with that truth and that kind of history.

This is in no way to devalue the real worth of the book here under review. On its own terms it provides enough of Walvin's 'raw data' for settling or supporting any number of arguments. The urgency of reducing the role of that scourge of the modern game, the penalty kick at goal, is reinforced by the calculation that while in 1953 the average number of penalty points kicked per game was 2.7 (and exactly 3.00 in 1963), the corresponding figure for 1983 was 16.8 (16.2 in 1982), an increase of 522 per cent. Historical geographers can plot the distribution of those clubs from which England for far too long chose to recruit most of their international players: they would appear to constitute a pretty narrow base (not least socially) of the Services, Oxford and Cambridge, and their London extensions. Not that Mr Godwin's book is all facts and figures. He provides us with a ration of photographs and his text is spiced with the odd anecdote. I always thought, though, that the telegram received by canned-foods tycoon Tony O'Reilly on his recall to the Irish side after a seven-year absence and 15 years after his first cap actually read 'Heinz meanz has beanz', thus retaining the flavour of a contemporary advertisement.

Finally, and with an eye to the publisher's blurb that this is a 'definitive record [and] history', the unsuspecting reader ought to be warned of the author's eccentric method of aggregating players' international appearances, which is to omit all non-Championship matches. This means that players like Llanelli's Handel Greville and Aberavon's Clive Shell, for instance, do not figure in any of Mr Godwin's many lists because they won their hard-won caps against Australia. It is indeed possible, if pedantic, to credit J.P.R. Williams, owner of the best-known initials in sport after lbw, with 44 Championship appearances, but he also won another 11 full caps against sundry Australians, South Africans and New Zealanders. Equally, to deny Prince Obolensky his historic appearance at Twickenham against the 1936 All Blacks only further confirms that a ledger can never comprehend a legend. I will not draw attention to the fact that Wales's first international was in 1881 (not 1883, p. xi), that it was Ireland who won the Triple Crown in 1948 (not Wales, p. 102), and that France's 'first-ever win in Wales' also happened in 1948 (not 1958, p. 276). I am glad to see the infamous Ringer incident at Twickenham in 1980 put into true perspective when 'Wales beat England by two tries to nil but lost the match' (p. 406), though I find it odd that there is nothing about the epic quality of the 1971 Welsh game in Paris, surely one of the greatest Championship matches ever, nor of Gareth's legendary lunging eighty-metre try against Scotland in 1972. These are minor slips in what is otherwise a most reliable and valuable 'record . . . of the Championship'. History, however, it is not.

Once or twice I have sidled up to rugby football. There is no doubt that in consideration of Welsh culture one has to conclude that this game, with its magnets of remembrance, has drained off much of the ardour that might have gone into a more sedulous cultivation of the arts.

Gwyn Thomas, *High on Hope*

INDEX/MYNEGAI

(italic figures denote Welsh-language references)